Kate Kraft

The nilometer and the sacred soil

a diary of a tour through Egypt, Palestine, and Syria

Kate Kraft

The nilometer and the sacred soil
a diary of a tour through Egypt, Palestine, and Syria

ISBN/EAN: 9783744745055

Printed in Europe, USA, Canada, Australia, Japan

Cover: Foto ©Andreas Hilbeck / pixelio.de

More available books at **www.hansebooks.com**

AND

THE SACRED SOIL:

A DIARY

OF A

TOUR THROUGH EGYPT, PALESTINE, AND SYRIA.

BY

Miss KATE KRAFT.

NEW YORK:
Carleton, Publisher, Madison Square.
LONDON: S. LOW, SON & CO.
M DCCC LXIX.

Entered according to Act of Congress, in the year 1869, by
GEO. W. CARLETON,
In the Clerk's Office of the District Court of the United States for the Southern District of New York.

THE NEW YORK PRINTING COMPANY,
81, 83, and 85 *Centre Street*,
NEW YORK.

To
JUDGE H. H. GOODMAN,

AS A MARK OF

FRIENDSHIP AND ESTEEM,

THIS BOOK IS RESPECTFULLY DEDICATED,

BY THE

AUTHORESS.

LAKE GEORGE, *Sept.* 16, 1869.

PROLOGUE.

In presenting this little work for the perusal of my friends, I beg to remind them that I have, as nearly as was consistent, adhered to the original design of giving a *"diary"* describing the manner of *"living"* and method of *"travelling"* on the Nile and through Syria, rather than entering deeply into incidents connected with the history of those countries.

To those more inclined to Biblical lore and the study of antiquities, the Bible will furnish sufficient food for the Holy Land, while the profound researches of Wilkinson, Lane, and others, will go far to satisfy the curious on the statistics and archæology of Egypt.

This interesting route of travel becoming more frequented, and consequently better understood, each succeeding year, naturally excites the curiosity of those having the hope of *"doing"* it yet in store; and, as a sequence, comes the question: How to do it?

The great point is to obtain a good dragoman; and, if fortune favors you in this particular, the success of your voyage is almost assured; whereas the constant annoyances and dissatisfaction arising from having a bad one will poison, if not mar, all your joyous anticipations.

Thus, on the Nile, we were happy in the selection of Mohammed-el-Adli, an Egyptian, who, we think, has not his superior; but it was far different in Syria.

The dragoman engaged for this part of the route, a Syrian named Joseph Mook, but for good and sufficient reasons best known to himself, had found it necessary to call himself Joseph

Carem,* gave us much trouble; and it was only through the conciliatory tact and management of Mr. Ferris that we succeeded in getting on.

Very little is necessary to take with you from Europe. Arms and ammunition excepted, I know of nothing that cannot be found either at Alexandria or Cairo.

A small supply of lettuce, parsley, and radish seed might be advantageously taken from Paris, and grown "*on the boat*," in board troughs arranged on the quarter-deck; and, in addition to the "*stock*," a supply of rockets and Roman candles, obtainable in Alexandria, would prove agreeable additions for grand occasions.

The necessity of publication was entirely an after-thought; as the idea forced itself upon my mind that, with only my written volume, a year's loaning would scarcely suffice to satisfy the demands of my numerous friends.

There are probably irregularities of language, and phrases decidedly "*Frenchy*," for which I beg their indulgence, as there must always be more or less surrounding difficulties for one writing in a "*foreign tongue.*"

* This man had commendatory letters from a gentleman of Boston, containing more religion than truth, which completely led us astray.

INDEX.

CHAPTER I.
                                                                         PAGE

Departure from Paris—Mont Cenis in a Snow-Storm—Turin—Bologna—Brindisi—Thence to Alexandria 0–24

CHAPTER II.
Alexandria in Egypt—Our Dragoman—Examining the Dahabeehs—Cleopatra's Needles—Pompey's Pillar—Dogs 25–32

CHAPTER III.
Alexandria to Cairo—The Delta—Pigeon Village—Charter of Vessel for Voyage on the Nile—The Contract—The Citadel—Old Cairo 33–43

CHAPTER IV.
Cairo—Its Mosques—Bazars—The Pyramids—The Tombs and Sphinx—Heliopolis—The Dervishes 44–59

CHAPTER V.
Our Dahabeeh—Its Crew—The Start—First Days on the Nile—Christmas Illumination—A Dangerous Weapon—Competition—Washing-Day 60–70

CHAPTER VI.
Voyage up the Nile—Races with the *Estella* and the *Crocodile*—Excursions on Shore—Egyptians as they are—Meeting other Boats—Excitement on Board—Is it a Crocodile or Lizard?—Arrival at Thebes—Grand Illumination—One Hundred and Ten Red, White, and Blue Lanterns—Mustapha Aga 71–88

CHAPTER VII.
Arrival at Esneh—Its Temple Three Thousand Years Old—City of Assouan—Island of Elephantine—Statue of an Egyptian King—Passage of the First Cataract—Three Hundred Nubians employed to pull our Boat through the Rapids—Arrival at Philæ 89–105

CHAPTER VIII.

Continuation of Voyage up the Nile—Lady Duff Gordon—Arrival at Wadi-Halfah—Arab Dance—Cataract of Batn-el-Hagar—Down Stream—Temples of Ferayg and Abou Simbel—Arrival at Derr—Nubian Wedding—Temple of Heron—Temple of Amada, built B. C. 2700—Temple at Dakkch—Kalabcheh, its Temple..106–118

CHAPTER IX.

Philæ, Beautiful Philæ!—Baron Hubner—Temple of Isis—Mementos of the French Army—An American Party—Impressions—Exciting Descent of the Cataract—Assouan—American Consul—Mussulman Sunday—Gebel Silsileh—Temple of Edfou—El-Kab—Ernent—Thebes again.........119–135

CHAPTER X.

Thebes—Temples of Medinet-Abou—Ramesium—Colossal Statue of Rameses—The Vocal Memnon—An Adventure—Koornah—Assasoef—Dayr-el-Bahree—Djalma—His Home—Washington's Birthday—Illumination........................136–155

CHAPTER XI.

Still in Thebes—Valley of Biban-el-Molouk—Tombs of the Kings—Petrified Clams—Great Sarcophagus—Belzoni's Tomb—Harper's Tomb—The Philosopher's Mistake—Karnak by Moonlight—Temple of Luxor—Departure from Thebes—Denderah—Dancing-Girls of Kenneh..................156–167

CHAPTER XII.

Abydos—The Cliffs of Gebel-Sheiek-Heredee—Orange and Lemon Groves—A Long Pull—Siout—Stabl-Antar—American Consul—Gebel-Aboofayda—Roda—The Palace—Tombs of Beni-Hassan—Minieh—Departure of Mr. R.—Benesoef—Floating Down—Aground—Memphis—Tombs of the Appis—Serapium...168–180

CHAPTER XIII.

Island of Rhoda—The "Nilometer"—Fatima—Woman's Rights—Good-by to our Crew—In Cairo again—Departure from Alexandria—Port Said—Suez Canal—Jaffa—The Convent—The Camp—House of Simon the Tanner—Selection of Horses—"The Sacred Soil"..........................181–194

CHAPTER XIV.

Our Caravan—Plain of Sharon—Lydda—Birthplace of St. George—An Accident—Ramleh—Mountains of Judea—Abou-Goch—David and Goliah—Mount of Olives—Bad Water—Jerusalem 195–206

CHAPTER XV.

Garden of Gethsemane—Grotto of Agony—Tomb of the Virgin—House of Mary's Parents—Procession for Mecca—Via Dolorosa—House of Pilate—Ecce Homo—Houses of Veronica and the Wandering Jew—Church of the Holy Sepulchre—The Tomb—Chapel of the True Cross—Calvary—Palm-Sunday—On the Walls—Lepers................................... 207–215

CHAPTER XVI.

Tomb of the Virgin—Tombs of the Prophets—Siloam—Fountain of the Virgin—Pool of Siloam—Mount Zion—Tomb of David—Wailing-Place of the Jews—Quarries—Joab's Well—Palestine Explorations—The Spring of the Arch—Tyropœan Valley—Ancient Halls and Aqueducts................... 216–226

CHAPTER XVII.

Mosque of Omar—Mosque of El-Axa—Solomon's Temple—Greek Fire—Rachel's Tomb—Hebron—Cave of Machpelah—Tomb of Abraham and Sarah—Abraham's Oak—Pools of Solomon—Bethlehem—Church of the Nativity—Birth of Christ.. 227–239

CHAPTER XVIII.

Convent of Mar-Saba—Shawaal—Arab Horsemanship—Dead Sea—Jordan—Pilgrim's Pass—Jericho—Fountain of Elisha—Return to Jerusalem..................................... 240–251

CHAPTER XIX.

Bethel—Jacob's Dream—Shiloh—Naplouse—Sichem—Sychar—The Woman of Samaria—Mounts Ebal and Gerizim—Sebastia—Samaria—Jezebel—Sepulchre of St. John the Baptist—Dothan—Djenin—The Marseillaise—A Storm—"Sir, your Revolver, the Bedouins!"................................. 252–265

CHAPTER XX.

Province of Galilee—Plain of Esdraelon—Mount Carmel—The Deserters—"The Turkey ate it, Sir"—Nazareth—Church of the Annunciation—Joseph's Workshop—Fountain of the Virgin—Rhapsody and Facts—Cana—Plain of Hattin—Tiberiade—Sea of Galilee 266–278

CHAPTER XXI.

Capernaum — Hospitality—Safed—Kedesh—Upper Jordan—Dan—Banias—A Cold Day on Hermon—Kefr-Haour—Tomb of Nimrod—Damascus—The Abana and the Pharpar—Naaman the Leper—Old Acquaintances—The Crooked Street called Straight—Massacre of Druses and Maronites............279-290

CHAPTER XXII.

Balbek...291-306

CHAPTER XXIII.

Beyrout—The Steamer—Retrospect—Rhodes—Smyrna—Ephesus—Constantinople—St. Sophia—Bosphorus—Black Sea—Golden Horn and Sweet Waters—Athens—The Acropolis—Parthenon—Eleusis—Messina........................307-816

INDEX TO PLATES.

The Nilometer	*Frontispiece.*
"The Oriental"	73
Island of Philæ	119
Temple of Isis	125
Absalom's Tomb	218

THE NILOMETER

AND

THE SACRED SOIL.

CHAPTER I.

DEPARTURE FROM PARIS—MONT CENIS IN A SNOW-STORM—TURIN—BOLOGNA—BRINDISI—THENCE TO ALEXANDRIA, EGYPT.

PARIS, December 1, 1867.

AGAIN gone! For two months and a half we have enjoyed our temporary home in dear Paris. The last week has been employed in preparing for our long journey to the East, and this morning at ten o'clock we left the Rue St. Honoré for the chemin de fer de l'Ouest, and arrived at half-past ten, where we found Mr. Rogers, our travelling companion, waiting for us. Our party of four, consisting of Mr. and Mrs. Thomas T. Ferris, of New York (my brother-in-law and sister), J. S. Rogers, of Paterson, New Jersey, and myself, are anticipating much pleasure from the glorious future. Aline and

Tom (Mr. and Mrs. Ferris) met Mr. Rogers about two weeks since, during a visit at the residence of Mr. E. Donnelly, and hearing of our intention to leave Paris shortly for Egypt, manifested a desire to join us, and coming the next day to look at out itinerary, felt much pleased with the splendid trip we were about to commence. So it was settled that he should leave Paris with us, and take the same steamer at Brindisi for Alexandria. At a quarter to eleven Messrs. Chagot and Lavigne, of Paris, came to wish us a safe journey, and remained until the last moment; new friends as they are, it was with regret we left them behind. Often will we remember the kindness they have shown us during our stay in Paris. The weather is dark and gloomy; it rains; yet the day has passed very rapidly. Mr. Rogers seems to be very agreeable and obliging. We have read this morning the newspapers sent by Mr. W. Warren, from Boston, containing an account of his voyage in Egypt, and which we all found highly interesting. We feel quite enthusiastic at the idea that we are going to tread the same ground so vividly described by that gentleman. We took our dinner in the cars, prepared by our cook in Paris the day before, and arrived at eight o'clock in Mâcon, Lamartine's birthplace. My thoughts have been often with him the past few days. As a young girl, I remember in reading his travels to the East how much I envied him. I never thought that the time would come when I also would be one of those happy few who have the good fortune to be able to roam through those sacred countries.

At last we have arrived at the Hôtel des Champs

Elysées, a very plain house, but the rooms very clean. Here we met with an American gentleman, Mr. O'Hara from Philadelphia, travelling with his wife, and whose destination is Rome.

Monday, December 2.

We were up at half-past four this morning, and at six o'clock left Mâçon for St. Michel, where we were to take the diligence to cross Mont Cenis. We reached that place at half-past twelve; the weather being intensely cold. After warming ourselves by a good fire we partook of dinner, and at half-past one Aline, Tom, and I took our places in the coupé of the diligence, Mr. Rogers having a seat in the interior. Notwithstanding the snow, which had commenced to fall, we soon felt very comfortable, being warmly wrapped up in cloaks, shawls, and blankets, and having hot water-cases at our feet. The diligence was crowded. On the banquette were eight men, among whom were several soldiers going to rejoin the Garibaldian army. They were very gay and patriotic, singing part of the time, and when passing through villages receiving marks of sympathy from the people standing in front of their doors. Being comfortably settled in our coupé, we soon began to appreciate the beautiful scenery unfolding itself before our eyes. It is said that few scenes can be more astonishing or more truly sublime than that presented to travellers crossing Mont Cenis; but how much more grand does it appear viewing it as we then did, a real winter scene, the snow falling rapidly, and covering the mountains with its white mantle, contrasting beautifully with the rich dark green of the fir; the villages strewed here and there, sometimes in the valley, sometimes on the mountain side, and inviting the eye to a quiet repose after having wandered so long on the peaks of these high Alps. It is supposed that Pompey was the first person who attempted a passage over this Alp; but it was not until the time of Napoleon that a roadway was completed, who, in 1810, ordered this stupendous undertaking to be executed, employing no less than three thousand workmen, at a cost of eight millions of francs. At eight o'clock we arrived at Lanslebourg, where the real ascent of Mont Cenis commences. The snow was falling faster and faster, the wind increasing in violence; eight horses were put to our diligence; night had come, and the road was only lighted up by a reflector lamp, fixed in front of the carriage. What a strange music the wind made, howling terribly, and dashing the snow violently against our window-panes, which were soon entirely covered. To attain the most elevated part of our route needed four more horses, twelve in all. It is a plain, six miles in length, encircled by the loftiest peaks of Cenis, and embellished with a beautiful lake, whose water in summertime reflects the surrounding heights. Here, before commencing the descent, ten horses were taken away, only two being left to the diligence. I was sorry it was night, as the descent into Italy is much finer than the ascent from Savoy; the road is similar to that of the Forca and the St. Gothard, which we passed last summer. The first gallery which presents itself is six hundred and fifty feet in length, and cut in several places through solid rocks of granite. We had hardly begun the descent when, all at once, and as we were commencing to sleep, the diligence gave a sudden and tremendous lurch, and lo! we were all on one side of the road. This was enough to awaken the whole party. The wind was blowing so terribly that we were not certain but that the horses, carriage, and all would be precipitated into the abyss. The drivers were swearing to their hearts' content, the poor horses were doing their best to recover the level of the road, and the travellers were asking themselves if they would not be obliged to regain the last post-house and pass the night as well as they could. At last the drivers did what they ought to have done in the beginning—put more horses on; and after a delay of five minutes more, we were *en route* again, descending with a frightful rapidity all the curves of the mountain. But that night it was ordained that everything should be against us, for the wind blew our light out, and we were enveloped in total darkness. We stopped half an hour, the drivers taking all that time to go to some neighboring house and have their lamp lighted again, and also probably warming themselves. Poor fellows! I do not wonder they felt the cold, as we heard that it was the first snow-storm of the season, and they were not yet accustomed to it; even our windows were all frozen up. Well, now that we are all right again, let us pursue our way. Down, down, down—if the horses were to stumble what would become of us! Half an hour's descent brought a complete change in the temperature. Our windows became clear, the snow ceased falling, the wind subsided, and soon after we had the moon shining in our faces, and the stars looking at us with their bright and lustrous eyes. After passing the plain of St. Nichólas is a gallery above two thousand feet in length, and cut through remarkably hard rocks. Here a wall of nine feet in height and six hundred in extent defends the gallery from earth and loose stones. It was half-past one in the morning when we arrived at Suza, at the foot of the mountain. Here a new annoyance was in store for us—the custom-house—and all our baggage was examined. Our intention was to take the train for Turin, but being too late, we decided to go to some hotel, pass the night as well as we could, and take the ten o'clock train in the morning for that city. Intensely cold, and at half-past two in the morning, we were drumming with all our strength at the Hôtel de France, a poor and gloomy-looking house. After having waited for about ten minutes, the door was opened and we were conducted to two rooms. Being tired we soon fell asleep, and only awoke at half-past nine.

TUESDAY, December, 3.

We hurried our dressing, but were ten minutes too late when we arrived at the station, and there was no other train until 4.50 in the afternoon. We breakfasted at the station, and afterwards seated ourselves before a bright and comfortable fire. At twelve o'clock I went out with Mr. Rogers, and took a walk of three miles, passing through two or three Italian villages. The weather was cold but dry, with a blue sky overhead. The sun shining on the snow-clad mountains gave a very pretty effect to the scenery. At 4.50 we left Suza for Turin, and at seven o'clock were luxuriously installed in a beautiful apartment at the Hôtel de l'Europe. One drawback to our anticipations was, that we had thought to find summer here, whereas the streets were all white with snow. We passed the evening near our fire, playing *bezique*.

WEDNESDAY, December 4.

Did not get up this morning until ten o'clock. Tom and Aline having visited Turin two years ago remained *at home*. Mr. Rogers and I took a guide and visited the Palazzo Royal. It is located in the centre of the city, in the Piazzi di Castello, a large, elegant square. Like all other palaces, the apartments are large and richly adorned. There are many paintings; some of Titian, Guercino, Albani, and Murillo. In the entrance, as you ascend the new and beautiful staircase, only finished last year, in honor of the king of Portugal, is a very fine equestrian statue of Amadeus I. The royal chapel is also very handsome; it contains among others a statue of Carlo Alberto, father of the present king, and one of Victor Emmanuel's wife, who died in 1856, and is buried in the church of La Superga. It is said she died heart-broken, and indeed her statue looks like desolation itself. From the chapel we had a fine view of the Duomo, which is the oldest of the sacred buildings of Turin. It was commenced about the year 602, by Agylulph, king of the Lombards, the interior of which is decorated with frescoes. From the Royal Palace we went to the Armoria Regia, which adjoins it. Amongst the curiosities is the cuirass worn by Prince Eugene at the battle of Turin; also a full suit of Duke Emmanuel

Filiberto, worn at the battle of St. Quintin; a great many flags, some from Solferino; others beautifully worked and presented by the ladies of Modena, Parma, Milan, etc., to Victor Emmanuel when he was named king of Italy. The Parliament House, which we next visited, is much inferior to the Parliament House in London, although the gallery of paintings contains a fine collection. Among the most valuable is the Madonna della Tenta, on wood, by Raphael; Pharaoh's Daughter finding Moses, by Paul Veronese; the Four Elements and a Holy Family, by Vandyck. Something that interested us much in the Museum of Antiquity was a plan of Jerusalem, with all the monuments yet remaining in the city. At the Palais Carignan we saw the room where King Victor Emmanuel was born. The church *del Corpus Domini*, which formerly belonged to the Jesuits, is very beautiful; the interior, both walls and columns, are all in marble and richly decorated. We afterwards took a carriage, and passing through all the principal streets, the Piazza di San Carlo, and the Piazza Victor Emmanuel, went to the public promenade (beautiful alleys of old trees along the Po), whence we had a magnificent view of the Alps!

> " Who first beholds those everlasting clouds,
> Seedtime and harvest, morning, noon, and night
> Still where they were, steadfast, immovable;
> Who first beholds the Alps, that mighty chain
> Of mountains stretching on from east to west
> So massive, yet so shadowy, so ethereal,
> As to belong rather to heaven than earth,
> But instantly receives into his soul

A sense, a feeling that he loses not,
A something that informs him 'tis a moment
Whence he may date henceforward and forever.

" To me they seemed the barriers of a world,
Saying Thus far, no farther! and as o'er
The level plain I travelled silently,
Nearing them more and more day after day,
My wandering thoughts my only company,
And they before me still, oft as I looked
A strange delight, mingled with fear, came o'er me,
A wonder as at things I had not heard of;
Oft as I looked I felt as though it were
For me the first time."

We regained our hotel at half-past four, delighted with our day's work, and waited patiently for Tom and Aline, who had gone out shopping. At half-past five we dined, and the weather being fine, we afterwards took a walk through the Arcades, which were brilliantly illuminated, and give a strange but pleasing aspect to the streets.

THURSDAY, December 5.

We left Turin for Bologna at a quarter of eight in the morning, and arrived there at three in the afternoon. The weather is very damp and rainy. On our road we passed Parma, Modena, also the battle-field of Marengo, and from the cars could see the fortifications. It was raining very hard when we arrived at Bologna. The city, with its low arcades, its narrow streets, its windows with iron railings, has a dark and gloomy appearance, impressing one with a feeling of sadness. As the evening arrived before we had finished our dinner, we postponed until the following day our visit to the churches, public monuments, and institutions.

FRIDAY, December 6.

The weather was very cloudy all the morning. We first visited St. Petronius' Church, which was commenced in 1390, and is built in the Tuscan-Gothic style. It is three hundred and eighty feet long, and one hundred and fifty-six wide; the chapels which surround it show signs of handsome frescoes, but are very much faded. The handsomest one is that of the Bachiochi, where Elise Bonaparte and her children are buried. On one side she stands hand in hand with her husband, while angels are crowning them, and on the other are her four children. They are all life-size, cut in beautiful white marble, the work of the two Franzoni. On the floor of the church is the meridional line, traced by the astronomer Cassini in 1653. I observed particularly the canopy of the choir, where the last German emperor, Charles V., was crowned by Pope Clement VII. We next visited the ancient University, founded in 1119 by Wernerus, called Suvena Juris. Upon entering you find yourself in a square court, with double arcades, having what appeared to be tombs on each side, with the armorial bearings of the families and inscriptions to their memory. We thought at first that we were in the Campo Santo, but the guide informed us there were no bodies buried here. All the inscriptions around us were only marks of honor to the celebrated dead.

The chapel has some beautiful frescoes. We went through the library, containing two hundred thousand volumes, and saw also a fine collection of antiquities. Bologna ranks among the first cities of Italy in her Academy of Fine Arts. The principal gems in the collection are St. Cecilia in Ecstasies, by Raphael; the Death of St. Peter and the Martyrdom of St. Agnes, by Domenichino; Samson Destroying the Philistines, the Madonna della Pieta, and the Massacre of the Innocents, all three by Guido. Before going back to the hotel we went to look at the two leaning towers,— when, by whom, or for what purpose built, no one now knows.

SATURDAY, December 7.

We left Bologna yesterday at four P.M. for Brindisi. Having to pass the night in the cars, we were glad to encounter two very agreeable travelling companions: an Italian gentleman, speaking French and English very fluently, and an English gentleman, Mr. Wales, going to Calcutta by way of Alexandria, and taking the same steamer as ourselves from Brindisi. The afternoon and evening passed pleasantly, talking on different topics, particularly of France, England, and Italy. Aline and I, having each two seats, could lie almost as well as in a bed, and slept very comfortably until morning. The hotels are miserable in this part of Italy; for breakfast that morning we had to content ourselves with an execrable cup of coffee and bread, the butter not being fit to eat. We arrived in Brindisi at half-past twelve, and had to cross the whole city on foot to go to the agency for our tickets.

It is a very ancient town, having a great many Roman remains, but particularly poor, ugly, and dirty; and the number of paupers is so great that before we left the shore we were surrounded by quite an army of them. After much difficulty in obtaining our billets, we hired a boat to convey us to the steamer, which is named the *Principe Tomasso*, and is very small. We have the best cabin on board, situated on deck, and aired by three windows, Tom having paid one hundred francs extra for it. The captain is an Italian, with a pleasant countenance, a counterpart to that of the doctor, who, not having any patients to take care of, employs his time in attentions to the ladies. There are very few passengers, and but two ladies besides Aline and myself. One is from Boston, and going with her husband to Calcutta; and the other is an Italian countess. The rest of the passengers are chiefly English, and their destination is Bombay. We remained on deck all the afternoon, but the weather was cold and cloudy. At four we took dinner with good appetite, but afterwards the sea became rough and compelled us to take to our berths, being overcome by sea-sickness.

SUNDAY, December 8.

All very sick until noon; the waves were very heavy, the boat too narrow, and rolling from side to side. What an awful feeling is sea-sickness! It takes all one's strength and spirit away. Lying languidly in our rocking-chairs, wrapped up in shawls and blankets, the Grecian Islands have passed before us without exciting any of those feelings of emotion which inspired

Byron to write his beautiful verses; and it was not until the following day, when the sea became calm and sickness had passed, that I could enjoy their reading.

THE ISLES OF GREECE.

"The isles of Greece, the isles of Greece,
   Where burning Sappho loved and sung,
Where grew the arts of war and peace,
   Where Delos rose, and Phœbus sprung;
Eternal summer gilds them yet,
But all, except their sun, is set.

"The Scian and the Teian muse,
   The hero's harp, the lover's lute
Have found the fame your shores refuse;
   Their place of birth alone is mute
To sounds which echo farther west
Than your sires' 'Islands of the Blest.'

"The mountains look on Marathon,
   And Marathon looks on the sea;
And musing there an hour alone,
   I dreamed that Greece might still be free;
For standing on the Persian's grave,
I could not deem myself a slave.

"A king sate on the rocky brow
   Which looks o'er sea-born Salamis,
And ships by thousands lay below,
   And men in nations;—all were his!
He counted them at break of day,
And when the sun set, where were they?

"And where are they? and where art thou,
   My country? On thy voiceless shore
The heroic lay is tuneless now—
   The heroic bosom beats no more!

And must thy lyre, so long divine,
Degenerate into hands like mine?

" 'Tis something in the dearth of fame,
    Though linked among the fettered race,
To feel at least a patriot's shame,
    Even as I sing, suffuse my face;
For what is left the poet here?
For Greeks a blush,—for Greece a tear.

" Must we but weep o'er days more blest?
    Must we but blush? Our fathers bled.
Earth, render back from out thy breast
    A remnant of our Spartan dead!
Of the three hundred grant but three,
To make a new Thermopylæ!

" What! silent still!? and silent all?
    Ah! no: the voices of the dead
Sound like a distant torrent's fall,
    And answer, 'Let one living head,
But one arise—we come, we come!'
'Tis but the living who are dumb.

" In vain, in vain: strike other chords:
    Fill high the cup with Samian wine!
Leave battles to the Turkish hordes,
    And shed the blood of Scio's vine!
Hark! rising to the ignoble call—
How answers each bold Bacchanal!

" You have the Pyrrhic dance, as yet,
    Where is the Pyrrhic phalanx gone?
Of two such lessons, why forget
    The nobler and the manlier one?
You have the letters Cadmus gave—
Think ye he meant them for a slave?

"Fill high the bowl with Samian wine!
    We will not think of themes like these!
It made Anacreon's song divine:
    He served—but served Polycrates—
A tyrant; but our masters then
Were still, at least, our countrymen.

"The tyrant of the Chersonese
    Was freedom's best and bravest friend;
That tyrant was Miltiades!
    Oh! that the present hour would lend
Another despot of the kind!
Such chains as his were sure to bind.

"Fill high the bowl with Samian wine!
    On Suli's rock, and Parga's shore,
Exists the remnant of a line
    Such as the Doric mothers bore;
And there, perhaps, some seed is sown
The Heraclidæan blood might own.

"Trust not for freedom to the Franks—
    They have a king who buys and sells:
In native swords, and native ranks,
    The only hope of courage dwells;
But Turkish force and Latin fraud
Would break your shield, however broad.

"Fill high the bowl with Samian wine!
    Our virgins dance beneath the shade—
I see their glorious black eyes shine;
    But, gazing on each glowing maid,
My own the burning tear-drop laves,
To think such breasts must suckle slaves.

"Place me on Sunium's marbled steep,
    Where nothing, save the waves and I,

May hear our mutual murmurs sweep;
There, swan-like, let me sing and die:
A land of slaves shall ne'er be mine—
Dash down yon cup of Samian wine!"

TUESDAY, December 10.

The time has passed more agreeably. The nearer we approach Egypt the more beautiful becomes the sky, which is of a deep blue. The sea is so calm we have hardly any motion. The captain says we will be at anchor to-morrow morning at three o'clock.

CHAPTER II.

ALEXANDRIA, IN EGYPT—OUR DRAGOMAN—EXAMINING THE DAHABEEHS—CLEOPATRA'S NEEDLES—POMPEY'S PILLAR—DOGS.

WEDNESDAY, December 11, 1867.

AT six o'clock A.M. I was on deck, looking at that Land of Egypt so often heard of, and so full of sacred and historical associations. God could not have given us a more glorious day for our entrance. Just one of those summer days, such as we have in New York. As our steamer glided slowly towards the port, the first objects which attracted my attention were Pompey's Pillar, the Pharos, and a quantity of windmills towards the west. The harbor was filled with numerous vessels of all nations. We were not yet anchored, when already shoals of boats were around the steamer, filled with dirty Egyptians, trying their best to get possession of baggage and passengers. So these are the descendants of the Pharaohs, the Egyptians among whom Abraham came to live, over whom Joseph the son of Jacob, originally a slave, ruled; the country where God told Mary and Joseph to take Jesus! "Out of Egypt have I called my Son." Here was the Island of Pharos, whose position first gave the idea to Alexander to build the city to which he gave his name, the witness of his triumphs, and also, later, of Cleopatra's beauty and wickedness. Indeed my heart felt sad in looking at thee, Egypt; so great at one time, so humble now! In reading notes about Egypt, I came across the document written by Amrou to the Caliph Omar, in the beginning of the Arabic conquest, towards 642 or 643. That prince had asked of him a description of Egypt sufficiently vivid and exact that he could imagine seeing with his own eyes that handsome country. I found it so beautiful I thought I would translate it, and give it place in my diary. He writes thus: "O Prince of the faithful! Paint thyself a barren desert and a beautiful country in the midst of two mountains; this is Egypt. All its productions and all its riches, from Assouan to Menchia, come from a blessed river which flows with majesty in the centre of the country. The moment of the rising and the retiring of the waters is also regulated by the course of the sun and moon. There is a fixed time in the year when all the sources of the universe come to pay to that King of the Rivers the tribute to which Providence has subjected them. Then the waters augment, come forth from the channel, and cover all the face of Egypt, to deposit a productive slime."

"There is no communication from one village to another except by the means of light boats, as numerous as palm-leaves. When the moment has arrived that the waters cease to be necessary to the fertility of the soil, the docile river re-enters the limits ordered by Destiny, so as to permit the treasures hidden by her in the bosom of the earth to be gathered."

"A nation protected by Heaven, who, like the bee, seems to be doomed to work for others, and without benefiting by the fruits of its labor. Open lightly the bowels of the earth, deposit therein the seeds from which to expect fertility, through the goodness of that One who makes the harvest grow and mature. The germ develops, the stem rises, the corn forms itself by the help of the dew, substitute of rain, and which preserves the fruitful dampness of the soil. Then, to the most abundant harvest, again succeeds sterility.

"It is thus, O Prince of the faithful, that Egypt offers, turn by turn, the image of a dusty desert, a liquid and silvered plain, a black and muddy marsh, a green and waving meadow, a garden-plot full of flowers, and a field covered with golden harvest. Blessed be the Creator of so many marvels! Three things, O Prince of the faithful, add essentially to the prosperity of Egypt, and the happiness of its inhabitants. The first is in not adopting lightly projects brought forth by Avidity, and tending to increase taxes; the second is in employing the third of revenues to the maintenance of canals, bridges, and banks; and the third is, only to raise taxes on the fruits produced by earth. Salut!"

In the midst of my thoughts Tom came to tell us that the boat was ready; and was followed by a dragoman who pleased us immediately. His name is Mustapha; and he has a very patriarchal face. He took care of our luggage, and, entering a boat, we proceeded to the custom-house, where we had to show our passports and have all our luggage examined. They seemed to be very strict, and even retained some of Tom's cartridges, which were sent to the American Consulate the next day. In waiting for the omnibus we had a first view of the crowds of donkeys, donkey-drivers, camels carrying goods, European carriages, and Egyptians, Greeks, and Turks, all mixed in an apparently inextricable confusion. We were assailed by men and boys, one wanting to carry an umbrella, another a bag, and one would have obliged us to take a donkey; but we stood firm, and after a few minutes were installed in the omnibus *en route* for the hotel. Our first impressions of Alexandria were not very favorable. We had to pass through narrow and irregular streets, the houses small, the shops and the people looking as dirty as possible. The *Hotel de l'Europe*, considered the best in the city, could not boast of extra cleanliness; and the cooking is miserable. It is situated on the *Grande Place* of the Consuls, which is the European centre. In looking from the window, if it were not for the animated scene—strings of camels, donkeys trotting gravely, some mounted by Bedouins, with their big sticks in their hands, others carrying Europeans, and followed by little boys in rags; Greek and Arabian faces; women dressed in loose blue skirts, with their faces half concealed, coming to get water from the basins, which are at the extremities of the *place*—you could hardly believe yourself to be in an Oriental city. The houses are without character; in front of all the hotels are handsome European carriages: so that, save the Egyptian features, you could imagine yourself in any other port of the Mediterranean. Upon inquiring of Mustapha about Mohammed El-Adli, the dragoman that Mr. Warren had last year, we were surprised to learn that he was his brother; and while we were dressing, they came together to our rooms. Mr. Warren had spoken highly of El-Adli, and we were much pleased with his appearance, as he was the first Egyptian we had seen who was well-dressed. He wore a handsome brown cloth embroidered suit, with a silk sash around his waist, and a white turban on his head, which well suited his expressive brown face. The gentlemen were in such a hurry to look at the dahabechs, or Nile boats, that, not waiting for us, they started with Mustapha. When at length we were ready, we went to sit on the balcony, and there met Mohammed, who asked us if we did not wish to join the governors, as he called the gentlemen. We said "Yes," and having chosen an elegant carriage, with a driver in Egyptian costume, our dragoman took his place near him, and we also went to see the boats. The atmosphere was so pure, and the sky so blue, that we enjoyed our ride exceedingly; and passing through new streets, entered an alley of large trees, seeing, for the first time in our lives, entire groves of palm-trees, which we found beautiful; and admired the bright flowers in gardens on the road-side. Soon we met Tom and Mr. Rogers; they had visited almost all the boats lying in the canal, but revisited them after joining us, and we all agreed that the "Cleopatra" was the largest, and, when newly arranged, the most comfortable; she was accordingly chosen. El-Adli asked £630 for three months, taking us to the second cataract and returning; we should have for that price all the comforts and the best cooking which could be obtained on the Nile.

After lunch we went to visit the bazars, which are far from being picturesque, and decidedly dirty; and purchased, in a Turkish bazar, two handsome scarfs for Aline and myself. Passing before the Latin Convent, and the new Protestant Church, we came to Cleopatra's Needles. These obelisks are before the ruins supposed to be the temple of Cæsar, and as it was erected by Cleopatra in honor of her son's father, it explains their traditional name. They are of rose granite, and were originally erected before one of the pylones of the great temple of Neptune, at Heliopolis. Only one remains standing, the height of which is seventy feet, and the hieroglyphics well preserved on two faces. The other, lying down, is nearly covered with earth, only one surface of about ten feet being discernible; and it might be taken for a flag-stone, were it not for the hieroglyphics seen upon it. Both bear the names of Touthmes III., of the XVIIIth dynasty, between 1625–1517 B.C. Indeed I must say that it needs a great deal of imagination to feel very enthusiastic before these ruins. The more remarkable monument—Pompey's Pillar—we found standing upon a mount, at a distance of a few hundred paces from the gate of the modern wall of Alexandria, which opens upon the sterile and desert country forming the narrow isthmus between the sea and the Lake Mareotis. It is a column of handsome red polished granite, of an elegant style, but the chapiter and pedestal are of inferior work, and have never been finished. It was erected by the Prefect of Egypt, Publius, in honor of the Emperor Dioclesian, after his victory, in 296 A.D., over Achillæus, who for five years had taken the title and insignia of imperial dignity. That Pillar, which has looked down upon all the changes that the memorable seat of art, learning, and commerce has through so many ages undergone, made only a sad impression on our minds. Our carriage was soon surrounded by beggars, both children and men, some of them blind, asking for backsheesh. We were glad to re-enter Alexandria, which we did by the Nile gate, and stopped at the Consul's, to whom Tom and Mr. Rogers had referred, for prices of dahabeehs. He said that El-Adli's price was not out of the way, so that the gentlemen, favoring Mr. Warren's recommendation, chose him as our dragoman, provided he should do all that the ladies desired. He asked us to go with him to the English and French shops, so that we could choose for ourselves the articles we wanted; and I suppose by the quantity purchased our table will be splendid, and easily satisfy any epicure we may meet with. They comprised ham, tongue, sardines, pickles of every kind, preserved vegetables, English and French preserves of all descriptions, best French confectionery, Mocha coffee, marquis chocolate, &c. In fact I cannot remember very well all he bought, but we were perfectly satisfied with the liberality which he displayed.

TUESDAY, December 12.

While taking our breakfast this morning the card of Mr. Tibbets, of Boston, was handed to us. Tom remembered that a friend had told him this gentleman was also going up the Nile, and perhaps would like to join us. He soon after made his appearance, and seems about sixty-five years of age, with beautiful white hair, and a pleasant cast of countenance; but we all felt that by reason of age and bad health he would not be a desirable companion; and were much relieved when we heard that his intention was to take the steamer. While Tom and Mr. Rogers were busy at the Consul's, settling the agreement with El-Adli, we passed the morning at home. On their return we heard with regret that after examination it had been found that the Cleopatra's bottom was rotten, and therefore unsafe; so that the best plan would be to leave for Cairo to-morrow morning, and there select the best dahabeeh to be had. In the afternoon we went to take a last look at the Cleopatra, to satisfy ourselves of the above fact, and thence drove to Moharembeh, a villa belonging to the Viceroy. The gardens are very handsome, and from them we had fine views of Alexandria, the surrounding country, and Mareotis Lake. All along the road are handsome villas, built in the European style, with gardens beautifully laid out, and belonging to the richest inhabitants of the city. In returning to the hotel by way of the Rosetta gate, we saw but a vast surface of naked ground, from which even the ruins have disappeared. We visited several ancient covered cisterns, so strongly constructed that they are still well preserved. Some are yet in use, and at the time of the inundation are filled with water from the canal. Alexandria can boast of having the greatest number of dogs found in any city: they go in troops, have no master, and at night seem to aspire in rivalry with the watchman in a low guttural barking which prevents one sleeping.

CHAPTER III.

ALEXANDRIA TO CAIRO—THE DELTA—PIGEON VILLAGE—CHARTER OF VESSEL FOR VOYAGE ON THE NILE—THE CONTRACT—THE CITADEL—OLD CAIRO.

FRIDAY, December 13, 1867.

WE took the eight o'clock train for Cairo; in the same carriage with us was the Italian countess, our travelling companion on the Tomasso. The trip from Alexandria to Cairo, by rail, occupies seven hours, and the road from the city runs between the Mahmoudieh Canal and Lake Mareotis. On the left we could see Pompey's Pillar, superb villas, factories, and Hollandish windmills on the edge of the canal, contrasting vividly with the mud houses. On the right, as far as the eye can reach, extends Lake Mareotis. This so-called lake was formerly very beautiful; but in 1801 the English, letting in the water from the sea, made of it an immense marsh, infecting Alexandria with pernicious miasma. The view of that uncultivated plain, bathed here and there by stagnant waters, which the wind hardly ruffles, makes a sad impression on one's mind. Damanhour was the first market town we came to, and we could see from afar its high octagon minarets; but upon approaching you find the place only a rude assemblage of unburnt brick habitations. Above Damanhour commences a landscape very much like Holland, if it were not for the palm-trees, the unut-

2*

terable azure of the sky, and the appearance of the population; and here the country of the Delta commences. Merruan thus gives a description of it:—"To an immense plain, where the horizon is not closed by any elevation of the ground, succeed fields admirably cultivated and intersected by a thousand canals, crossing in all directions, and which one could compare to the meshes of a net thrown on the ground. Here rise villages, composed of about thirty huts constructed with mud; there, stone villas surmounted by minarets and cupolas, shaded by palm groves. The population is active and laborious; not like the negroes, lying down like lizards, with their backs to the sun, during working hours; some draw up water for the irrigation of the earth, while others tie up the germ of corn. We have never seen human habitations giving a more perfect idea of a working bee-hive than such a village with its narrow and winding streets, where our eyes embrace the view from the height of the cars, without finding it possible to trace any sign of idleness." Near the village of Dahare we came in view of the Rosetta branch of the Nile. The river is very wide at this place, and the iron bridge between the two banks very ornamental. At Benal-Assal, one hour from Cairo, on the shore in a handsome situation, is an Italian palace belonging to Abbas-Pacha, but trees are wanting. What struck us as something singular was, on our right, a village built expressly for the breeding of pigeons; no other inhabitants but these dwelling in it. It is constructed of mud, and the palm-trees which surround it give it a peculiar and picturesque aspect. Near Cairo we had a faint view of the pyramids of Gizeh, and the two chains of mountains, the Lybian and the Arabic. It was two o'clock when we came in sight of the city. Cairo was built in 969 of the Christian era, by Gowler, general of the Sultan El-Moez, after the conquest of Egypt in the name of the Fatimite sultan of Moghareb. In commemoration of his conquest he named it El-Kabirah (the victorious), from which the French have made Caire. In leaving the station we had a strange scene;—the crowd was very great, the place filled with donkeys, carriages, and camels. We could hardly move; and Aline and I were carried by our dragoman, El-Adli, to the carriage which was to convey us to our quarters, the new English hotel; a commodious and beautiful building, situated on the Esbekyeh, the largest plaza in Cairo, surrounded on all sides by houses and palaces; handsome walks planted with sycamores, under the shade of which are many little café houses. The new hotel was commenced three years ago, but is far from being completed. How comfortable, clean, and luxurious we found it, compared to the one we had left in Alexandria. The table is excellent, the rooms large, airy, and fully furnished. As soon as we had taken lunch we selected a carriage for use during the time we should pass in Cairo. We chose a handsome open barouche, lined with cherry-colored silk, two large gray horses, an Egyptian driver with the customary yellow silk turban on his head; and with our runner dressed in white, some distance in front, we proceeded to Embabeh, or Boulak, to look at the dahabechs. There is no comparison to be made between Cairo and Alexandria; the latter has too much of the European character, while

Cairo is essentially Oriental. The road to Embabeh was through a large avenue occupied by foot-passengers—Greeks, Egyptians, Copts, and Europeans, all in their national costumes—while donkeys, camels, and carriages made it hard for them to perambulate. Such noise, such confusion! we were for some time amazed at it; still, being something new to us, we rather liked it. The port of Boulak is very animated; there were about thirty dahabeehs, all of which we visited, and our choice fell on the Pelican, which we baptized the Oriental. We engaged her after the owner had agreed to make all the changes suggested, and she will look well when all is ready. Night had come before we returned to the hotel, and we were just in time for dinner. The evening was passed by Aline and Mr. Rogers reading, while I dictated to Tom the agreement with our dragoman furnished by our Consul. As it may be found interesting for my friends in the New World to know on what conditions and in what manner a Nile voyage is made, I will transcribe it here.

"This contract, made this fourteenth day of December, in the year one thousand eight hundred and sixty-seven, between Thomas T. Ferris and J. S. Rogers, citizens of the United States of America, parties of the first part, and Mohammed El-Adli, dragoman, party of the second part, witnesseth:

"1. The said Mohammed El-Adli agrees to act as dragoman for the parties of the first part (consisting of said Ferris and Rogers, Mrs. Ferris and another lady, Miss Kraft, four persons altogether), at and from Cairo, up the river Nile to the first or second cataract, as may be decided by the parties of the first part, and back to Cairo; making such stops and excursions as said parties of the first part may direct.

"2. The said Mohammed El-Adli agrees to furnish in clean and excellent order, for the use of said parties of the first part, the dahabeeh named Oriental (now Pelican), already selected for the voyage; the same to be equipped complete with beds, lights, table, wash, and bed linen, cooking utensils, a complete first-class canteen, and all furniture usual or necessary for the complete comfort of the voyagers. To furnish all meats, vegetables, fruits, preserves, tea, coffee, and provisions of the best quality, such as will compose the most perfect cuisine known on the best Nile boats; to furnish a small boat or dingee, with oars, to be used as said parties of the first part may direct; to furnish a good crew of twelve men, besides a competent reiz, rudderman, and boy; to furnish a first-class cook and waiter, all of whom shall be at all times subject to and obey the orders of said parties of the first part, and none of whom shall at any time leave the dahabeeh without the order or consent of the said parties of the first part previously given.

"3. The said Mohammed El-Adli agrees that throughout the voyage the cabins, rooms, and everything shall be kept clean and orderly; bed, table, and wash linen changed as often as may be directed by the parties of the first part, and the clothes of the voyagers washed and ironed whenever desired.

"4. As to the management of the dahabeeh, it is agreed that in ascending the river the dahabeeh shall sail day and night when the wind is fair, and that when the wind is unfavorable, or there is a calm, the crew shall track or tow the dahabeeh from sunrise to sunset. In descending the river, the men shall row continuously day and night during a calm, shall sail when the wind is fair, and shall be allowed to float down during a head-wind. At all times when sailing, the sheet shall always be held in the hands of one of the crew, and not tied or fastened. And the dahabeeh shall be provided with sufficient ballast for entire safety and security.

"5. The said Mohammed El-Adli agrees to furnish meals at such hours and of such dishes as may be directed by the said parties of the first part. The said Mohammed El-Adli will pay for all provisions and eatables, wages of cook and servants, as well as for the dahabeeh, all guides, tribute and backsheesh, for all donkeys or other means of conveyance, at each and every place visited. The wines and liquors, however, will be provided by the said parties of the first part at their own expense.

"6. The said Mohammed El-Adli agrees that the decks shall be thoroughly washed every day before eight o'clock (A.M.), European time, and will appoint some suitable person of the crew to attend to this duty. He agrees further, to make himself responsible for the correct and respectful behavior of the reis, crew, cook, and servants. Should the conduct of any of these become offensive to any member of the parties of the first part, the said Mohammed El-Adli agrees to discharge the offending person or persons and substitute others.

"7. No other passengers or merchandise shall be

taken on board the dahabeeh without the express consent of the said parties of the first part.

"8. It is agreed that in ascending the river the dahabeeh shall stop one day for baking bread at each of these two places, Siout, and Esneh, but no other stops are to be made, except such as said parties of the first part may direct.

"9. In case the voyage is continued to the second cataract, the whole expense of carrying the dahabeeh across the first cataract will be borne by the said Mohammed El-Adli.

"10. In consideration of the faithful performance in all respects of this contract on the part of the said Mohammed El-Adli, the said parties of the first part will pay to the said Mohammed El-Adli as follows: For the voyage to the first cataract and back, four hundred and twenty pounds sterling; or for the voyage to the second cataract and back (in case the said parties of the first part should choose to go to the second cataract), six hundred and thirty pounds sterling. These sums to be in full payment in each case, unless the said parties of the first part should detain the dahabeeh at any place or places, for the purpose of sight-seeing or their own pleasure, more than thirty days altogether, which are allowed for stoppages in case of the full voyage to the second cataract and back; or twenty days allowed for stoppages, in case of the voyage to the first cataract and back. The days of stoppages to be computed from sunset of one day to sunset of the next following day. Odd hours to be reckoned as parts of a day. The voyage will begin when the dahabeeh actually starts from Cairo to ascend the river. It is expressly agreed, however, that the dahabeeh shall be ready at Cairo, at the disposal of the parties of the first part, on the nineteenth instant.

"In case the said parties of the first part should require stoppages more than thirty days in the full voyage, and in consequence of such stoppages the full voyage is prolonged more than ninety days, then the said parties of the first part will pay for every such day in excess of ninety days, or sixty days, as the case may be, at the rate of seven pounds sterling.

"11. The sum of three hundred pounds sterling will be paid in Cairo on signing the present, and the residue in Cairo after the completion of the voyage.

"12. It is agreed between both parties that the parties of the first part may adjoin one or two more persons for the present voyage on paying eighty pounds sterling for each for the full voyage to the second cataract, or fifty-three pounds sterling for the voyage to the first cataract.

"13. It is agreed by both parties that any dispute which may arise as to the interpretation of this contract shall be referred to the American Consul-General for Egypt, or his representative, whose decision shall be final.

"In witness whereof the said Ferris and Rogers, members of the party of the first part, have hereunto signed their names, and Mohammed El-Adli has hereto affixed his seal, the day and year hereinbefore mentioned.

"Thos. T. Ferris.
"J. S. Rogers.
[Seal] "Mohammed El-Adli.

"Consulate-General of the United States of America for Egypt. This fourteenth day of December, 1867, personally appeared before me, Charles Hale, Consul-General of the United States of America, the within-named Thomas T. Ferris, citizen of the United States, and J. S. Rogers, citizen of the United States, who signed the witnessed contract in my presence, and Mohammed El-Adli, who affixed his seal in my presence, all of whom acknowledged the within contract to be their free act and deed.

"Witness my hand and seal of office,
"CHARLES HALE."

[CONSULATE SEAL OF THE UNITED STATES.]

SATURDAY, December 14.

Ten o'clock striking, and we are hardly through breakfast. "Too late, too late," says Tom. "If you want to see Cairo you must keep better hours and be off at nine o'clock." Very well, sir, we will. While the gentlemen were out shopping, and ordering the flags and streamers, I read to Aline the description of Cairo given in the guide-books; but what book can give a correct idea of the motley crowd and their animated features,—such a view as that which we had from our windows on the balcony fronting the Esbekyeh? Tom says it is quite impossible to give an accurate description to others of the vivid scene we have constantly before us. I have found it so, and know that all I can say will seem poor compared to the reality. The governors, with Thaddeus, our guide, came back at three o'clock P.M., and we being ready, spent the rest of the afternoon visiting Old Cairo. We followed the occidental part of the city until Bab-es-Seideh-Zeineh, a quarter entirely Arabic, with a number of little mosques and a few pretty Arabian fountains; and we particularly admired a mosque, so very picturesque, with its stone door and its handsome clump of trees. Then, leaving on our left high heaps of rubbish, which bounds Cairo on the south, we came to the head of the aqueduct of the citadel. A heavy building contains the sakyeh, which is used to raise the water, and near by is an old sycamore, under whose shade, protected from the hot rays of the sun, lounge the camel and donkey drivers; a pretty group for a painter. Following a shaded avenue we arrived at Old Cairo. This city was founded by Amrou, general of the Caliph Omar, at the time of the conquest of Egypt, A.D. 640. As he was besieging a castle called Babylon, his tent was planted a little to the north of the place invested, and his wish was that in commemoration of it the city, whose construction was commenced on the place where he had encamped, would take the name of Fostat, a word in Arabic meaning tent. Fostat remained the Mussulman capital of Egypt until the foundation of Cairo, in A.D. 969. In 1168, at the time of the irruption of the crusaders into Lower Egypt, the Saracens, fearing that Fostat would fall into the hands of the Christians, set fire to it: it burned fifty-four days, and this was its definitive ruin. There is a population at present of almost three thousand inhabitants, nearly all of whom are Copts, who are the last broken remains of the ancient Egyptian race. They have kept their Christian faith unbroken, and thus perpetuated the old Pharaonic nationality, as well as the language and the name of their race. One hundred and fifty thousand Copts, scattered over the land, are all that remain of the people of Sesostris and of the Ptolemies. We passed through narrow and irregular streets, some of them covered with matting as a protection from the rays of the sun. The shops are very small, not more than five feet wide, and few of them are clean. We remarked also in Cairo, still more than in Alexandria, that a large proportion of the children were afflicted with sore eyes; the number is incredible. We asked Thaddeus the cause, and he replied that until two years of age no mother thinks of washing her child, being afraid that if it were clean and pretty, the evil eye would look upon him. What profound ignorance and barbarism! These people must be hard-hearted, or how can they endure the sight of these poor little sufferers, who almost all the time are obliged to hide their faces, not being able to endure the rays of the sun. How can they allow the accumulation of matter to close the eyelids, and the flies to settle thereon as they do? Sometimes the eyes are covered with them, and it is a disgusting sight. Feelings of anger, sadness, and pity creep over you in looking at it! Are we not in the nineteenth century? Shame be on the government which, instead of trying by all means in its power to enlighten the people given by God to its keeping, leaves them each succeeding year to sink lower and lower in degradation and abasement!

CHAPTER IV.

CAIRO — ITS MOSQUES — BAZARS — THE PYRAMIDS — THE TOMBS AND SPHINX — HELIOPOLIS — THE DERVISHES.

SUNDAY, December 15, 1867.

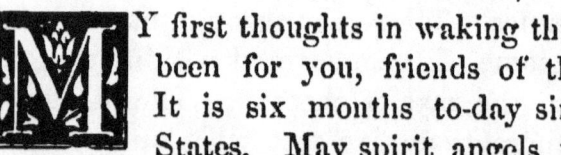

MY first thoughts in waking this morning have been for you, friends of the New World. It is six months to-day since we left the States. May spirit angels with their rapid wings bring to you our good wishes and kisses! We breakfasted at eight, and at nine our carriage took us to the Citadel. The weather was cold and pleasant, like an autumn day in America; the sky of an azure blue. The Citadel dates from the end of the twelfth century, and is the work of the celebrated Youssouf-Salah-Eddin (Saladin), who also had a palace built there, near a mosque. This palace, which afterwards became the residence of the sultans, was remarkable for a large square hall, supported by thirty-two rose granite columns taken from the most ancient Greek and Roman temples, and which were surmounted by as many Pharaonic chapiters brought from Memphis. This building, which was allowed to go to ruin, was entirely destroyed in 1829, to give place to the new mosque of Mohammed Ali. Our first visit after passing under the heavy doors of the Citadel, where we were saluted by soldiers presenting arms, was to this elegant mosque. Woollen slippers were put over our shoes, and we proceeded to the yard, which is surrounded by columns cut in handsome alabaster. In the centre is the fountain of ablution, of an octagon form, but the ornamentations are too heavy. On the northwestern gallery is a square tower, or Chinese pavilion, black and gold above, holding a clock which was presented by King Louis Philippe to Mohammed Ali; rather a poor present, and we did not admire it. Within, and near the entrance door, is a gallery supported by a row of small columns, to the right of which is the tomb of Mohammed Ali. The mosque itself is surmounted by a great cupola flanked by four half-cupolas, with four little octagon domes, one in each angle. The cupola is supported by four large pillars, parts of them of that elegant oriental alabaster whose amber tint and transparency has the character and appearance of the opal. The decorations are green and gold. When we entered, some Moslems, with their faces on the ground, were making their devotions. The open windows permitted the sunbeams to enter; numerous birds have built their nests in the mosque, and by their song were also praising the King of creation. We felt that never had we entered a church whose music impressed us with a more religious feeling than the song of these birds. Having remained sufficiently long to examine the interior, we left by another gate leading on to a platform, whence extended a magnificent view far away beyond and beneath us. At our feet lay the *Place* Roumeilch, with the Sultan Hassan Mosque; a little farther to the left that of Touloun, and above it the great city, bristling with minarets. In the confused mass of terraces, the streets have only the appearance of dark fissures. Large white palaces make a show near the bushy trees of the Esbekyeh, which seems to touch Boulak. Beyond, the Nile flows slowly in its wide bed, edged by a line of rich green, and disappears in the plains of the Delta; while farther off still, imposing even at such a distance, are the pyramids of Gizeh, d'Abousir, and Sackarah. On our way to visit the Viceroy's palace we stopped at the spot where the massacre of the Mamelouks took place, in 1811. The chief, Emir-bey, to escape death, spurred his horse over the parapet, a fearful descent of over fifty feet, and although the horse was instantly killed, the rider was not only uninjured but sprang up and ran away—the only one who escaped the dreadful power of the ambitious Ali. The only two things worthy of remark in the Viceroy's palace are the alabaster bath-room and the council chamber, in which (on a *dais*) Ismail Pacha's chair is surmounted by a crown richly studded with real stones. Leaving the palace, we next visited Joseph's Well. Some persons, not remembering particularly the story in the Bible, confound this with the place where Joseph's brethren threw him, after having sold him to the Egyptians. But the account of historians is, that this well was discovered and cleaned out by Saladin Joseph. It is dug out of the solid rock, square, and having a depth of three hundred and forty-nine feet. There is an inclined plane which circuits about the shaft, gradually descending at quite a steep angle, by means of which men, and even animals, can reach the bottom, which is thought to be below the level of the Nile. The descent is two stories, and quite dark, rendering it necessary to be helped by the Arabs. A sakyeh, propelled by two oxen, elevates water to the first level, whence a second one brings it to the surface. From the Citadel we went to the Sultan Hassan Mosque, which is on the Roumeileh *plaza*. It is said to be the handsomest and oldest in Cairo; and indeed we found it so old and broken down that we took but a cursory view of it, and from a balcony observed with much more interest the strange spectacle which Roumeileh *plaza* presented.

It was market day; the crowd compact and noisy. Stores of all kinds, on all sides of the plaza, presented to the public a strange assortment of goods, while numbers of merchants, carrying their merchandise on their backs, were offering it at cheap prices. One had common cashmere, another fez caps, and others bright dresses or loose robes. It was curious to see a dirty fellow exchanging a filthy cap for a bright new one, making the contrast with his faded suit still more apparent. Women, with their long, ugly black masks, were beating down the prices of new dresses; men, with water in *goulis*, were offering it to the thirsty; while boys leading donkeys, loaded with sheepskins filled with water, were sprinkling the streets. The varieties of costumes, the noise, crowd, dust, and I may say the dirt, made it a curious picture to look upon. From Hassan Mosque we went to that of Touloun, and then took a ride through the bazars. Here the occupants are also busy-looking, presenting the same variety of costume. The streets are narrow; many having matting spread overhead to protect the inhabitants from the burning rays of the sun; and the oriental houses, alternately red and white, present a similar appearance to the mosques. The first story is of stone, and the upper ones of brick; the windows have wire lattices of diversified patterns. We can now see the use of having a runner; the crowd is so dense, and the streets not being paved, one cannot hear the tramping of the horses; the runner halloos "Place! place!" and the crowd disperses as if by magic; men and donkeys stand close to the walls or stores, and we pass without hurting anybody. In the Turkish bazar the streets are so narrow one can only pass on foot or on donkeys; we therefore alighted from the carriage, and walked through. Tom bought himself a handsome suit, which becomes him exceedingly. We returned to the hotel for lunch at one o'clock, and in the afternoon went to Choubra, a pleasure-ground of the late Mehemet Ali, one hour's ride from Cairo, on the shore of the Nile. The road leading to it is planted with acacias and sycamores, forming a charming avenue impenetrable to the sun. The gardens of Choubra are laid out in straight alleys, and are remarkable for the quantities of flowers, orange, lemon, and date trees. A beautiful basin, of Carrara marble, surrounded by a balustrade, also in marble; a colonnade with kiosques advancing in the water; while at each angle a parlor richly decorated, excited our admiration. In one of the parlors was the portrait of Mehemet Ali, also an elegant vase of Sèvres, a present probably of the King of France. We heard that this garden had been designed and ornamented to serve as a pleasure-ground for the harem of Mohammed Ali. When it was the Pacha's wish, his ladies were permitted to come here and enjoy one or two days of liberty, and their principal amusements at such times were rowing in small boats on the water of the basin, or propelling little carriages on the pavement at the sides.

MONDAY, December 16,

Was passed in shopping and looking at the preparations on our boat.

TUESDAY, December 17,

Was a day whose remembrance will be sweet in after years. At seven o'clock we mounted on donkeys chosen by Thaddeus, and, followed by several guides, left the hotel to visit the great Pyramids of Gizeh. The weather was cold, but clear, much the better for the donkey ride of eight miles we had before us—five miles to Old Cairo, and, after crossing the water, three miles from the village of Gizeh to the Pyramids. We took the great avenue of Ibrahim Pacha, which is planted with majestic-looking trees, and *"au galop"* swift gazelles. What a glorious ride we had! it was the first time that we had mounted these light, strong, and gracious animals during our stay in Egypt, and we were delighted with them; our gallop would not have been despised by any good horseman. After passing the bazars of Old Cairo we stopped on the shore; our guides helped us to dismount, and Thaddeus went to make arrangements for crossing the river on one of the ferry-boats. But here we had a scene which was not at all pleasant. About twenty boats are

3

employed crossing the river at this point, each one in turn. It appears that it was not the turn of the one which was to take us over, and the boatman had a fight with those who considered their rights invaded. The Egyptians are very noisy and loquacious, and soon the battle became general. The two opponents seized each other by the throat, in the midst of the screaming and gesticulations of thirty or forty around, who gradually became more excited, until all joined. After half an hour of pushing and jolting they separated, either from fatigue or mutual consent, and as nobody was hurt we succeeded in getting the right boat, and crossed the river among a crowd of natives. We looked upon it as an Egyptian scene, and were much amused. Arrived at Gizeh, we remounted and pursued our way. My saddle required arrangement, and consequently, when ready, I was the last, with only my guide and Thaddeus. While galloping through the village to overtake the party, my donkey stumbled and fell, but, happily, I was able to disengage my foot from the stirrup, and jumped to the ground without being hurt. Thaddeus helped me to remount, and soon we rejoined the others. Leaving Gizeh, we passed through an irregular plain, planted with groves of palm-trees, and scattered here and there were a few Arabian villages; we followed the road straight to the Pyramids, having on our right the battle-field of Napoleon. The more you advance, the more the three great monuments increase in size and in imposing aspect, especially as you see them between the palms. Nothing grander can be conceived than this vast green plain, with its rich groves, and behind as background the three colossi, detaching themselves from the fawn-colored border of the desert, overflowing with light. A new road, intended for a railway, has been lately built, said to be for the purpose of conveying the Empress Eugénie to the Pyramids, when she will pay a visit to the Pacha; it was the first news we had of it. Before arriving at the Pyramids, the water of the Nile not having all disappeared from the canal, we had to cross it three times, carried by the Arabs, who were there in numbers, awaiting the arrival of travellers. We were each of us compelled to have four of them, and it was no easy job for either party. The water in some places was so deep that they were up to their waists, and we did not feel perfectly safe on their shoulders. I know, for my part, I was afraid that at any moment I might accidentally take a cold bath, but there was probably no danger, and we arrived safely at the Pyramids, after walking for nearly half an hour in the desert. I cannot say that I like its monotonous appearance, nor do I participate in the pleasure which some persons find in crossing it; and for two, three, and four weeks, having no other view than the sand reflecting the rays of the sun. We rested for some time at the foot of the Pyramids, surrounded by fifty Arabs, each one anxious to help us in the ascent, and, while we were waiting, wishing to display their skill in going up and down the great Cheops. Their language was very amusing, and it is astonishing how readily they pick up foreign tongues. Some of them spoke French, German, English, and Italian well enough to be understood. "Want to see Arab go up the Pyramid in five minutes, up and down; want to see it? a shilling." When we sought for the cleanest of them to help us, they chattered, "Me clean, me a good Arab; leeve over there in one of these villages; have a clean house." Well, we made our choice and commenced the ascent, which is very difficult, the steps being high and rough, some of them measuring about three feet and a half, so that it is hard to make the ascent without help. Mr. Rogers went first; I followed; Tom and Aline came last. The Pyramid is very steep, and measures four hundred and twenty-two feet vertically. Each of my hands was taken by an Arab, while two behind pushed me. After going up ten or twelve steps I commenced to feel quite nervous, and was afraid of getting the vertigo; so looking neither right nor left, but straight before me, I ascended as quickly as any lady ever did, to the astonishment of my four Bedouins. I had the fortune to choose good ones, who did not pull me too rudely, nor annoy me by continually asking for backsheesh. They have an amusing song with which they treat you during the ascent and descent: "Me have a good mistress; if she satisfy, me satisfy; give Arab plenty of backsheesh." I only rested once, and arrived on the platform of the Pyramid in twelve minutes. Mr. Rogers was there two minutes before me. I sat down, and needed at least four minutes to regain my breath. Tom then made his appearance, having been detained looking after Aline, who, after going up part of the way, found it too difficult, and returned. The view we had from the platform was admirable, the sun coloring the immense, attractive, and fascinating panorama.

Before us the Nile was stretching forth in the midst of a great carpet of verdure, where, strewed as gray spots, are seen the narrow, straggling villages of Gizeh, Fostat, and Boulak; beyond, the tall minarets and domes of Cairo, its high citadel, and the summits of the Makattam; on the right, the Pyramids, and the fields where Memphis once was; at all the other points of the horizon, a desert waste. Nothing is more striking than the contrast of the green valley of the Nile against the warm tints of the sand, which offers to the view an extensive, knobbed, and rugged surface, dotted with undecided-shaped red and fawn-colored hills, in the midst of which the playing light produces effects the most powerful and unexpected. Having descended, we found Aline waiting for us at the entrance to the interior chambers, in a great state of excitement. It appears when she desired to go down, the Arabs, thinking they would not get any backsheesh, pretended they did not understand her; they pulled her so much that her dress was torn, and it was only by promising them "many" backsheesh she could manage to be obeyed. We took our lunch amid the confusion created by the noise and chattering of fifty Arabs standing around; when speaking together, it always seems as though they are quarrelling. All had some curiosities and antiquities to offer for sale. We bought a few, as a reminiscence of Cheops, and, attended by our guides, visited the interior chambers. One is called the king's chamber, the other, the queen's. In the former is still a sarcophagus, without ornaments or hieroglyphics, in which the royal mummy was deposited. The rooms were so close and warm, and also so difficult of access, that we were glad to make our exit and breathe the fresh air again.

Near the Pyramids are situated numerous tombs and the Sphinx; the principal of the former being near the small pyramids, on a large esplanade of basaltic rocks, is literally honeycombed with sepulchral pits, which in the centre are disposed six rows deep. The greater number belonged to high functionaries and eminent personages of the first Pharaoh's court. To the east of the second pyramid is the celebrated Sphinx. The accumulated sand of ages covers all the inferior part; but the face, though mutilated and broken, is still grand. It is the representation of a lion *couchant*, with a human head and neck, measuring from the chin to the tip of the forehead about thirty feet, cut in a mass of rock, and dates from the XVIIIth dynasty. At three o'clock we took leave of our escort, having given twenty dollars of backsheesh, and yet were asked for more. We again mounted our donkeys, and on our way back, asked ourselves which had most amused us: the Pyramids or the Arabs? At five P.M. we arrived at the hotel, very tired; I particularly so, not being accustomed to riding much on *donkey-back*. Before dinner we took a bath, in order to free ourselves of any Egyptian plagues, that might have domiciled themselves on our persons; and passed the evening in company with Mr. Tibbets, and Mr. Forrest, the agreeable proprietor of the hotel. Aline amused herself in playing billiards with Mr. Forrest and Tom; but I felt so fatigued that at eight o'clock I retired.

THURSDAY, December 19.

Yesterday and to-day have been passed in looking at the preparations on the boat, and shopping.

It is not unusual that parties proposing to ascend the Nile, having made selection of a satisfactory boat or dahabeeh, are not pleased with the name adopted by the owner, or perhaps selected by the occupants of a former year. Our boat, as I have previously stated, was named the Pelican, which by general consent we changed to Oriental. As there are no European painters in Cairo, it is necessary to give the owner of the boat an exact copy of the lettering desired, and a half sovereign. The Arab artist daubs it on as well as he is able, without comprehending in the least what he is doing. Our " Oriental," indeed, was executed so badly that Tom and Mr. Rogers were compelled to turn sign-painters, erase the Arab's work, and repaint the name, which they did in a really artistic and workmanlike manner. An English party who had engaged a neighboring craft were not so successful. Determining to rechristen her the Sphinx, they had given a slip of paper with the word carefully printed thereon to the owner, who promised to have it ready the night before their departure. Imagine their horror, upon arriving the next morning, and everything complete, to find the name very cleverly painted ˙xᴎɪΗdS

FRIDAY, December 20.

In the morning we drove to Heliopolis, which takes about two hours to reach from Cairo, and is the prettiest drive we have yet taken in Egypt. Nothing is left of the once beautiful city; no remains are to be seen of the handsome Temple of the Sun, and the long avenue of sphinxes and obelisks. Several of them have been taken to Alexandria, and those known as Cleopatra's Needles came hence; one is in Rome, and some say that the one in Paris also came from Heliopolis, which is a mistake, however, as it came from Luxor. The only obelisk remaining is twenty-one metres in height, and the most ancient in all Egypt. Returning to the city, we stopped at Matarieh to see the Virgin Tree, a beautiful sycamore, under which it is said Joseph and Mary, with the Holy Child, rested during a night as they were travelling into Egypt. Whether true or not, the roots are of an incredible age, undoubtedly from the fact that century after century they seem to be renewed by shoots succeeding the decaying trunk. The present tree is an irregular bunch of trunks grown together, making a circumference of over thirty feet, with a comparatively scanty foliage on its huge limbs.

In the afternoon we went to see the whirling dervishes. The room in which the religious waltz takes place is similar to a dancing-room or theatre. A floor smoothly waxed, and surrounded by a balustrade, is in the centre; light colonnades support a gallery for the women and true Mussulmen, the Europeans being seated on chairs around the balustrade. We there met Mr. Tibbets, and several other persons from the hotel. After waiting some time, the dervishes made their appearance, preceded by a high priest, who, with his hands crossed upon his breast, walked solemnly to a piece of carpet spread on the floor, and, after bowing twice, sat down upon it. His followers, after bowing respectfully to him, took their places, and for one or two minutes kept a profound silence, with their heads leaning on their breasts. The head-dress of these Mussulman monks consists of a thick brown felt cap, looking exactly like an inverted flower-pot. A vest and waistcoat of unbleached muslin; an immense plaited skirt of the same color; and narrow white drawers complete their costume. The prayer commenced, and with it the genuflexions, the prostrations, the ordinary affectation of the Mussulman worship, which would be laughable were it not for the conviction of their sincerity and the gravity of the faithful. For a while Aline and I could hardly restrain ourselves, and it was only by the exercise of great self-control that we succeeded in keeping serious. The psalmody of the Koran was accompanied by flutes and darboukas; the latter marking the rhythm, while the flutes performed in unison a chant, in an elevated tone and of infinite sweetness. Immovable in the midst of the enclosure, the dervishes seemed to be intoxicated with that music so delicately barbarous. After a time one of them opened his arms, raised them, and commenced to turn slowly, then faster, and still faster; a second, then a third one imitated him, until at length all of them joined in an irresistible whirling, making us feel quite dizzy looking at them turning so monotonously, and we did not understand how they could continue it so long. It was amusing to notice the profound exaltation expressed on their faces, their eyes fixed towards heaven, the hands crossed on the breast, turning and turning—they seemed to be in a perfect ecstasy. All at once they

3*

stopped, and remained quiet for a few minutes; then, the music commencing again quicker than ever, they recommenced their waltzing, excited more and more by the singing of the imaums above in the gallery. Thaddeus told us it would continue thus until the end, so we retired, and, entering our carriage, did a little shopping, and afterwards made a visit to our boat. Everything will be ready by to-morrow. We reached the hotel in time for dinner, and were surprised to find a band of music, which gave us as many tunes as we had courses. About nine o'clock in the evening all the ladies and gentlemen were invited to the dining-room, "*sans cérémonie,*" to have a dance. Tom renewed acquaintance with Lord Francis Conyngham, who visited America ten years ago, and had often been entertained by him. Lord Francis was delighted to meet him again, and introduced him to his lady, the daughter of the Marquis of Tredegar. They arrived yesterday, with three English gentlemen, Rev. Mr. Wight, Rev. R. W. Yukes, and Mr. Hamson. They intend going up the Nile as far as the first cataract only, their time being limited, and have engaged two dahabeehs, the " Bund " for Lord and Lady Conyngham, while the other gentlemen will occupy the " No Name "! Their boats will probably be ready by next Tuesday, and if the wind fails until that time, perhaps we will start together. Tom introduced us to Lord Conyngham, who invited us to dance: Aline accepted, but I had to refuse, feeling still too fatigued from my Pyramid ascension to indulge in a waltz. An American family named Messenger, from Brooklyn, consisting of father, mother, and two daughters, has just arrived, and intend going up the Nile as far as the second cataract. At dinner, to-day, we were joined by Mr. Forrest and an English General, on his way to India, whose name I have forgotten, and among the guests whom Mr. Forrest pointed out to us was the celebrated Lady Franklin, also *en route* for India.

CHAPTER V.

OUR DAHABEEH—ITS CREW—THE START—FIRST DAYS ON THE NILE—CHRISTMAS ILLUMINATION—A DANGEROUS WEAPON—COMPETITION—WASHING-DAY.

SATURDAY, December 21, 1867.

ALL our morning and part of the afternoon were devoted to shopping, and I do not know when we will finish; so many little things are required for so long a journey. At four o'clock we left the hotel, after thanking Mr. Forrest for all his kindness to us during our stay, and arrived at five with our baggage on board our dahabeeh. El-Adli was not there, but we were received by the crew in a respectful and pleasant manner. Abousaid, our private servant, had the table set ready for dinner, and everything appeared truly oriental, except our *salon* and table: they looked so cheerful and Parisian that we felt at home at once, and sat down to the best dinner we had eaten since leaving Paris. We had soup, four courses, pastry, and dessert—counting eleven dishes. The quality and style of the cooking, the neatness and taste displayed, relieved us of any apprehension regarding the merit of our cook and waiters. Our cook Gabriel is second to none on the Nile, very neat, prompt, and good-natured, abstaining like all the crew, captain and servants, from intoxicating drinks. After dinner we arranged the state-rooms which had been assigned to each of us, and El-Adli having arrived gave orders that the "Oriental" should be moored in the stream, ready to take advantage of the first fair wind. We afterwards went on deck, and enjoyed exceedingly the loveliness of our first evening on the Nile, while twenty lanterns lighted up and fixed to the yard marked the event. Two dahabeehs were moored not far from us: one, named the "Crocodile," under English colors, having two gentlemen on board with whom we became acquainted while at the New Hotel; the other, named the "Estella," under German colors, with a party of four—two English and two German—and we will probably all start together. What a lovely evening! The sky, of a deep blue, is lighted up only by the stars. Our fifteen men, dressed in dark loose robes, white trousers, with white and red turbans, are seated in a circle playing on drums and tambourines, an accompaniment to their peculiarly plaintive Arab song. Our dragoman, the reis, steersman, cook, and boy are grouped around them on the deck, and the lanterns under the awning light up the dusky countenances of the crew, forming in all a very interesting study. We took the small-boat and rowed down the river, to take a look at our dahabeeh, while the song floats to us from afar. The "Crocodile" and "Estella" have hung up some lights also. At ten we return to our boat and retire for the night.

SUNDAY, December 22.

We arose at eight o'clock, took a very good breakfast at nine, consisting of three courses and fruits, with excellent coffee. At ten, Thaddeus having arrived with the carriage, we drove to the English chapel in Cairo, where the Rev. Mr. Wight, assisted by the Rev. Mr. Yukes, was to preach. Being a little late, we found upon entering that the congregation were assembled and prayers already commenced. The sermon was poor, but the hymns were sung beautifully, and, as we were strangers in a foreign land, selected most appropriately for the occasion. After church Mr. Forrest invited us to take lunch at the hotel, but we declined, fearing to spoil our appetites for dinner. We drove to the hotel, however, and, attended by several gentlemen, among them Lord Conyngham, went on top of the house, which affords a view almost as beautiful as the one we had from the Citadel. At two we were back at our new *home*, of which I shall now give a description.

Our dahabeeh is built of wood, with a large saloon, four state-rooms, and a small saloon in the stern—the whole occupying about one-half the length of the boat. She is very neatly painted and decorated, perfectly clean, very nicely furnished, with blue and gold damask curtains, and similar draperies at the doors; divans and chairs to match; tables, large French mirrors, pictures, rich carpets, and an excellent and full supply of dinner and kitchen ware, bed and table linen, silverware, etc., etc. The closets, bath-room, water-filterer, pantry, and lastly the kitchen, on the bow of the boat, are all in perfect order. The quarter-deck is well supplied with woollen damask divans, marble-top table, chairs, etc. We found her measurement to be 96 feet in length, by

14½ in breadth; the saloon, 12 by 12; state-rooms, 6 by 4 feet 8; after saloon, 9 by 10. She draws about thirty-three inches of water, has the cabins sunk twenty-eight inches below deck, the height of which is six and a half feet. The gunwale is eleven inches above deck, and twenty-nine inches out of water. She carries, on a mast stepped well forward, a large lateen sail, extending on a spar 120 feet in length, which is lashed to the head of the mast, and shifted forward of it. A smaller mast is stepped entirely aft of the helm or tiller, on which a similar sail, less than a quarter the size of the foresail, is lashed in the same manner, and the sheet runs through a projecting boom from the stern. She has twelve oars, and a crew consisting of the captain, second captain, twelve men, steersman, cook, and boy. We have a far greater provision of flags than any boat we have seen on the Nile. From the peak of the main-yard our streamer, of which the first twenty feet is blue and stars, with the rest white and red, waves seventy-two feet from its halliard. A similar extra one is attached to the small yard, being thirty-six feet long, the ordinary length of those in use. From the small mast aft waves the American flag, 7 by 12. A red flag, 7 by 12, with the word *Oriental*, in white letters, is hoisted generally below the long pennant, while a huge white flag, twenty feet by nine feet, with the words *New York*, in black letters, is hoisted on extra occasions on a halliard extending half way up the main-yard; and one hundred and ten red, white, and blue lanterns are ready for illuminations.

MONDAY, December 23,

Finds us still at anchor, with a light head-wind. After lunch Tom and Aline went again to the bazars shopping, while Mr. Rogers and I remained on board. At three the wind changed. We perceived the *Estella* and *Crocodile* preparing to spread their sails; how unfortunate that Tom and Aline were out, for it delayed us several hours in starting. All our sailors returned from shore; suddenly El-Adli arrived in great haste, and gave the signal of departure. He had sent a man of the crew to find Mr. and Mrs. Ferris, with instructions to meet us at Old Cairo. So at half-past three, half an hour behind the *Crocodile* and *Estella*, we tripped anchor and commenced our voyage. I went upon deck to enjoy the sight, with all my enthusiastic feelings at their height. How splendid does our dahabeeh look! how gracefully do our streamers fly in the air! Our bellying sails, with a dark border, look beautiful. What a pity Tom and Aline are away! how they would enjoy this too! What a glorious sunset! I have seldom witnessed one so brilliant. The little sails on the opposite shore are reflected clearly on the water; the sky, from blue, changes to more than twenty colors, until finally the orb sinks below the horizon towards Gizeh and the Pyramids, coloring all the surroundings with a golden tint. The wind was fresh, but Mr. Rogers and myself did not move from the deck. No twilight intervening between day and night, we were soon enveloped in total darkness. The time was nearly six, and I was going to tell Mohammed to light our signal lanterns, when I thought I recognized the voice of Aline coming from a little boat on the river. We called loudly, and were answered. Having waited for more than one hour at Old Cairo in an open carriage, being cold and tired, they resolved to come in search of us, and happily had crossed our way. We took a late dinner and then went upon deck to enjoy the sailing; but the wind had died out, so we anchored a short distance beyond the island of Rhoda, having passed the *Crocodile*, while the *Estella* was still ahead of us.

TUESDAY, December 24.

The weather beautiful, but calm; the men tracked or towed the boat all the morning. At ten o'clock, the wind having changed, we spread our sail, and soon passed the *Estella*, which had run aground on a sand-bank. We enjoy our quiet life, a correct idea of which will be found in the following extract from Mr. Warren's description of "Life on a Nile Boat":—"The charm of the life on a Nile-boat is not to be met with in a steamer, or in any other way of locomotion. It consists of the traveller being a perfect king on his dahabeeh, master of her movements, stopping when and where he pleases, with servants to do his bidding. If he is fond of sporting, myriads of wildfowl abound along the banks of the river. His boat has, besides all the comforts of a hotel, professed cooks that excite his wonder by the variety and quality of the dishes served up by well-trained and painstaking servants. The air is balsamic, the sky clear, such as is only experienced in Egypt; the climate is perpetual spring, without a drop of rain, while the insensible gliding of the boat along the stream invites to charming recreation in writing, drawing, reading, etc. Such a home on the Nile, with its serene cheerfulness and freedom from all restraint, has a charm and novelty for its season without satiety. Cut off as it were from the world (except now and then meeting a friend afloat), business, politics, cares of all kinds, everything is forgotten but country and friends left behind, in this slowly moving of the panorama of a world so full of wonders, containing the monuments of an age and people challenging the admiration of every beholder." We stopped tracking at six, tied up to the shore, and slept at Sorfaye.

Wednesday, December 25.

A beautiful morning, the sky of such a deep blue, and all of us in fine spirits. "Merry Christmas to all!" Breakfast being over, we read together a portion of the Bible relating to the birth of Christ; then Tom went upon deck and fired a salute in honor of the day, after which he and Mr. Rogers employed themselves preparing the lanterns for the illumination, Aline in reading the Bible, and I in writing. The day passed away quietly, with a head-wind, and at five we were served with a splendid dinner, worthy of more guests than our poor selves. Vermicelli potage, fricassee of chicken, roast lamb and cauliflower, peas, an enormous turkey with salad, dessert composed of twenty-two dishes, and four kinds of wine, the last of which was champagne, composed our Christmas feast. In the afternoon the men decorated our boat, and in order to go ashore we had to pass through an awning of palm-leaves. In the evening we had a splendid illumination—one hundred and ten red, white, and blue lanterns gracefully trimmed our boat, while the men all joined in singing their Arab songs and choruses, and thus passed away our pleasant evening.

THURSDAY, December 26.

We arose late; both Aline and I had a slight headache, which was probably the effect of the champagne yesterday. Tom was up at sunrise, and took a photographic view of the boat, and after breakfast passed his time in drawing. I sat down on the deck and sketched an Egyptian house, with some palm-trees. Just as I was finishing, we received a visit from the two Englishmen of the *Crocodile*, whose boat is anchored half a mile below, with the *Estella* near them. We remained tied up, as the head-wind was so strong it prevented the men tracking. The view we have before us is very poor; a mud village, with a few palm-trees. At four o'clock we commenced to track, but the adverse wind still continued so strong that we tied up for the night only a quarter of a mile beyond our position of the preceding day.

FRIDAY, December 27.

We arose at eight A.M., took breakfast at nine, and prepared for a walk on shore. Before leaving the boat, as Tom was examining his pistols, one of the side chambers of the old one suddenly exploded, and the ball, after striking against the wood of a chair, ricocheted on a divan. We were standing near him, and it was a benediction of God that one of us was not wounded or killed. The pistol was evidently not in good condition, and we felt how thankful we ought to be for our escape. How near is sorrow to happiness! death would have met one of us laughing.

Our walk was not very pleasant, as the furious wind blew the sand about us until our eyes were filled with it. Notwithstanding, we passed through the village of Chaobak, a very dirty place; the men lazily lounged on the ground, and a crowd of children followed us; our guides, with their sticks, had much trouble to prevent them coming too near. Having gone as far as the dahabeeh *Crocodile*, we there met the gentlemen of the *Estella*, but as the path to go on board was very steep, we concluded to let Tom pay his visit alone, and pursued our walk. The annoyance of the dust, though, soon tired us, and we returned to our dahabeeh, and passed our afternoon sewing and reading. At six o'clock a light breeze sprang up, and we commenced to sail; but it only lasted until eight, when we tied up, leaving the *Crocodile* and *Estella* some miles behind.

SATURDAY, December 28.

This morning, early, Tom went shooting, and killed two pigeons. After breakfast we all went out walking. The weather so delightful, the sky so resplendent, the air so pure and calm; what a charming climate during the winter months! The men having stopped tracking, Tom took a view of our dahabeeh, but still it did not prove to be as good as he would like it. He then went shooting again, and killed three more pigeons and some other birds. A slight breeze sprang up at twelve, and we got under way, but, lasting only for an hour, we tied up for the night at Kafr Laïet. In the evening, while playing *bézique*, we heard men shouting, and going on deck found it was the crew of the *Estella*, who, having missed the *American boat*, when daylight broke this morning, helped by a good breeze and the tracking of their men, followed until they had overtaken us, and tied up behind us for the night. A little later we went on deck, to listen to our men singing to the accompaniment of their music. They already perform much better than at first, and have dropped much of their timidity as we ascend the Nile. A pleasant evening, and we retired at ten.

SUNDAY, December 29.

An unusual sight—the sky is slightly clouded and it is quite cold. We tracked from seven till ten, and stopped for the men to take breakfast. Tom took a photographic view of the three dahabeehs; ours ahead, the *Crocodile* after, and the *Estella* last, which proved to be very good. He also took one of the upper-deck, with us all seated there. At twelve a slight breeze sprang up and we commenced sailing. One hour after, our reis (or captain), instead of sending the little boat, ran the dahabeeh ashore to get eggs and vegetables, brought by some women, and thus allowed the *Crocodile*, and afterwards the *Estella* to pass us, much to our annoyance. But the *Estella* soon ran aground, and we repassed her; and although Mr. Laming, one of her party, shouted to us that we would soon be aground also, we kept ahead, and at half-past five tied up near the *Crocodile*, with the *Estella* still behind us. During dinner, however, the *Estella*, contrary to the etiquette of the river, tracked past both boats and moored half a mile ahead of us.

Monday, December 30.

We had a slight wind from the south; the men tracked all the morning, while we went ashore for a walk. Tom took his gun, and killed several doves. Having a bad headache, I was compelled to retire to my berth in the afternoon. At six P.M. we tied up at Rakkah, or Rigga.

Tuesday, December 31.

Until three o'clock in the afternoon we remained tied up, being washing-day. There was no wind, and the *Estella* and the *Crocodile* tracked out of sight. Here was an amusing scene. Four men were washing, others fixing poles in the ground, and attaching ropes thereon, whilst Aline and I busied ourselves making starch. It was the first time we had ever attempted it, but we succeeded admirably. Tom thought it a very curious sight to see us all so industrious, and said he ought to take a photographic view of us in our new vocation. At three, a slight breeze having sprung up, the men brought their tubs, soap, and clothes on board, and we spread sail— but the fickle wind lasted only a short time, and at half-past five we tied up for the night.

CHAPTER VI.

VOYAGE UP THE NILE—RACES WITH THE ESTELLA AND THE CROCODILE—EXCURSIONS ON SHORE—EGYPTIANS AS THEY ARE—MEETING OTHER BOATS—EXCITEMENT ON BOARD—IS IT A CROCODILE OR LIZARD?—ARRIVAL AT THEBES—GRAND ILLUMINATION—ONE HUNDRED AND TEN RED, WHITE, AND BLUE LANTERNS—MUSTAPHA AGA.

WEDNESDAY, January 1, 1868.

A BEAUTIFUL bright morning for New-Year's Day, but yet no wind; so we commenced tracking at seven A.M., while Tom fired a salute in honor of the day. The scenery on the Nile, thus far, has been very tame, and I may say very uninteresting; but the weather has been so delightful that we enjoy our new mode of life exceedingly. At length a breeze sprang up, and at eleven we came in sight of the *Estella* and *Crocodile*, although, having stopped eight hours the day previous, we did not think we should overtake them so soon. At half-past eleven we passed the *Zarifa*, bound down, with an American family on board, Col. Rathburn, wife, and sister—who were recognized by Mr. Rogers as acquaintances. We saluted them by dipping colors, and they answered in the same manner. They have only been to the first cataract. Poor Mohammed-el-Adli felt quite disappoint-

ed that we had not told him before that this was New-Year's Day, as he wanted to give us a dinner similar to that on Christmas; but we told him we had plenty with our ordinary meal, which is always excellent. The wind increased, so that we passed the *Crocodile* at one o'clock, and at half-past one the *Estella*. Her people must have been annoyed, for they cannot bear the idea that we should be ahead of them. At three we ran aground, and the *Estella* also; but she got clear first, for her captain and steersman seem to be a great deal smarter than ours, and she took the lead, her party feeling very happy. While we were trying to get clear the *Crocodile* passed us, and we followed her half a mile astern, but rapidly gained on her, and at a quarter past three passed her. Came in sight of Benessoef at six P.M., and El-Adli asked us if we wished to stop: but as the wind was good we told him to keep on. Benessoef looked very pretty from the boat; we had not seen so much vegetation or so many trees since leaving Cairo. We continued sailing until one A.M., when we overtook the *Estella*, and tied up near her.

THURSDAY, January 2.

Clear, bright morning, but light wind. We were under way at seven A.M., when the *Estella* poled past us, while the *Crocodile* was nowhere to be seen. The morning passed very quickly; in fact, at twelve o'clock, when we arrived at Bebah, we had hardly finished dressing. We took a pleasant walk to the village, through groves of palm-trees and fields of beans and corn. It was market day, and the crowd of people

THE "ORIENTAL."—*See page* 73.

was very picturesque, and here for the first time we saw children entirely naked. While Mohammed purchased lambs, the gentlemen being with him, we remained in the shade, with our guide, to wait for them. Soon we were surrounded by a crowd of men, women, and children, curious to see Europeans. Our guide drove the men away, but the women and children remained to gaze at us. At last, Mr. Rogers coming back to us, and feeling tired of being objects of so much curiosity, we returned to our dahabeeh, and as we could see Tom nowhere in the crowd, thought he had gone shooting. We were escorted to our boat by nearly fifty persons, and when we arrived found Tom stretched out on the sofa on deck, laughing heartily to see us coming thus attended. The weather being exceedingly warm, the gentlemen dressed themselves in Egyptian costume, which made them look cool and comfortable. Tom then occupied himself by taking several views of our boat, with groups of Arabs on shore and palm-trees behind. We tied up a quarter of a mile above the village, with the *Estella* in advance of us. For several nights we have had clear moonlight, and as I prize it much I remained on deck, lying on a sofa, and conversing with Mr. Rogers until half-past nine.

FRIDAY, January 3.

Clear morning and no wind; nothing remarkable in the scenery. Passed our time ironing, braiding, and reading. The *Estella* is still ahead of us.

SATURDAY, January 4.

Tracked until nine A.M., when we, as well as the *Estella*, tied up for the crew's breakfast. A passenger steamer stopped with a party of Americans on board, and Tom and Mr. Rogers went to speak to them. They informed them that on the way up they had passed five American and three English boats, while they reported the *Crocodile* a short distance behind us, and Mr. Messenger and family, in the *Messenger Bird*, at Benessoef. The steamer wanted twenty-two guineas to tow the *Estella* to Siout, but as the price was exorbitant, they declined, and we continued tracking together. A light wind sprang up from the north at six P.M., and at half-past seven we passed the *Estella* by fair sailing, but soon she took the lead again by poling. At eight P.M. both boats tied up until midnight, when the wind arose, and enabled us in two hours' time to reach Cosaneh, where we again tied up.

SUNDAY, January 5.

We got under way at nine A.M., with a good breeze; the *Estella* passed us a half hour later. At half-past ten we were abreast the Copt convent, situated on the hills upon the eastern bank, called "Gebel-y-Tayr" (The Hill of the Birds). Two good Christians, at least so they assured us, swam out from the shore, and getting into our yawl called lustily for backsheesh. These men are Coptic monks; are they a benefit to, or an excrescence on, the Christian religion? A large new dahabeeh, called the *Memphis*, under the Russian flag, which our dragoman says belongs to the Russian Consul, and which has been in sight all the morning, overhauled and passed us at noon : from the number of women that we saw, we supposed that gentleman had adopted oriental life. We passed Mineah at half-past twelve, where the Memphis stopped. Passed the tombs of Beni-Hassan at five P.M. The wind being favorable, we postponed our visit until our return. At half-past six came to anchor; no wind, the sails hung in folds, and the *Estella* came abreast of us, tracking. At seven a light breeze sprang up, when we tripped anchor, and made for the western bank, where we found the wind better. The *Estella's* lights were visible where she was tied up, becalmed on the opposite shore. We covered our cabin windows in order to steal a march on her, and continued sailing with a light breeze until midnight, when the wind died out and we tied up at Esbet.

MONDAY, January 6.

With a light breeze we got under way at seven A.M.; at nine quite calm again, and the men on shore tracking. The *Estella* was nowhere in sight. Aline, who has been a little indisposed for two days, was better this morning, and joined us on deck again. We passed Antinous at one, and Roda at two P.M. Roda looks beautiful, and is the first pretty scenery we have had on the Nile; the country being well cultivated, with plenty of trees, the brown Lybian hills make a fine background, while the skies are as usual of a deep blue. These places are very interesting, but we will stop to visit them on our return. While writing, Mr. Rogers came to invite me to take a walk, and as the country looked so tempting I cheerfully acquiesced, as all around is so green and bright. For the first time I found some wild flowers, which I gathered to put in our albums. The sakyehs were in great number, while several fields of sugar-cane were in sight. The gum-trees are plentifully mixed among the sycamores, the acacias, and the palm, and two to three hours slipped away agreeably before we regained our boat. In the evening I read "O'Donoghue," an Irish story, by Lever, which transported me to familiar scenery. The remainder of the evening passed playing *bézique*.

TUESDAY, January 7.

On looking out of the window at seven A.M., we found that the *Estella* had tracked up to us during the night, and was tied up in front. We heard that the dragoman was much annoyed when he found in the morning that the *American boat* was again gone, and gave his crew one pound to catch us, which induced them to work nearly all night. I wrote to-day until four P.M., when I went on deck to enjoy the lovely scene. Our boat was gliding gracefully over the water; some of the men were sewing, some busy at the sails, while others were praying. It is their Ramadan, and for thirty days, from sunrise to sunset, they cannot touch food. Their religion has much poetry in it. When they pray,— which they do repeatedly during the day, with their faces towards Mecca,—having previously washed their hands and faces, they prostrate themselves to the ground several times and kiss it, then crossing their hands, their eyes turned heavenward, implore devoutly the King of creation. We tied up for the night at Tel-el-Amarna.

WEDNESDAY, January 8.

The *Estella* has employed a steamer to tow her as far as Siout, and left us at sunrise. Good-by to our competitor! There is no wind this morning, and we are tracking. With a good breeze we could reach Siout to-morrow, but with a calm or head-wind it will take us a week. At eleven A.M. we passed the dahabeeh *Lincoln*, under the American flag. The Arabic chain of mountains is commencing to be very picturesque, and looks beautifully by moonlight.

THURSDAY, January 9.

Morning somewhat cloudy; light wind, and men out tracking. Thus we continued until half-past three, when a breeze from the north sprang up, and we unfurled our sail; but alas! the wind soon failed again. At eight P.M. we were under and abreast the rugged cliffs of Aboofayda; the moon shone brightly; we shouted, and called names, and the cliff called back; a bark came down the river; her men, about six in number, talking all together, and the echoes answering as if there were a thousand. As Aline was still sick, we asked her to look out of the window, while Tom fired his gun; the rattling echoes were grand, just like a volley of artillery. We continued tracking until we arrived at the next village, and tied up at nine P.M.

FRIDAY, January 10.

We tracked during the whole morning, but at a

quarter past two p.m. a northerly wind sprang up and we soon passed the village of Manfalout. Aline felt somewhat better during the afternoon, and remained on deck reclining on a sofa. One of the crew, in coming from the tombs opposite Manfalout, found a piece of petrified bone, which he gave to me. We continued sailing with a fresh breeze until nine p.m., when the wind died out and we anchored four miles from Siout.

SATURDAY, January 11.

We tracked during the morning until nine, when a breeze sprang up, and we arrived at Siout at eleven, where it was necessary to stop twenty-four hours to bake bread for the crew. Aline is still quite unwell and incapable of going out, so I passed the morning writing home. At noon Tom, Mr. Rogers, and I took donkeys and went into the city to make several purchases. The country around Siout is beautiful, but we did not spend much time looking at it, as we feared Aline would get lonely during our absence. We went first to the hospital for some medicines which we had neglected to obtain before leaving Cairo, and thence to the American consulate to deliver our letters. The consul was not at home; but going through the bazars we met his son, a very handsome Egyptian, who spoke French. He was very polite, took charge of our letters, and expressed his regret that he was not at home when we called on his father. The bazars are in long narrow streets, covered at the level of the house-tops with matting, to resist the heat of the sun. The Egyptians here, as elsewhere, are not particularly clean; in fact, the beggars were so dirty and surrounded me in such numbers that I was compelled to use my riding-whip to get rid of them. We passed the afternoon in company with Aline, and the evening on deck, admiring the moonlight.

SUNDAY, January 12.

After breakfast I read some chapters in the Bible. Tom then went to take a photographic view of Siout, while Mr. Rogers and I took a walk in the Pacha's garden. Having found a pretty spot, a summer-house surrounded by tropical plants, I sketched it. When we returned home Tom showed us his view of Siout, which proved to be a good one, and then went with me to the garden, to ascertain if my drawing was correct, and showed me how to get proper proportions. At one P.M. we left Siout with a good breeze. The *Crocodile* arrived just as we started, and we heard that the *Estella* and an American boat left on Friday.

MONDAY, January 13.

Light breeze, and got under way at two A.M., passing Abouticg at six, and Tartah at four in the afternoon. Observed several persons in European costume at the latter port, who, our dragoman informed us, are Greek and Italian merchants, come to purchase the wheat in advance of its growth. This section of the country produces large crops, and the banks where now only a dozen boats are moored, six weeks hence will be lined with a thousand busy craft, each loading for a northern market. At half-past four passed Gebel-Sheick-Hereedeé, and continued sailing until three in the morning.

TUESDAY, January 14.

At three A.M. the wind died out, and we anchored three miles below Menchich. A small fishing-boat passed this morning while we were at anchor, and reported three dahabeehs twelve miles astern. One must be the *Crocodile*, and the other two, having had fair and strong wind, could not have stopped at Siout to bake, but will probably push on to Girgeh. Heard also that the *Bund*, with Lord and Lady Conyngham, the *No Name*, with Rev. Mr. Wight and party, were at Siout, while four days ago the *Messenger Bird* was at Minich. Under way again at seven; the wind light, but favorable. Passed Menchich at ten A.M. An unburnt brick town; the upper stories of the houses white-washed and used for pigeons, while the dwellings are below. Passed Girgeh at half-past three this afternoon. This was formerly a large city, but the river has gradually washed the greater part of it away. Several minarets without mosques, and about a hundred houses, are all that remain. As the wind continues favorable, we will not visit the ruins of Abydos until our return, nor stop at night. While passing some of the high eastern hills, where the river approaches close to their base, the uncertain wind, as it came in fitful gusts, gave our men much trouble; and the yawl annoyed us exceedingly through the night, by occasionally coming with a thump against the stern, and waking us all up. It is a very dangerous pass. We got aground several times, requiring the united efforts of the crew to get afloat again.

WEDNESDAY, January 15.

Continued sailing with a favorable wind until five P.M., when we tied up at Dendera, for the purpose of letting our dragoman cross the river to Kenah, to purchase chimneys for our lamps, the only two we had being broken. Before dark we saw upon the opposite shore two dahabeehs; one under the French flag, bound down, the other with no flag up. The reis informed us that an English gentleman, with his wife and maid, were on board, who left Cairo several days previous to our departure. We met such a family at Alexandria, and have no doubt but that it is the same.

THURSDAY, January 16.

We got under way at three A.M., and made good distance before daylight, but the wind died out at seven. Going on deck before breakfast with Tom, we found there were two dahabeehs behind us that we had overtaken and passed during the night; there is still another a short distance ahead; all under the English flag. The weather is delightful; and as our men were out tracking after breakfast, the country looked so rich and inviting that we went on shore; Tom, as usual, with his gun, and Mr. Rogers for the first time carried his. Aline is not very strong yet, and was compelled to take Mohammed's arm, keeping near the shore, to be able to go on board when tired. I followed the gentlemen, carrying my album, hoping to find an opportunity of taking a sketch. We had not been on shore ten minutes when we came upon a flock of wild pigeons, which afforded an occasion for Mr. Rogers to try his luck, and he killed two with a single shot. Soon they became so plentiful that Tom killed five at one shot; we brought eighteen back with us, and if Tom had had more cartridges he could have killed double that number. We passed a great many places where the men, naked except a rag tied about their loins, were busily engaged drawing water with buckets and poles from the river, to irrigate the land. This primitive arrangement is called the "shadoof." Thus it was in the days of Abraham and the Pharaohs; thus it is to-day; thus will it be for another thousand years, unless a more civilized race shall overrun this fair land, spoil the Egyptian, and teach a new order of things. Beginning to feel tired, and finding the sun very hot, we passed through a village on our way back to the boat, and as usual I was a curiosity here, and we were followed by a crowd of men, women, and children, some of the latter entirely naked, asking us for backsheesh. We sought a shady resting-place, for our boat was far behind, and waited for it to come up. What a beautiful sycamore! Some natives were seated beneath its shade, and near it was a shadoof. Tom observed that it would make a pretty picture, but I felt that I was too much of a novice to undertake it; so we kept on walking, still followed by our primitive escort. I remarked some distance ahead a scheik's tomb, with palm-trees before it and a sycamore near. Thinking it would look pretty in my album, we directed our course towards it; and while Mr. Rogers and Tom seated themselves under the shade of the trees, I took my position on a heap of doura stalks, to commence my drawing, helped by Tom's observations, and at times much annoyed by the natives who surrounded us. Having returned to the river-bank, we had to wait some hours for our boat, and the *Adelina*, an English dahabeeh, passed before us while seated on the shore. We addressed a gentleman whom we saw near, but he was an Italian, and did not speak a word of French; his dahabeeh, which he pointed out to us, was near ours; she had no name, but there must have been some English on board, as the flag was of that nation. It was four o'clock before we were again on board, very much fatigued, having walked some seven miles. Our trophy was a white ibis, which, after Mrs. Ferris had admired, had the river for its grave. We tied up at El-Arabat, seven miles from Thebes, surrounded by five dahabeehs.

FRIDAY, January 17.

Commenced tracking before breakfast. We heard that the boat which was on the opposite shore last evening, and which has crossed to this side this morning, is called the *Zingara*, and contains an English party. While the two boats were abreast, Mr. Rogers held a conversation with the gentlemen, who informed him that they left Cairo on the 12th of December, and have been stopping on their way up. The *Gazelle*, and the *Union*, both under the English flag, passed on their way down this morning. The *Gazelle* has on board the Duke and Duchess of St. Albans, who have been to the first cataract. We observed this boat particularly, as it is the one spoken of so highly by Mr. Warren; she is a fine vessel, wider than ours, but not so long. Having head-wind, and the weather being cold, Aline and I remained in the cabin sewing, while Tom basked in the sunshine on deck; the men were out tracking, when suddenly we heard them shouting "Hup, hup, hup!" Tom rushed into the saloon, seized his gun, saying, "It is a crocodile!" We felt a little alarmed, and expected to see a monster twenty or thirty feet long; however, our fears soon subsided when we saw a small reptile, measuring only as many inches. Tom killed it with a single shot, and one of the men brought it on board. A closer examination showed it to be only a species of lizard, and it was thrown into the river. A light breeze having sprung up, we anticipated an early arrival at Thebes. We soon came in view of that place, and when nearly there fired a salute of thirteen guns. Several dahabeehs were anchored, and among them we recognized with pleasure our old friend the *Estella*. The British and American flags were flying from the top of the ruins of an ancient temple; and we learned that this was the British and American Consulate. We tied up on the opposite shore of a small cove, so that our boat presented a broadside to Thebes, while all the others were moored near the town, excepting the *America*, which was directly ahead of us. She looked very well with her five little flags flying, bearing the initials of the party; but nothing in comparison to our craft, decorated with the pennant seventy-two feet long, the American, the Oriental, and the huge "New York" flags, besides three large Turkish ones of El-Adli. What do you say of the Americans, Messrs. Englishmen? Do you not think these two boats well represent their nation? After pitching our tent on shore, and as we were on the point of starting out, we received a call from General Darling of the *America*, a very pleasant gentleman, and who told us they had also arrived in the afternoon, and seeing our white flag with New York written on it (Tom's idea), and being of that city himself, he was delighted to meet some of his countrymen. After a pleasant conversation and social drink with the gentlemen, at leaving he invited us to pay a visit to their boat, and become acquainted with the ladies. So Aline and I remained home to dress, while Tom and Mr. Rogers went to pay a visit to the U. S. Consul, Mustapha Aga, from whom they received letters. There they met the Governor of Thebes, who, with the Consul, was invited to visit us. While taking dinner El-Adli had all the lanterns prepared; we kept dark until we knew whether any of the other boats were going to illuminate. One English boat did, but with only a few lanterns, all of them white. Having lighted our one hundred and ten—red, white, and blue, one third of each color—Tom and Mr. Rogers went to help the men, and suddenly a string was run up to the peak of the main-yard, another string to the after yard, and a third string on halliards arranged half-way up the main-yard; a row commencing on the extreme bow, and running to the end of the jigger-boom; another row six feet above that, and also running the entire length of the vessel; a third row around the railing of the quarter-deck, and a fourth row above that, hung to the rope that secures the awning; three lanterns still higher on the three flag-staffs for the Turkish flags, and others at prominent points. After all had been arranged and lighted, we put on our shawls and were going to take a row in our little boat, to observe the effect and to pay our promised visit to the ladies of the *America*, when El-Adli came into the saloon to announce a visit from the Consul, the Governor, and also Mr. Laming, of the *Estella*. Mr. Rogers therefore wrote an invitation to the party on the *America* to join us, and to meet our distinguished visitors. The three gentlemen—General Darling, Major Roessle, and Major Moller—came, expressing their regrets that the ladies were unable to do so. Chibouks were presented to the guests, together with cigars, coffee, champagne, cakes, and confectionery. Aline and I could not look enough at the Governor[*]; he is about twenty-five, and has the most beautiful face one can imagine. His complexion is of course dark, but his eyes! One might well be envious of such eyes! So large, so bright, so languid, and with eyelashes so long and thick and black. His nose is rather too thick, but his mouth, with its black, silky moustaches, is very expressive. His dark brown hair is worn long, and curled. He is of a good size, has a very *distingué* air, and wore his costume (a white cashmere shirt, a striped silk vest, with a cashmere scarf and wide brown drawers of embroidered cloth) with unequalled grace. His coiffure was very picturesque; a yellow silk foulard falling in folds around his

---

[*] We afterwards ascertained that this was not the Governor, but a government official.

head, with a small turban of gold and black wound around it; several chains hung to his waist, while his little finger was adorned with an emerald surrounded by diamonds. He only spoke the Egyptian language, but we had no difficulty in entertaining him, having El-Adli as an interpreter, as well as Mustapha Aga, who speaks English fluently. The three gentlemen of the *America* gave us some details of their passage of the cataract, while Mr. Laming complimented us on our illumination. After the Consul and General Darling and his party had left, Mr. Rogers remained to entertain Mr. Laming, while we, with the Governor, went to take a view of our craft. All the evening little boats with parties from other dahabechs were rowing about looking at it, and the Governor complimented us by saying it was the flag-ship of the squadron. He remained quite late with us, and invited us ladies, upon our return, to pay a visit to his wife. We were much pleased with the idea, and promised ourselves much pleasure in accepting it. Soon a good breeze sprang up, and Mr. Laming was requested to return to his boat, as they were preparing to leave. When will we meet the *Estella* again?

SATURDAY, January 18.

After breakfast the boat was made ready, and we called on the *America*, but found nobody *home*. They had left early in the morning for Karnak. Their boat, which was named the *Victoria* last year, is a fine one, and, as we learned, the handsomest of all on the Nile; much more elegantly furnished than ours. General

Darling having arrived at Cairo the 14th of November, had his choice, and very naturally selected the best. Having left our cards, we called on the Consul, who received us with much courtesy, and treated us to syrup and the gentlemen with chibouks. The temple in front and above his house is remarkable for the beauty of its pillars, which still give you a good idea of the strength and solidity of ancient monuments; but a great part of it is buried by the sand. Mustapha presented us with several handsome specimens of antiquities; and having received his promise to give us a letter to the Governor at Assouan, we bade him adieu, returned on board, and as the wind was fair, immediately got under way. In a quarter of an hour, a horseman, mounted on a fine Arabian steed, and dressed in flowing robes, was seen swiftly approaching. It was the bearer of the promised letter; he delivered his charge, and away, as in a fairy tale, flies steed and rider. The wind died out, and we remained at anchor until the morning.

CHAPTER VII.

ARRIVAL AT ESNEH—ITS TEMPLE THREE THOUSAND YEARS OLD—CITY OF ASSOUAN—ISLAND OF ELEPHANTINE—STATUE OF AN EGYPTIAN KING.—PASSAGE OF THE FIRST CATARACT—THREE HUNDRED NUBIANS EMPLOYED TO PULL OUR BOAT THROUGH THE RAPIDS—ARRIVAL AT PHILÆ.

SUNDAY, January 19, 1868.

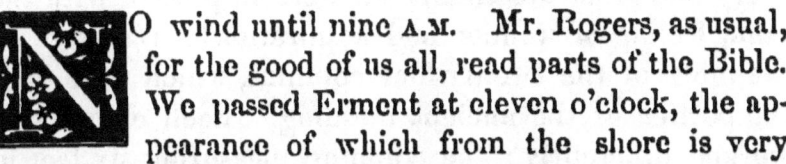O wind until nine A.M. Mr. Rogers, as usual, for the good of us all, read parts of the Bible. We passed Erment at eleven o'clock, the appearance of which from the shore is very pretty, and here are large establishments for the manufacture of sugar. Aline, Tom, and Mr. Rogers went on shore for a walk, but I remained on board, and passed the afternoon on deck, enjoying the quietness of the declining hours. Gébélem, two mountains forming an isolated group, with the tomb of an Arabian scheik, make a pretty picture, and we greatly admired it. At five we ran aground, and took our dinner, enlivened by the song of our men's singular chorus, as they endeavored to get the boat afloat, and it was nearly eleven when we arrived at Esneh.

MONDAY, January 20.

We were up at half-past six this morning, and as soon as breakfast was over, went to visit the Temple, the great ancient monument of this place. The entrance is by a small alley-way, and only one-third of the columns are above the street. Before 1842 it was almost entirely hidden beneath a mass of rubbish; but Mohammed Ali, passing through the city, gave orders to have it cleared. You descend by a rude staircase of about forty stone steps to the interior. For a moment every one of us was silent; all were impressed with the same feeling of wonder and admiration! We were in the midst of the twenty-four columns, which were only the portico of the ancient building. Each chapiter is worked differently; the columns, measuring six feet in diameter, as well as the walls, are entirely covered with hieroglyphics. Before it was open to the admiration of the world, probably some Arabs had made their dwelling in it, for the greater part of the ceiling and the chapiters are blackened by smoke; still the hieroglyphics are as well preserved as if made recently. How beautiful must have been the temple whose portico gives so grand an idea of it! What a wonderful people these Egyptians must have been! What means had they, and how could they, not only transport, but also elevate these heavy stones to their respective places, are questions which naturally come to the mind of the curious. Three thousand years have passed away; their descendants, oppressed and ruled as slaves, bring to your heart a feeling of pity; but these monuments of their ancestors, though mutilated, are still there, an appealing voice from the spirit world telling you: "*If not crushed and oppressed by the rude hand of war, what might we not be!*" We were accompanied in our visit by a German from Elberfeld, Prussia. He is a missionary, speaks a little English, and was delighted to find some persons who could converse in his native tongue. While we were admiring the Temple, a party of gentlemen arrived, who entered into conversation, and informed us that they had passed us yesterday during our dinner, in a steamer furnished them by the Viceroy. They were accompanied by a dragoman of his Highness' household, and who was with the Prince of Wales on the Nile six years ago. Tom exchanged cards with two of the gentlemen, Messrs. Cailles and Perrier, who are French, and invited them to come on board our dahabeeh; they declined, however, as their steamer was ready to start, but expressed the desire of meeting us in Paris. We afterwards took a long walk through the city, which shows, by the mounds of rubbish with which it is filled, sites of ancient buildings. We admired a handsome minaret in passing, which I would have liked to sketch, but was afraid of the dirty crowd which would have collected around us. We visited also the Pacha's garden, but the sun becoming very hot, soon returned to our dahabeeh. We had not been back half an hour when the whistle of a steamer was heard; she was coming down the river, and stopped near us. It proved to be the same vessel that had passed us with American passengers on the 4th of January, near Benesoef, and presently two of the gentlemen called on us. They announced themselves as Mr. Fisk and Mr. White, from Syracuse, N. Y. After remaining an hour with us, and partaking of champagne and cake, they returned to their steamer, which had only stopped a short time to take in coals. While we ladies retired to rest, Tom took his materials and started off on a sketching expedition, and at four o'clock, in company with Mr. Rogers, I went to see his drawing. It is of an old Roman wall which protected ancient Latopolis from the encroachment of the river, while the trees above, and a portion of our boat protruding from behind a clump of rocks in the distance, make a pretty picture. At five the German missionary came to dine with us, by invitation. Having lived here three years, and speaking the Egyptian language, he is well acquainted with the life and customs of the present inhabitants, and gave us some valuable information. He is a kind and good-hearted fellow, trying his best to bring some of these poor souls to Christ, but has had much trouble to succeed. He left us early to join some Copt women, who come every evening to his house to hear from his mouth the word of God.

TUESDAY, January 21.

This morning, on rising, we found that we were under way with a good wind. It is now eleven o'clock A.M., and we are all on deck, the boat gliding noiselessly on the water, with a clear sky as usual. But shut your eyes and listen,—hear the cocks crowing, the hens cackling, the doves cooing,—surely you can imagine yourself in a barn-yard; but no, it all proceeds from our extemporized yard at the stern of the boat, where our live-stock is placed, ready at short notice to contribute to the luxury of our table. We continued sailing all day and evening until eight P.M., when we ran upon a sand-bank, just above Edfou, and notwithstanding the efforts of the crew, were unable to get off until morning.

WEDNESDAY, January 22.

At seven A.M. regained the channel, and continued our voyage with a good northerly wind.

At half-past eleven A.M. we passed one English and three American boats. The English vessel is called the *Undine;* Mr. Lawrence and family, of Boston, occupy two boats; and Messrs. Morse and Dwight, of Jersey City, with two Swedes, the third, named the *Zelica.* As we approached we fired a salute of six guns, which compliment was duly acknowledged and returned, flags mutually dipped, etc. Continued sailing, and in another half-hour the four boats are out of sight, the excitement is over, our ordinary life is resumed—reading, sewing, writing—the delightfully balmy breeze fanning us, our craft gliding swiftly, silently, steadily, through the waters, green banks on either side, sown with lupins to the water's edge, the gray hills in the distance; thus do we continue as we are gradually nearing Gebel-Silsileh. Pass Gebel-Silsileh at three P.M. Here the hills approach close to the river, leaving no cultivatable ground. On the west the rocks are full of tombs, grottos, and quarries, while on the eastern side are quarries, wherein are evidences of huge stones having been taken. We shall not stop however until our return, when we will examine the entire *vicinage.* It is at once evident that the Nile has broken away the rocks at this point at some remote period, thereby probably changing the entire character of the lands above. At half-past four we passed the American dahabeeh *Manhattan*, having on board Messrs. Phœnix and Pomeroy of New York. The gentlemen were on shore, and saluted us as we raised our flag *New York*, while their dragoman came on board to ask for letters. Continued sailing until eight, when we ran aground, and remained hard and fast until morning, about ten miles below Assouan.

THURSDAY, January 23.

No wind. Our boat had gradually cut her way through the sand, and we are again afloat, but waiting for some of the men who are out in the yawl, fishing for an anchor they had lost during the night in the effort to get her off. At eleven the wind sprang up, we spread our sails, and hope, if it continues, we will arrive in Assouan in two hours. At twelve we passed the steamer given by the Pacha to Messrs. Cailles and Perrier, going down the river, on their return from the first cataract. Salutes were exchanged, flags dipped, and the gentlemen doffed their hats as they glided rapidly past. At two we noticed some children running along the shore, and whose numbers gradually accumulated. They were some distance off, but evidently anticipated the arrival of our dahabeeh. Soon they were joined by numbers of men and women, and upon inquiry we found that some of our sailors lived here, and that we were to stop, as they will have leave of absence for a day, and join us at Assouan. A touching meeting took place, friends meeting friends, kissing, greeting, and saluting them. We delivered into the arms of his mother, who seemed overcome with joy, a little boy whose father remained in Suez, and gave him in keeping to one of our men to take home. Now we are *en route* again, and will be in Assouan in an hour. At three we arrived in view of that place, and fired a salute of twelve guns. The Nile here is very narrow, the two mountains—the Lybian and the Arabic—show to advantage. The modern city is on the eastern side, in a hollow, and covered with groves of date-trees and gardens, while the houses are all built of crude brick. The harbor where we stopped was spacious, and on one side protected and nearly closed by rocks; while opposite is the Island of Elephantine, appearing very green, and whose shores are covered with palm and dom trees, which greatly add to the beauty of the landscape. After we had anchored, Tom and Mr. Rogers went to take a walk, while Aline and myself remained on deck, watching an Abyssinian merchant surrounded by slaves, who were all busy sorting his merchandise. A number of children and men came to offer us the curiosities of the country,—silver bracelets, fox-skins, baskets, ostrich feathers, and Nubian dresses (a single fringe which they wear around and below the waist). The expense attending the dressing of a Nubian belle is not great, as one of these garments costs about fifteen piasters (seventy-five cents), and will probably last a year or two :—a pleasant contrast with an American or French beauty. A poor blind man, with a withered arm, sat down on the sand and sang; his appearance was so sickening that we sent him away with a backsheesh, yet he did not deserve it, for Mahommed told us that, miserable as he appears, he has two wives. How can he support them? As we were making our observations on the strange customs of this strangest of all countries, we saw the Englishman and his wife coming towards us whom we had met at Alexandria, and who arrived here a few days ago; they took a look at our boat and returned. Not very social, these English! The gentlemen arrived as we commenced our dinner, and brought us several ostrich feathers, of which only a few are very good.

FRIDAY, January 24.

We hurried through dressing to go to the island of Elephantine. The wind not being good, and the *Estella* moored ten miles ahead, waiting for a fair wind to pass the cataract, we will be obliged to remain here all day. We took our drawing materials with us, and also the photographic instrument. The weather being delightful, while our men were rowing and singing, I enjoyed the scenery. The ruins here and there on the hills, the green island we were approaching, the habitations shaded by palm-trees, the curious formation of rocks, rendered the *tout ensemble* picturesque and full of interest. As soon as we landed we were surrounded by men, women, and children asking for backsheesh. Two of the little girls were dressed in the Nubian fashion, bead necklace, bracelets, ear-rings, hair plaited in a hundred little braids, and *that* fringe around their waists made them look strange and singular. Tom took a photographic view of a sakych built on an ancient wall, and afterwards we visited other parts of the island. Desolation all around you! The ancient city has disappeared; the rubbish forming a large hillock of seven to eight hundred yards in circumference, and the soil heaped with fragments of pottery; here and there are a few columnar remains of two ancient temples, which have tumbled down, and heavy stones covered with hieroglyphics very well preserved. In a hollow, going towards the shore where our boat was lying, we saw a statue of an Egyptian king, probably on the site of an ancient temple, represented seated, with his hands crossed upon the breast. There he sits, all alone, looking with eyes of stone on the changes which have succeeded to so much fame!

"Vanity, vanity, all is vanity!"

We took our seats in the boat amidst the shouting of the inhabitants of the village, who had followed us in our examination of the place, and crossed to the opposite shore to take a sketch. I forgot to mention that while we were on the island we saw an English dahabeeh entering the port. It was the *No Name*, with the English divines and Mustapha, the brother of our dragoman, on board. They left the *Messenger Bird* and the *Bund* at Siout. We afterwards conversed with Mustapha, who does not seem to be very well satisfied with his party. Mr. Rogers called on them, and they told him that they thought the *Bund* and *Messenger Bird* were now at Luxor. While we were busy with our drawings, Aline, who had returned on board, passed her time most agreeably. A steamboat provided by the Pacha arrived with several gentlemen, two of whom were with us on the *Principe Tomasso*, and had called with their friends, a gentleman from Smyrna, and a Greek, I believe.

5

I had just commenced writing when Abousaid brought in a card, announcing the Rev. Andrew Jukes and Mr. Hamson, from the English boat *No Name*, and soon the Rev. Mr. Wight followed.

Mr. Rogers and I entertained them for an hour; but while listening to their conversation I could not help comparing the life on their boat with that on ours.

While basking in the sunshine of that wondrous climate, and elevating our minds in the midst of those marvels of antiquity, we had seen with regret day after day pass never to return; while they complained of passing dull and monotonous weeks, and were only too anxious to reach Cairo again.

When they had taken leave Mr. Rogers smilingly remarked: "How is it possible for three crabbed old bachelors [Mr. R. is himself '*one of them*'] to pass ninety days together without wearisomeness and *ennui* creeping in? To light up and enliven '*Life on the Nile*' requires the presence of ladies. Woman is the good fairy distributing smiles and sunshine around her."

In the evening we received another visit from the gentlemen of the *Tomasso*, who were soon "*at home*" with us, smoking chibouks and sipping coffee. With them was the private dragoman of the Pacha, a very well-educated person, speaking French and English fluently, and who loves his country, Egypt, as much as Mr. Rogers does America. We listened with pleasure as he gave us better ideas of the agriculture of the country than those we had, and of the cotton crop particularly. It was the first time he had ascended the

Nile, and, like many others, had been disappointed in the scenery; yet one true thing he said; that travellers coming to Egypt were sure to find not only health but knowledge. He seemed quite enthusiastic about the wondrous Nile, and the richness of the soil compared with other countries.

"Where," said he, "will you find another favored land like this, watered annually by the overflowing of the Nile, enriching by its deposit, and preparing the soil for the fruition of the seed?"

"Yes," replied Mr. Rogers; "but how do you continue the necessary moistening of the land? Manual labor is required at your shadoofs from the planting time until the harvest."

"True," said our Egyptian friend; "but do you not do the same?"

"Certainly not; God does our work, while man does yours. He gives us plentiful showers as the soil and plant require it."

This was a poser, and he was forced to admit that competition could not take place between Providence and humanity.

It being our first meeting with such an educated Egyptian, we listened with much pleasure to the general information he gave, and the evening passed pleasantly until ten, when they all wished us good-night and a happy voyage.

SATURDAY, January 25.

We did not at first know whether we could begin our passage of the first cataract to-day, it being the end of

Ramadan, the Egyptian Christmas. But our dragoman was anxious to start, and promised backsheesh; so after breakfast, with a very light wind, we spread our sails, and commenced to pass between the rocks which cover the river, forming a great many channels. The scenery is quite different from all we have yet seen; the rocky islets presenting curious formations. We increased our force of men when leaving Syene, or Assouan. Some time before we arrived at Schail the eddies, produced by the rocks which obstruct the river, were so strong that some of the crew went in the yawl, and attached a rope around a rock a hundred yards ahead, thus helping us to pass. Schail is the first interesting island we approached, and is situated at the first gate or rapid. There we found a hundred Nubians waiting for us; fifty of them came on board, while fifty others went farther off, to pull the rope when ready. A curious scene was then presented. Nubians, the best swimmers we ever saw, jumped in the water, rode astride a light log, and carrying the rope around their necks, or between their teeth, took it to the men who attached it to the rocks, while the Nubians on the *Oriental*, all the time singing, pulled at the rope, passing in turn before the excited scheik, who is dancing and whirling a stick about his head. These naked Nubians, with the hot sun shining on their copper skins, floating on the water with the current, or swimming against it as easily as if walking, brought to my mind the imaginary picture I had often formed, when on Lake George and Lake Champlain, of the Indians in their canoes in by-gone times. The first gate is passed; the men stop to rest, clapping hands and dancing, their manner of showing their satisfaction. After we were through the second gate, we beheld Messrs. Jukes, Hamson, and Wight on the shore. They manifested a desire to come on board and witness the performance; so we sent our yawl, and could not help admiring the manner in which the sailors took advantage of the eddies to reach the dahabeeh. Refreshments were presented to the gentlemen, and all our attention was again given to the third gate; which took a long time to pass. Here the rock, which cuts transversely a part of the course of the river, can be compared to a dentated wall, whose crest shows itself above the water at short distances, and forms a series of islands and shoals. The Nile, being pent up by these obstacles and driven back, raises itself and overleaps them, and thus forms a number of little cascades. At five o'clock we anchored, and the gentlemen took leave, thanking us for the pleasure they had enjoyed.

SUNDAY, January 26.

We breakfasted at seven o'clock, so as to be through before the swarm of Nubians should arrive. To-day there were three hundred, for we had to pass through the most difficult part, which occupied three hours and a half. At one moment it was very exciting; the passage through the rocks and rapids is so narrow, we were uncertain as to whether our dahabeeh could be taken over safely. Five enormous ropes were attached to as many prominent rocks, so that in case one or two should give way, we might yet be held by the others, and not dashed to pieces. I must say that I did not see the danger;

Tom explained it to me, but I thought from all accounts it would have been more terrific. At the last gate is the strongest and heaviest rapid of all; but they succeeded in passing through without accident. It is now one o'clock, and during all the time of the passage a party of Europeans had been witnessing the operation. We thought the picture must have been admirable from the shore: the dahabeeh dancing on the brawling torrent; the men scattered about the rocks, with their picturesque dresses; while others are pulling at the ropes to force the boat to pass; our sailors, armed with strong poles, watching to ward off the shocks; while naked Nubians, as strong as Hercules, their backs to the boat and their feet as buttresses, are also acting as fenders. Mohammed informed us that the party on shore was the Russian Consul and lady, with their attendants, from the dahabeeh *Memphis*, who must have been very much interested, as they remained during the three hours of our passage, notwithstanding their exposure to the burning rays of a mid-day sun. When we arrived near them, we sent our cards inviting them on board to partake of some refreshments; but the lady being afraid they declined the invitation.

The view in approaching Philæ was enchanting. This island (with its green vegetation), covered with ancient temples, is the most beautiful point in all Egypt, whose extreme limit it is, and merits a particular description, which I shall give when we return, as we propose then to pitch our tent and remain three days. We only delayed a quarter of an hour, just long enough for our dragoman to pay the *reis* of the cataract; while Tom made use of the delay to go on shore and take a general view, and soon we were off again.

Nubia, which we have now entered, is much grander and bolder in its scenery, thus far, than Egypt. Dinner was announced, but we were in a beautiful bay, and were determined to stay on deck until we had passed it. The weather for two days has been very warm, 105° in the sun; it is evident we are nearing the tropics. At eight o'clock the wind died out, and we anchored on a pretty shore, where the crescent moon shone brightly through the palm-trees.

MONDAY, January 27.

We have had four hours' sailing during the night, and it was cold this morning. We commenced breakfast at eight o'clock, but left it unfinished to go on deck and admire the bold scenery. As we near Kalabshee, the mountains which fringe the two sides of the Nile contract so as to leave no passages along its banks; rocks appear thickly above the surface of the water and form little rapids, affording a view grander than when passing the cataract. At Kalabshee we saw the ruins of the temple, which we will visit on our return.

TUESDAY, January 28.

We were under way at half-past five A.M., with a good northerly wind. At half-past six passed the British boat SPHINX, on her return, and at seven another dahabeeh, also under British colors, bound down, without a name. At half-past seven, passed the ruins of the temple of Dakkeh, and a few hours later two American dahabeehs, named the *Thetis* and *Heron*. We tied up for the night at Wadee-el-Arab.

WEDNESDAY, January 29.

A faint air is stirring, but from the south, and the men are out tracking. I think Nubia is the poorest land I have ever seen. The hills approach almost to the river, consequently there are no plains to overflow; and the only cultivatable lands are the banks, after they are left bare by the receding waters. Here are a few beans, lentils, lupins, and a little wheat. Occasionally one sees some palm-trees, and these suffice for the few wants of a primitive population in a climate where little or no animal food is required. Last night we heard the cries of the jackals that came to the river for water and plunder; a stray lamb or chicken is the great desideratum, but sometimes they have been known to attack a man. At eleven A.M. a small steamer passed us on the way down, with some passengers on board, who fired a salute, which we acknowledged by dipping our colors. This vessel was hauled over the first cataract, by order of the Pacha, during the high water, in anticipation of the visit of the Duke and Duchess of St. Albans, to convey them from the first to the second cataract. After having performed the allotted task, the Pacha gave orders that any two or more voyagers, who were willing to pay twenty pounds each, might have the use of the boat for the same purpose. We tied up for the night at Sabooa.

THURSDAY, January 30.

No wind until ten A.M., when a moderate northerly breeze sprang up, and we made good time during the day, passing the same kind of country. Wind died out during the afternoon, and we tied up at Korusko.

FRIDAY, January 31.

Here the river makes a bend, and our course hence to Derr, about twelve miles, is almost north. In this reach the wind is almost always adverse, and it is necessary to track. Our case proved no exception to the general rule, and as the movement was very slow, particularly against a fresh breeze, we all went on shore for a promenade. We tied up in the evening opposite Hassaya, not having made, during the whole day, more than five or six miles.

5*

CHAPTER VIII.

CONTINUATION OF VOYAGE UP THE NILE—LADY DUFF GORDON—ARRIVAL AT WADI-HALFAH—ARAB DANCE—CATARACT OF BATN-EL-HAGAR—DOWN STREAM—TEMPLES OF FERAYG AND ABOU SIMBEL—ARRIVAL AT DERR—NUBIAN WEDDING—TEMPLE OF HERON—TEMPLE OF AMADA, BUILT B.C. 2700—TEMPLE AT DAKKEH—KALABCHEH, ITS TEMPLE.

SATURDAY, February 1, 1868.

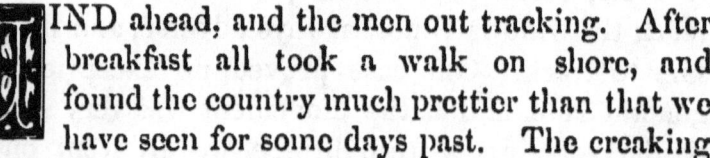WIND ahead, and the men out tracking. After breakfast all took a walk on shore, and found the country much prettier than that we have seen for some days past. The creaking of the sakyeh, or water-wheel, is never out of hearing, as they are placed in continuous rows, from one hundred and fifty to two hundred feet apart. Just as we arrived at Derr we saw a dahabeeh approaching, which proved to be the *Estella*, and Mr. Laming came in the yawl to pay us a visit. They have only been to Abou-Simbel, and are now on their way back to Assouan. He offered to take letters, which he would mail for us in Thebes, but, unhappily, not expecting to meet him so soon, we had none ready.

SUNDAY, February 2.

Very good wind all day until eight o'clock this

evening. In the afternoon we met the dahabeeh of Lady Duff Gordon, bound down the river, who sent her dragoman to inquire if we had letters for her. We had none, but sent our cards and a copy of the "London Times," given to us at Assouan by the French gentlemen. She is an English lady, living in Thebes, where she has adopted many Oriental fashions. Strangers are always anxious to see her, and we will probably pay her a visit on our way back. The weather, though beautiful and clear, has been quite cool for two days, and El-Adli says we will find it very cold in Wadi-Halfah. We have moonlight nights again, and yestereven, as I could not go to sleep for a long time, I passed half an hour looking out of my window. All was quiet, and the starry heavens presented a glorious sight, yet the scenery around was so tame that I could not help contrasting it with a moonlight night we passed last 13th of August, in a new Swiss châlet at Frutigen, after coming down from the Gemmi. Being wearied, we retired early, but waking in the middle of the night, I found my room so light that I arose, and stepping out on the balcony, could hardly repress a cry of admiration. The Kanderthal, surrounded by lofty peaks, the Birren-horn, the Weisse Frau, the Doldenhorn, the Gellihorn, the Niesen, were lighted up by a full moon, leaving here and there some deep shadows, while other places appeared as if illuminated by the sun. The Kander was running at my feet; its music was sweet to the ear; the painter was God! Each time I enjoy a moonlight scene, I see the snow-clad mountains of Frutigen shining before me.

MONDAY, February 3.

We have had a good wind all day, and Mohammed thinks we will arrive at Wadi-Halfah to-night. This morning at nine o'clock we passed the magnificent temple of Abou Simbel. At one o'clock an American dahabeeh came in sight; soon a yawl, with the dragoman, was seen approaching; he was a Maltese, and inquired if we had letters for his party, a Mr. Rodman, wife, and daughters, of Boston, who left Cairo on the 5th of December. They have had adverse winds all the time, and will stop only two days at Philæ, and one week at Luxor, where we will probably meet them. As we came in sight of Wadi-Halfah, the delighted men took their tambourines and commenced to play and sing, and for the first time, as is customary in arriving here, they improvised a dance—the most comical thing we ever witnessed. When they had finished they came to shake hands with us, and congratulate us on arriving at the end of our journey.

TUESDAY, February 4.

At twenty minutes past eight we took our pilot and three other men on board the yawl with us, and started for Abouseer, four miles and a half above Wadi-Halfah. The rock of Abouseer, our destination, is about two hundred feet above the level of the river, from whose summit you have a scene savage beyond description; north, east, and south, stretches before you the cataract—Batn-el-Hagar (The Stone Belly) as it is called by the Arabs. Thousands of black rocks obstruct the current of the river, which finds as many narrow channels impassable to boats. The gushing water is not so terrific as Strabo describes it, who stated that he was deafened by the noise. What would he have said of our Niagara? The cataract extends six miles; on its shores are neither villages nor habitations—all is silent and deserted. We sat down in the shade of Abouseer; for carpet our feet had the sand blown hither by the wind from the desert of Abou-Solom, and on our right stretched a chain of rocks, whose summits are frequented by wild-pigeons. A salute of thirteen guns was fired by the gentlemen, which disturbed the wild-fowl and vultures in their repose. At twelve we took a very good lunch, with red wine and champagne, in which our men participated; and before leaving, Mr. Rogers having written a few lines from Walter Scott appropriate to the occasion:—

> "Breathes there the man with soul so dead
> Who never to himself hath said—
>   This is my own, my native land!
> Whose heart hath ne'er within him burned,
> As home his footsteps he hath turned
>   From wandering on a foreign strand?
> If such there breathe, go, mark him well;
> For him no minstrel raptures swell.
> High though his titles, proud his name,
> Boundless his wealth as wish can claim,
> Despite those titles, power, and pelf,
> The wretch, concentred all in self,
> Living, shall forfeit fair renown,
> And, doubly dying, shall go down
> To the vile dust from whence he sprung,
> Unwept, unhonored, and unsung."

enclosed them in a champagne bottle, and directed it, with our names, as well as that of the boat, to any American who should hereafter visit the place.

We were back on our dahabeeh at two o'clock, and found dromedaries waiting for us to ride, and although a little frightened at first, when once mounted, thought it a pleasant method of locomotion. Tom tried to take a picture of us, but the animal on whose back I was seated was so restless that he had to try again, still without success. Since our arrival our boat has been put in readiness for the return trip: the crew have taken off the sails, lowered the yards and arranged them ;—the long one fastened fore and aft, from mast to mast, just overhead, and the short one aft shifted to the foremast, to carry sail sufficient for steering ;—the current and our twelve sweeps, manned by as many "sinewy-armed men of bronze," being the only motive power used on the Nile in returning. We left Wadi-Halfah at five o'clock P.M.

WEDNESDAY, February 5.

The men rowed all night ; the wind was neither good nor bad, yet, helped by the current, we soon arrived in sight of Abou Simbel, and took the yawl to visit the small temple of Ferayg, consisting of a hall supported by four columns and two side chambers. It has the name and sculpture of Amenophis, of the XVIIIth dynasty, and was constructed about sixteen hundred years B.C. It was during the XVIIIth dynasty that the most beautiful temples and monuments of Egypt were built. The temple of Ferayg was afterwards used as a

Christian church. In entering we saw upon the ceiling a rude painting of Christ, dressed in a long-brown robe, and his curly hair surrounded by an aureola. If the stones could speak, how much they would have to tell of the numbers of the faithful who have there knelt down! We have now entered a region of ruins which succeed each other almost without interruption. After leaving Ferayg we rowed down the river, and arrived at the same time as the dahabeeh before the two beautiful temples of Abou Simbel, which are cut in the rock; date from the reign of the great Rameses II., 1311 B.C.; are the handsomest remains in Nubia and except Thebes, in all Egypt. Mr. Rogers and I first visited the smaller temple; but as we had forgotten to take candles, could not see the chambers in the rear. We afterwards, however, all inspected it together. The façade is ornamented with six colossi, each thirty-six feet in height, representing Rameses and his wife Nofriari, with their children. The interior has three divisions; the first room is supported by six pilasters, with chapiters having Isis' heads sculptured on them, which are perfectly preserved; and all the walls are decorated with sculptures, but much injured by time and the hand of the spoiler. We then explored the great temple, a wonderful work of ancient times. The exterior is remarkable for the four most beautiful of all Egyptian colossi; representing Rameses II., seated on thrones attached to the rock, and the faces, of some which are fortunately well preserved, evince a beauty of expression the more striking as it is unlooked for in statues of such dimensions.

Their total height is about sixty-six feet, without the pedestal: the ear measures three feet five inches; fore-finger to the fork of the middle finger, three feet; from inner side of the elbow joint to the end of the middle finger, fifteen feet. The total height of the façade of the temple may be between ninety and one hundred feet. About thirty years ago Mr. Hay cleared to the base of the two colossi on the south side of the door; of which circumstance he made an inscription over the door-way. He also exposed to view the curious Greek inscription of the Ionian and Carian soldiers of Psammeticus, first discovered by Mr. Banks and Mr. Salt, as well as some interesting hieroglyphic tablets, which still remain in sight.

We found before the entrance at least fifty Arabs, men and children, busy taking the sand from the door-way, yet we had to stoop down and crawl into the interior, which comports well with the grandeur of the façade. The grand hall is immense, and supported by a double row of eight Osiride columns eighteen feet high, without the cap and pedestal; only one of which is entirely visible, the others being partially buried in the sand. The second room has only four square pillars, without statues, and to it succeeds a corridor, and the adytum, with two side chambers. Eight other rooms open on the grand hall, but they are very irregularly excavated, and some of them have lofty benches projecting from the walls. In the centre of the adytum is an altar, and at the upper end are four statues in relief. The walls are entirely covered with very well preserved sculptures, representing military expeditions from the time of Rameses. The heat was exceedingly oppressive, augmented by the resinous torches held by our men, and we were glad to get some fresh air. The rays of the sun being intense, Aline and I went back to our dahabeeh, while Tom, attended by Mr. Rogers, took a view of the great temple. The men are again rowing, and our boat is gliding over the water.

THURSDAY, February 6.

It is the first cloudy morning we have had. We arrived at Derr at a quarter before two P.M., where we tied up and went on shore. We passed through the town, which is entirely built of unburnt brick plastered with mud; and groves of date-trees give it a picturesque appearance. The temple here, having a depth of one hundred and two feet in the rock, is also from the reign of Rameses II. A great part of the portico is gone, the excavated portion alone remaining; while the sculptures are inferior to any that we have yet seen, and very much injured. This temple was consecrated to Amoun-Ra, from whence the city took the name of Pe-ra, or the city of the sun.

In leaving it we were surrounded by the natives, particularly women, offering to sell straw baskets coming from the White River. We have not yet found any of the Nubian women dressed as we had anticipated, *i.e.*, solely with the fringe: on the contrary, unlike the Egyptian women, who have part of the legs bare, they have long, wide drawers, falling almost to the feet, and wear loose dresses trailing on the ground. They are about the color of Indians, and have a peculiar mode of plaiting the hair in short braids which hang all around the head; nearly to the eyes on the forehead, and about six inches down the back. The end of the plait has a little bit of clay fastened on it, tending to keep it in place, while the hair is so plentifully smeared with castor-oil that the odor is far from being pleasant.

On our return we stopped before a house where a wedding was being celebrated. Some of the people brought us chairs, and about two dozen of the women, old and young, but all very ugly, commenced a sort of dance, to the music of a pair of drums. The time they kept was good, and the scene was certainly novel; that day they were probably more decorated than usual. Bits of metal were hanging from the braided ends on their foreheads, other bits were formed into necklaces and bracelets, while a few especially *élégantes* went so far as to have ear-rings and a nose-ring with coral pendents through one side of the nose only. After amusing ourselves with this sight we distributed some backsheesh, and left them to their enjoyment, followed by all the boys of the town.

We left Derr at twenty minutes past two, and were floating leisurely down stream, when the dragoman came to ask us if we were ready to go ashore. We were approaching the temple of Amada, which stands near the river, whose high banks were overgrown with gum-trees. It is built of large stones, but almost buried in the sand. The rooms, columns, and walls are covered with sculptures which have been painted, remarkable for the preservation of their colors; some being quite vivid.

The foundation of this temple seems to belong to the reign of Ousertasen III., 2,700 B.C. The names of Thousmes IV. and Amenhotep II. of the XVIIIth dynasty are also mentioned. In the first century of the Christian era this temple was transformed into a church, which explains much of its degradation, but still it is elegant in its style. Soon we are again floating down the river. The sunset is glorious, resembling the one we witnessed the day we left Cairo. The sky is flecked with silver and golden clouds, and as the sun declines towards the west, the pale moon is showing herself in the east.

FRIDAY, February 7.

No wind through the night. We expected to arrive in Dakkeh this morning, but at two o'clock we are still on our way. At six this morning we passed an American dahabeeh moored to the shore: none of her people being up, we could not ascertain who was on board, nor was any name visible. In the afternoon we took a walk, and found the country to be poor; some scattered mud-houses and the desert behind, sand everywhere, and one or two palm-trees, were all we met with, except some ten or twelve natives, who, as usual, followed us to our boat. In the evening we passed close to a dahabeeh, and as we asked the name, were answered: "Henry Williamson," probably an English gentleman.

SATURDAY, February 8.

We arrived at Dakkeh at one o'clock in the night, tied up to the shore, and early in the morning went to visit the temple; but I felt too unwell to appreciate its beauty. It is situated on the hill, five minutes from the river; has been quite extensive, and was built at different periods; first commenced in the time of Ptolemy Philadelphus, by the king of Ethiopia, Ergamene, and continued by two others, and even by the Romans under Augustus. During the time of the Christians, when all the idols were thrown down, this once so remarkable temple was much injured, and looks as though an earthquake had shattered it. Tom and Mr. Rogers examined it very carefully, while Aline and I sat in the sun and amused ourselves looking at all the antiquities offered by the natives.

I must say the contrast between their ancestors; what they have been, and the present inhabitants as they are; always pains me. Not feeling well I returned to the boat, carried by *fidèle* Osman; the sand being too heavy to permit me to walk. Before leaving Dakkeh, Aline and Mr. Rogers amused themselves giving backsheesh to all the children who had accompanied them, a scene always amusing. In the evening, at ten o'clock, we came in sight of Gerf-Hassayn. As the moonlight was brilliant, Mr. Rogers and Tom, with Mohammed and five men, went to visit its temple; and returned at midnight, not much pleased with the ruin, which is very rude and almost wholly destroyed.

SUNDAY, February 9.

We arrived at Kalabcheh at noon. This village, situated under the tropics, must once have been a very considerable city: the remains of whose temple, extending to the river, are perfectly wonderful. What is left of two great staircases and the high stone embankments attest what it once was. The masses of ruins are very imposing, of which three rooms still remain. First is a court, surrounded by columns, but only one of them now standing; then an immense hall, with noble doorways and columns, the chapiters and walls handsomely wrought; the figures showing better proportions than the generality of those we have seen in other temples. We sat down on a large shaft in the great hall; back of us was another chamber, probably the sanctum; but we left Tom and Mr. Rogers to inspect the remainder, as all the rooms are so full of huge stones that it was too difficult for us to climb over them.

After Aline had left us, with Mahommed, to return to the boat, Tom went on the side hills to seek a good position for a photographic view. After a while he returned and told us he had discovered part of a mummy, and wanted us to go and look at it; but this was not the only one, for we were among the mummy-pits, dug like small caves in the rock; and we took from one, as reminiscences, two feet, part of the lower jaw-bone, and a few pieces of cere-cloth. Aline did not much approve our antiquarian treasures, and it is true that their appearance is not very inviting. As usual, an amount of backsheesh was distributed, and at half-past five we left Kalabchch, much admiring its position among dom and palm trees.

We passed an hour in the evening on deck, listening to the songs of our sailors, accompanied by the splashing of the oars in the water. The night was calm, the water still, and the pass of Gebel-Kalabchch enchanting.

MONDAY, February 10.

I am still indisposed, and for the present do not enjoy much our Egyptian life. This morning, at ten, Tom, Aline, and Mr. Rogers went to visit the temple of Debout, built by an Ethiopian king; but it is so small and so rudely constructed that they did not take much interest in it. The weather was warm and invigorating, and we thought it probable we would arrive at Philæ before dark. At five we came in sight of it, and soon tied up to the shore, as we expect to stay three or four days. To-night, for more than two hours, we remained on deck, waiting for the appearance of the moon: it rose slowly from behind the hills opposite, and soon the entire globe was reflected brightly in the water, spreading its mantle of light on the romantic ruins of the island.

ISLAND OF PHILÆ.—See page 119.

CHAPTER IX.

PHILÆ, BEAUTIFUL PHILÆ!—BARON HUBNER—TEMPLE OF ISIS—MEMENTOS OF THE FRENCH ARMY—AN AMERICAN PARTY—IMPRESSIONS—EXCITING DESCENT OF THE CATARACT—ASSOUAN—AMERICAN CONSUL—MUSSULMAN SUNDAY—GEBEL SILSILEH—TEMPLE OF EDFOU—EL-KAB—ERMENT—THEBES AGAIN.

TUESDAY, February 11, 1868.

ABOUT one o'clock we received a visit from a party on board a small steamer, which we had observed lying on the opposite shore, and which we had supposed to be a tax-boat. There were four persons: consisting of Baron Hubner (celebrated in Austrian politics), Count and Countess of Schönbrun, and one of the state ministers of the Pacha. They were very agreeable, spoke much about Nubia, and were particularly interested in Tom's views. Refreshments were offered, and after stopping an hour, they left to take sketches of the Temples: and at three P.M. Mr. Rogers and I also went to visit the island. Beautiful Philæ! yet how much more beautiful with its splendid buildings and surrounding groves and gardens, now a mass of ruins, a picture of desolation, in the midst of which you silently pass, feeling sad at heart. It occupies a space of about twelve acres; and is elevated sufficiently above the river to be protected in the time of high water. The buildings are of sandstone, and all that remains is still admirable. They were commenced under the reign of Ptolemy Philadelphus (285–247 B.C.), and completed by his successor, Ptolemy Evergetes (247–222 B.C.). The principal temple, dedicated to Isis, is composed of a first pylone, a court-yard, a peristyle (on the left of which is a side temple), a second pylone, a portico, several halls, and the sanctuary. The width of the façade of the first pylone is one hundred and thirty feet; its height, fifty-six feet. The temple is everywhere ornamented with sculptures, but a great part of them were barbarously destroyed in the time of the early Christians. In the court-yard are the remains of several granite sphinxes. Near the terrace is a small but exceedingly interesting room, the four walls of which are decorated with hieroglyphics and symbolic figures; representing the various processes of embalming the dead; as well preserved as if they had been finished yesterday: being in a retired part of the temple, they have escaped mutilation from barbarous hands.

Under the first pylone I found a commemorative inscription, engraved by the French in 1799: and copied it just as it is. Above it in black letters is written:—

"Une page d'histoire ne doit pas être salie.

L'an VI. de la République le 13 Messidor
Une armée française, commandée
par Bonaparte, est descendue
à Alexandrie.

THE NILOMETER AND THE SACRED SOIL.   121

L'armée ayant mis vingt-jours
après les Mammelouks en fuite
Aux Pyramides.
Desaix commandant la
première division les a
poursuivis au-delà des
cataractes où il est arrivé
le 13 Ventose de l'an 7.

———

Les généraux de brigade
Davoust, Friand, et Belliard
Doubelot chef de l'état major
Latournerie Comm^{dt} l'Artillerie
Eppler chef de la 2eme legèrè
le 13 Ventose an VII. de la Républic
le 3 Mars an de J^s Cst 1799.

Gravé par Castex, sculpteur."

In the court, before passing the second pylone, in a corner on the left, we found also an inscription written by the scientific expedition of the same epoch:—

"R.F.
An 7.

Balzac.	Coquerel.	Corabœuf.
Castaz.	Coutelle.	Lagerière.
Ripault.	Lépère.	Mechain.
Nouet.	Lenoir.	Mectoux.
St. Genis.	Vincent.	

Longit. depuis Paris 30° 16′ 22″
Latitude boreale   24° 3′ 45″ "

The two colonnades to the south, forming an avenue in front of the grand temple, are of the time of the first Cæsars. On the riverside to the east is an edifice dominating all the others, open at the top and sustained by columns richly worked; the remains of a temple built by Nectanebos I. (378–386 B.C.), thirty years only before the conquest of Alexander. It is the most ancient monument on the island, and was dedicated to Isis. We passed hours in our examinations; but for a lover of antiquity, and one skilled in the knowledge of hieroglyphics, a month in Philæ would not prove too much.

WEDNESDAY, February 12.

It is now three o'clock. Ever since breakfast Tom has been busy taking photographic views, while Mr. Rogers, Aline, and I went on the island. I sat down in the little room near the terrace and tried to take a sketch of two Egyptian figures, but after several attempts gave it up in despair. During the afternoon our boat was moved to the other side of the island, and moored at the foot of the great temple. The slope of the hill on which it is situated is covered with palm and gum trees; and the depths of the shadow alternating with the light which the moon reflected, and the temple on the height, bathed in its silvery radiance, produced a charming effect: and I could not but indulge in deep and serious feelings while contemplating it, and went to sleep to dream of the past grandeur of Egypt. How hidden and mysterious are human destinies!

THURSDAY, February 13.

I feel a great deal better to-day; for a week everything in my eyes had assumed a gloomy aspect. This morning the cloudless sky, the singing of the few birds on the island, the gracious flight of our doves happy to be at liberty again, the good-humored laughter of our sailors, the limpidness of the water, with the reflection of the trees, the sweet air, the sun, all and everything find an answering chord in my heart, which is full of thankfulness to God, who has permitted me to come hither. Glory to Him!

At twelve o'clock, and just as we had finished lunch, Mohammed came to inform us that a party of Americans had arrived at Philæ, and were visiting the great temple. We soon saw them at the entrance, observing our American colors. Mr. Rogers and Tom went to speak to them, and learned that they arrived at Assouan the day before, on two dahabeehs; being a party of nine persons. One of the dahabeehs is the *Cleopatra*, the boat first chosen by us in Alexandria, and which has since been put in order, and Tom says that both gentlemen and ladies seem to be very sociable. He invited them to lunch with us, but the ladies were afraid to descend the steep hill, and expressed the desire to meet us in Thebes, where we will be about the same time. Several of them are from New York, others from Massachusetts, and a lady and two daughters from Cincinnati.

At three o'clock all of us went to pay a last visit to wonderful Philæ; and although I cannot agree with Warren that it is the loveliest island in the world, it *is*, perhaps, the most interesting, with all its ancient associations; yet it lacks its once beautiful gardens, now filled with rubbish; and no flowers but a few wild ones are to be found. Clear away the debris; prop up yon falling column; support that tottering entablature; plant shrubbery in its midst; thus making the ancient temples look still more grand, more sublime.

Beautiful Philæ!—as beautiful still, in your ruins, as you were in ages gone by! The sun of an eternal summer still gilds your shores, and the same pale moon that called to their midnight orisons the kingly priests of yore, still shines with its silvery light, awakening in the breast of the pale-faced stranger, who has wandered hence from his far home in the cold North, feelings of awe and reverence for Him to whom time is but a span in the circle of eternity!

Beautiful Philæ! Glimpses of the indistinct outlines of your temples are seen through the vistas of the waving palms; the shining river at your feet, the mountain heaps of boulders beyond, piled up at play by the giant descendants of the angels, long, long ages before the dark-skinned men of Ethiopia knew the land. Beautiful Philæ!

We left at half-past four, and moored near the cataract, so as to be ready to start as early as possible tomorrow morning, before the wind should commence to blow, otherwise we would be detained until it had subsided.

FRIDAY, February 14.

At a quarter before seven we were up and taking breakfast. The reis of the cataract, with his two steersmen and ordinary escort of men (at least fifty), had arrived. We went upon deck; and with much clamor the men commenced to row toward the rapids, of which there are three. The first is the largest, being at least

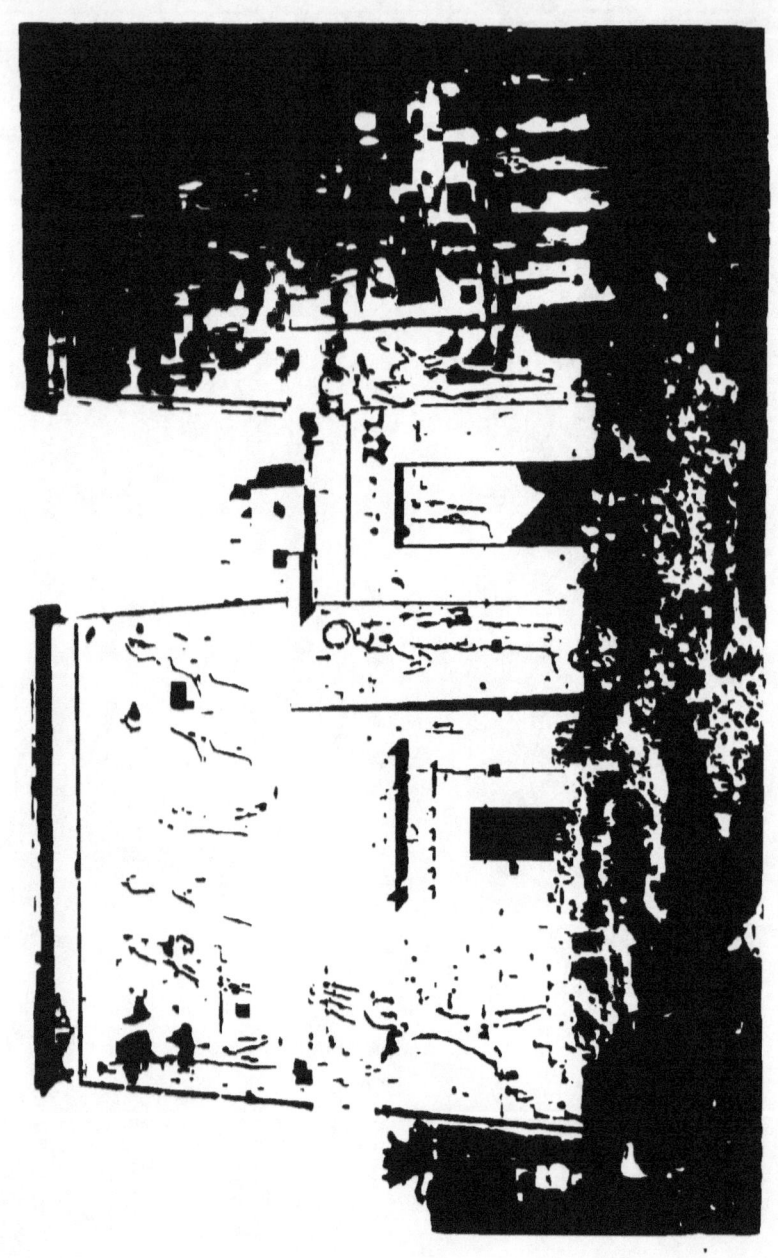

TEMPLE OF ISIS.—*See page* 120.

thirty-three feet high, with the waters boiling against the rocks; the most splendid, exciting, admirable, and frightful scene we had ever witnessed, being a different channel to that by which we had made the ascent. If by the least error we miss our course, our boat will be dashed to pieces, and we shall be inevitably lost; but we descended successfully, and only struck a rock after we had passed through. How I wish Mr. Chagot had been there, to reproduce our boat as it was dancing on the whirling waters, seemingly attracted by the rocks, but held by a sure hand, and passing with incredible rapidity between them. The two other gates were far inferior to the first, yet were quite exciting.

We arrived at Assouan at half-past nine, and found two dahabeehs moored to the shore: one very small, which we had seen at Cairo, called the *Morning Star*, under British colors, and another, the *Fawn*, flying the American flag. While Tom and Mr. Rogers were inspecting the quarries, we went with Mohammed to buy feathers. After examining the bazaars, which are the cleanest we have yet seen in Egypt, we returned to the boat, and soon after received a call from the American Consul. We accepted his invitation to visit his wife and daughters, which we propose to do with the gentlemen.

Upon the return of Tom and Mr. Rogers they report the quarries as well worth seeing. From here were taken all those huge blocks of hard granite so plentifully strewn throughout the land in the form of statues; and there is still to be seen an enormous obelisk, a hundred feet in length, which has never been detached from its parent bed on account of a flaw, only discovered after the work had proceeded thus far. Peculiar marks upon the surfaces of the rocks, about a foot apart, showing where cuts had been made, about six inches wide and nine deep, are still visible, indicating that something had here been inserted to split off the desired portion. Was this water, dry wood afterward wetted, or wedges of iron, upon which a number of workmen, equal to the number of wedges, would incessantly strike until the rock parted? Whatever the great power employed to cut the huge stones, convey them hundreds of miles, and set them up in their new places, no doubt it was exceedingly simple.

Having taken lunch, we went to the Consul's, and were shown to the back part of the house, into what might be called the parlor—a small room with a ceiling, enclosed only on three sides, the fourth, opening upon a yard, full of doves and other birds. The room was carpeted, and a very wide divan, with cushions, occupied the greater part of it. The Consul's son, a handsome Egyptian, introduced us to his wife and sister, the former being a young and pretty woman of about nineteen, but the sister having nothing very pleasing in her countenance. We were certainly more of a curiosity to them than they were to us; for, after shaking hands, they passed their time inspecting us, and commenting on our peculiar fashion of dress. They wore loose robes of silk, with mantillas on their heads, and loads of gilt necklaces and bracelets. Soon the gentlemen came in, preceded by the father, who is a Copt, which explains his admitting strangers, and particularly gentlemen, to his house. The two women were very bashful, the sister particularly so, and hid her face whilst the gentlemen were present. Coffee and dates were handed around, after which the Consul presented us with two red Egyptian vases and several drinking-cups made of the mud of the country: but as they would have occupied too much space in our moderate-sized trunks, we were not able to take them to Paris. After leaving the Consul's we went through the bazars again, and stopped at the one we had visited in the morning while looking for feathers; it being new and handsomely built, we wished Tom and Mr. Rogers to see it. The owner, who is a merchant, and the richest one of Assouan, has several similar ones. We found him in his store, dressed in a blue silk wrapper, and were received by him most cordially, taking us to the top of the house, and showing us everything. It being a Sabbath-day with them, we left him washing his feet to go to the mosque, and in the bazars we found many doing the same thing. The mosque being open, we could see Mahommedans kneeling down on the ground praying. We had hardly reached the boat when the Governor of Assouan, with his clerk, who carried the customary inkstand hanging on his breast, and the captain of a steamer which was lying in port, came to call on us. We entertained them as well as we could, and before they left the governor caused his clerk to write his name, and the date of his visit to us, in Egyptian characters, in my journal. We left Assouan at about three o'clock P.M., and Mohammed says we will be at Kom-Ombos to-night. The guide-book informs us that very little is left of it, that the ancient city as well as the two temples, or rather what remains of them, are nearly buried beneath the sand, so that we have decided not to visit that scene of desolation, but to push on to Gebel-Silsileh.

SATURDAY, February 15.

The most cloudy day we have yet experienced on the river. We passed Kom-Ombos at five o'clock this morning, whence our little boat brought Osman on board, one of our crew who had been visiting his parents. At ten o'clock we came in view of the *Cleopatra*, which had left Assouan twenty-four hours before us, and we learned that she had been aground since yester evening. We exchanged salutes, and then sent ten of our crew to help theirs, and after an hour and a half hard labor they succeeded in getting afloat again. They thanked us through our men, who returned delighted, each one having received a bottle of wine for his work. We commenced to row again, and soon arrived at Gebel-Silsileh, where the *Cleopatra*, *Rachel* (which we had also overtaken), and *Oriental* tied up near each other; and Tom introduced us to the two parties, who are the same that came to visit Philæ while we were there. On the *Rachel* was Mrs. Potter, who is in deep mourning, her two daughters, a governess, and a courier; and on the *Cleopatra*, Mr. and Mrs. Prentiss Dow, Mrs. Sherrer, Mr. Briggs, son of the ex-Governor of Massachusetts, and his mother-in-law, a remarkably active old lady, certainly seventy years of age.

The name Gebel-Silsileh, applies to a defile of the

valley, where the two parallel chains of hills which border the river approach each other until they are only five hundred yards apart. The Arabs have a tradition that in by-gone times the river was closed by means of a chain, extended from one shore to the other, and thus the name had its origin—Silsileh in Arabic signifying chain. There are in the rocks a great many grottoes or sepulchres. The most remarkable of these excavations presents at the exterior a façade, supported by four pillars, and among the hieroglyphical inscriptions are the cartouches of the kings of the XVIIIth dynasty, and of the following ones. The bass-reliefs, as well as the hieroglyphics, are much defaced, and it is very difficult to decipher them. Tom obtained a very good picture of the façade of the temple, cut in the solid rock, with Aline, Mohammed, and myself sitting in front.

What renders Silsileh very interesting is the immense sandstone quarries, which in former times furnished enormous stones for the erection of the temples in all Egypt. They are very extensive, but all now is silent. Centuries ago the chisel of the workman ceased to resound, and you pass on gravely, with nothing to disturb your thoughts except your own voice, which, as you speak, is repeated by sonorous echoes. Egypt! Egypt! with wise and powerful men at thy head thou yet couldst become a rich and mighty nation!

We left at four o'clock for Edfou. Tom sent invitations to the parties of the two boats to come and pass the evening with us, which they accepted; and after dinner our deck and the door of the saloon were decorated with red, white, and blue lanterns, in honor of our

6*

visitors, who arrived at eight o'clock. We passed a very agreeable and social evening, while amid a general conversation tea, champagne, lemonade, crackers of all descriptions, and French confectionery were offered, and we had the satisfaction, when our visitors departed, to hear that this was the pleasantest evening they had passed on the Nile. We arrived at Edfou at eleven o'clock at night.

SUNDAY, February 16.

We started as soon as we had finished breakfast to visit the temple of Edfou, which is certainly the most beautiful we have yet seen in Egypt. Its grand and imposing aspect impresses you with a feeling of wonder and admiration; and it is not only the grandest, but the best preserved of all the temples of High Egypt. Eight years ago the whole of the interior was concealed by the houses of the modern inhabitants, so that a very small part of it was accessible, through a narrow aperture, and could only be examined with the assistance of a light; at all times annoyed by the troublesome importunities of the people. Under the orders of Mr. Mariette it has been entirely excavated, and is protected by the government, which has placed a guard, with twenty-five men under his control, to keep it in order. The door leads into an immense court, supported in front by nine columns, and on each side by twelve—thirty-three in all—covered with hieroglyphics and sculptures; thence to the temple, with a portico of twelve immense columns; the chapiters, as in Esneh, being each differently worked. The naos, or sanctuary, with a granite altar, where the gods were placed, is surrounded by nine lateral rooms, the walls of which are covered with sculptures and hieroglyphics, all in perfect preservation. We went down by a narrow passage to the well formerly used by the priests and their attendants, and which is still filled with water. The building is full of secret staircases, long corridors in the walls, without apparent issues, but which certainly have some hidden ones. We ascended to the top of the temple by forty-two steps, and there had a splendid view of the green fields, the river, which here forms a considerable curve, and the city, consisting of at least three hundred houses, all built of crude bricks; and as they have no roofs, we got a glimpse of their interiors, all very dirty. They contained no furniture, and only straw for bedding, while the sheep are joint occupants with the people. The pigeon-houses are much better built than the habitations, and present a very pretty appearance from a short distance. The parties of the two boats joined us in our visit, and agreed with us that it was worth coming to Egypt, if only to see and admire this temple. We remained six or seven hours, and during the heat of the mid-day sun, the long galleries, supported by columns in the great court, afforded us a cool and pleasant retreat, while the sculptures on the walls and columns were interesting to examine. Probably it has served the same purpose to the priests of ancient times. We left Edfou in the afternoon, and arrived at El-Kab at eleven o'clock at night.

Monday, February 17.

The *Rachel* has left the *Cleopatra*, and is on her way to Thebes. After breakfast we, in company with the party of the *Cleopatra*, started to visit the celebrated grottoes of El-Kab, which village marks the site of Elethya, opposite Hieracopolis. As we were riding our donkeys we could see before us, the walls of the ancient city, constructed of hollow bricks; and numerous mounds, formed by quantities of rubbish, covering a considerable space which was formerly occupied by private residences. A few remains of temples have alone escaped the raid of time; but they were so distant, and the weather so warm, that we decided not to examine them.

We visited the most curious and important remains of Elethya,—her grottoes, cut in the heights which terminate the plain, and overlook the site of the ancient city. Near a great rock called El-Mohamid, several of these hypogees, ornamented with sculptures, date from the first kings of the XVIIIth dynasty; and are certainly tombs of high dignitaries and puissant lords. The sculptures on the walls, as the subjects they represent, are highly interesting; the coloring being still in perfect preservation. All the details of agriculture, fishing, hunting, embalming, and preparation of mummies are represented. The owner of the tomb is seated on a handsome chair, with his wife near him, and a favorite monkey at his feet; a great number of his friends are seated near them, smelling the lotus; while others are playing on instruments of music.

We left El-Kab at eleven o'clock, on our way to Thebes, where we expected to find letters from home. At half-past four we arrived at Esneh, and as our dragoman stopped to have coffee ground, Aline, Tom, and Mr. Rogers went on shore, to take a walk in the Pacha's garden. During their absence Mr. Dow came to invite us to pass the evening with them, while floating down the Nile. At six P.M. the *Cleopatra* got under way, but we had to wait for the return of Mohammed, who did not get back until after nine; and consequently abandoned our intended visit. A strong wind having risen from the north, rendered it impossible to make any head-way; we therefore remained at Esneh until morning.

TUESDAY, February 18.

Only once before have we had such a cloudy sky since we have travelled in Egypt. We had head-wind all day, and heard that the *Cleopatra* was obliged to stop on that account, and lay all night behind the Pacha's garden. Under way in the afternoon, and reached Ermont at ten o'clock at night.

WEDNESDAY, February 19.

At nine o'clock we took donkeys, and went to visit the temple of Ermont. It was at least three miles from the dahabeeh; but we enjoyed the ride, as the country was beautiful and abounded in trees. Half of the way we passed through an alley, with a row of acacias on each side; on our right and left were groves of palms, while beyond were fields of wheat, peas, etc., of an emerald green. We heard that all that section of the country belongs to the Pacha, which accounts for the good farming.

Very little is left of the temple of Erment. The village marks the site of ancient Hermonthis, which name it still retains. The ancient temple of the time of Thousmes III., of the XXIIId. dynasty, has entirely disappeared. One hundred years before the Christian era, a second temple was built by Ptolemy Alexander, and his mother, Cleopatra. It is situated on the left of the mounds, and there now remain only three or four columns, probably a part of the portico, and near them a room in which the hieroglyphics are well preserved; but it was so filthy we could hardly go through it.

We left Erment at eleven o'clock, and, favored by a strong wind, "*made*" Thebes at half-past two. The *Cleopatra* and the *Rachel* had arrived yesterday. One English boat was also here, and two steamers, of which one was that of Baron Von Hubner, the Austrian Minister, and Count and Countess of Schönbrun; the other, a passenger steamboat. Tom and Mr. Rogers went at once to the Consulate, to inquire for letters. Mr. Ferris found a great many for him, but there were none for me. Mr. Dow, having met them, asked after us, and we resolved to go and pass the evening with them. We met there an American gentleman, Mr. Smith, an antiquary, who has lived here ten years, and has a collection of Egyptian antiquities, which he sells at exorbitant prices, a single scarabee being sometimes valued as high as five, six, and even seven pounds sterling. In conversation with us, he corrected the impression received from some of Warren's remarks regarding Lady Duff Gordon, who, he asserted, is not at all as eccentric as represented in his book.

CHAPTER X.

THEBES—TEMPLES OF MEDINET-ABOU—RAMESIUM—COLOSSAL STATUE OF RAMESES—THE VOCAL MEMNON—AN ADVENTURE—KOORNAH—ASSASOEF—DAYR-EL-BAHREE—DJALMA—HIS HOME—WASHINGTON'S BIRTHDAY—ILLUMINATION.

THURSDAY, February 20, 1868.

WE were up early, and at eight o'clock met the *Cleopatra* party on the opposite bank, and all started at the same time for Medinet-Abou. The first ten minutes of the ride was through sand; and the wind being very strong made it quite unpleasant; but soon we came to a green and cultivated part of the country. The two temples of Medinet-Abou (the name is Arabic) are situated about four miles, or about one hour's ride, from the shore. At the time of the Mussulman conquest a small Copt city being near it, the inhabitants had appropriated, for the culture of the Christian faith, several of the halls of the great temple. On the approach of the enemy they fled to Esneh, and since that time it has been deserted.

The houses had been built on the monticules of rubbish, which were so high that in some parts they were on a level with the highest points of the temple. Mr. Mariette, the director of the Museum at Cairo, has had the *débris* that had accumulated within the temple in part cleared away; but the work is far from being completed. The smaller temple was commenced by Thousmes I., of the XVIIIth dynasty, about 1660 B.C., and terminated by his successors Thousmes II. and III. The royal pavilion and the great temple belong to the reign of Rameses III., the founder of the XXth dynasty, toward the year 1280 B.C. All these buildings face the Nile.

I shall not attempt to describe the small temple of Thousmes I., because it loses all of its importance near the large one, whose ruin is still very impressive. Seated all together on the top of the second pylone, we had a fine view of the whole edifice. In front was the great court, one hundred and ten by one hundred and forty-five feet, having on one side a gallery formed of seven pillars, with caryatides, and on the opposite side eight large columns. The walls of the houses of the ancient village formerly filled this yard. Mr. Mariette had a part removed, but half of it is yet choked with dirt and bricks; and the columns are buried within six feet of the top. The caryatides are almost all either broken or buried; two are covered with mud; two others are badly mutilated; two again broken to the waist, and another to the knee. On each side of these are small statues, coming only as high as their knees. In our rear, the great court is superior to any we have yet seen; its portico was one of the handsomest existing in Egypt, being 125 × 135 feet. The galleries which surround it were formed, on the right, by eight pillars, which formerly supported caryatides; on the left, similar ones; while on the north and south were corresponding numbers: in former times, painted and ornamented with emblematic figures. I counted twenty-four columns, but they were all broken at about the height of five feet from the surface. The walls of the gallery on each side are covered with sculptures and hieroglyphics, and the painting on some of them is very fresh. The rest of the temple is a mass of ruins, so that I could not follow the traces of the former edifice.

Leaving Medinet-Abou, we visited the palace of Rameses II., which was known for a long time under the name of Memnonium; but since the reading of the inscriptions by Champollion, no doubt remains about the constructor of this once magnificent palace, and its true designation. The reign of Rameses II., the Sesostris of Grecian historians, is placed between 1407 and 1341 before the Christian era. The palace, when it stood in its glory, was composed of a monumental entrance, a large court ornamented with a double row of columns, forming a gallery; two large halls, supported by numerous columns, and by a suite of apartments forming the extremity of the edifice. A dromos and an alley of sphinxes added to the grandeur of the palace, while the interior was ornamented with sculptures, paintings, and colossal statues. The last have been broken, the greater part of the walls and columns thrown down, the paintings obliterated, and what remain of the sculptures mutilated.

All this was the destructive work of Cambyses, who avenged himself on a conquered people, and at the same time annihilated the record of victories over the Persians, whose remembrance they perpetuated. The two pylones which formed the façade are partially standing, but the bass-reliefs thereon are almost defaced. The colossal statue of Rameses, cut in rose granite of Assouan, is badly broken, and its pieces cover a large part of the court. Its size, when entire, confounds the imagination; for, although seated, Wilkinson says that it was more than forty feet high, being nearly eleven times the natural height, and was cut from a single block. It is calculated that its weight was more than a million of kilos, or eight hundred and eighty-seven tons. The hall following the yard, where the statue of Rameses is lying, presents only a scene of destruction; two broken statues of black marble have fallen on the ground, the head of one of which is still perfect. Of the rooms at the rear of the edifice, there is only one entire, supported by eight columns; back of these we walked on monticules of rubbish, and from time to time next to a pit; and one hundred and sixty feet farther on we found some vaulted arches, built of brick, as well as bases of columns, and probably the construction of the palace extended beyond these.

On our return we stopped before the two colossi of Memnon; which seated on thrones, and of the same immense proportions, are seen for miles off on the plain. They were cut from coarse, hard grit-stone, and the faces are much mutilated. Twenty-seven years before the Christian era one of the statues was broken in the centre, attributed by Eusebius to an earthquake, from which the monuments of Thebes suffered much: and in the third century, under the reign of Septimus Severus, the injured part was rebuilt by means of blocks of sandstone placed one on another, as seen to-day. It was known under the name of the vocal statue of Memnon, because it was said that every day at sunrise it would utter an harmonious sound. A little boy climbed up, and striking against a large stone lying in the lap of the statue, it emitted a metallic ring; and this stone undoubtedly has some connection with the ancient tradition.

When we were almost in sight of the dahabeeh, I perceived that I had lost one of my sleeve-buttons, and then remembered that while I was looking at Rameses' statue I had heard something fall on a stone, without knowing what it was. I valued them highly, as they were given to me by a dear friend; and having informed Aline of my loss, I ordered my guide to come with me, and galloped my donkey all the distance back, about three miles and a half. The guide was very obliging, but was afraid night would come sooner than I expected, and while showing me the sun, just setting behind the hills, he excited the donkey to gallop faster and faster. It was a glorious ride, such as I never had enjoyed before, and not amiss either in emotions; for on arriving at the ruins, and being surrounded by a dozen Arabs, I began to reflect that it was not very prudent for me to have come thus by myself; yet I showed no signs of fear, and looked for my button. I did not find it, but as soon as I offered a dollar reward, it was given to me by an Arab. While returning at full gallop, and about half-way back, I met Mr. Rogers coming to find me, afraid that something might have happened to me alone among these people. It was dark when we reached our boat, and Tom and Aline had commenced dinner.

FRIDAY, February 21.

We started at ten o'clock for Kournah, a temple north of Medinet-Abou, which was commenced by Rameses I., king of the XIXth dynasty, 1460 B.C. It looks beautifully from afar, surrounded as it is by trees, but loses much of its beauty as you approach it. It was rudely built, and is far from having the grandeur of Medinet-Abou. Its dimensions are small; three doors under a vestibule give entrance to the interior. The room in the centre is sixty feet in depth, and the roof was supported by six columns, but the interior is so full of stones and rubbish that we could hardly pass through it; the sculptures on the walls and the hieroglyphics, however, are well chiselled. On the right and left are three small chambers, while at the extremity are some others; but the degradation of the edifice is such that you can with difficulty distinguish their location. A fine view presented itself from the top of the temple which faces the east. To the south was Medinet-Abou; the figure of Memnon and its companion out in the plain; then the Palace of Rameses II., with his overthrown colossal statue. Behind us were the Lybian hills, honey-combed with the tombs of the ancient inhabitants; so numerous indeed, that it would consume weeks to visit them all. Looking to the east over the river we saw the ruins of Luxor, and farther to the North, those of Karnak. The plains between the river and the temple were covered with a growth of green and luxuriant vegetation, with here and there interspersed groves of palm and acacia-trees, and nearly at our feet, a short distance to the north-east, were several sheiks' tombs.

Three hours during the afternoon were employed by the gentlemen in visiting the tombs, among which were those of Assasoef; but the odor within was so unpleasant, owing to the enormous quantity of bats with which they are filled; that Aline and I preferred to stay in the fresh air. As we were taking our lunch near the ruins of the temple of Dayr-el-Bahree, we met the Governor, whom I have christened "Prince Djalma," and who had come there to sketch. He followed us to the Ramesium, where Tom went to take a view, and upon his invitation we stopped at his house, which was on our way to the dahabeeh.

We first entered a room encircled by blue satin divans; several *étagères* were filled with Egyptian antiquities, and a rich Turkish carpet covered the floor. A servant soon entered, carrying a waiter covered with an embroidered velvet, bordered with silver fringe. The master of the house removed the cloth, which had concealed sherbet, and taking a tulle napkin, also embroidered with silver, and having a similar fringe, presented a glass to Aline. While she was drinking he stood before her, napkin in hand, and when she had finished, gave her the napkin to wipe her mouth; then coming to me he did the same, and afterwards to the gentlemen. A few minutes later the servant again came in with little cups of excellent coffee, each one in a silver holder; then, chibouks having been presented to the gentlemen,

Effendi Djalma invited us ladies to enter his wife's apartments. She is as handsome a woman as he is a man, and was robed in a magnificent costume: large and flowing purple silk brocade drawers, embroidered with a flower in gold, and a similar tunic trimmed with little tassels of gold, and over it, with wide sleeves, a velvet coat, also richly embroidered with gold. Her long, lightly undulating hair was flowing gracefully around her face, and plaited behind; a little toque of purple crape was fastened on the side by a diamond aigrette; her ears and fingers were also adorned with diamonds. Her skin was not very dark, and she had long, soft, languishing eyes, with black curved eye-lashes, a Grecian nose, a little mouth, showing such teeth as are only seen here. How handsome she was! and we found her to be equally graceful and amiable. She would not sit until we had seated ourselves, and only took her cigarette after Aline had smoked it a moment, and presented it to her. We remained with her an hour, speaking more by pantomime than otherwise, as our Egyptian vocabulary did not exceed ten words. Her joy to see Europeans was extreme. She wanted to have us remain to dinner, and every time we rose to take leave would make us sit down again. No other man than her husband ever sees her; she never goes out but at night, and then with a mask on her face. We bade her adieu, after having promised to come again; and her nurse, who was with her during our visit, in bidding us "Good-day" and "Good-by," almost knelt down in kissing our hands.

After our return, and while dining, we received an

invitation from Mrs. Potter to pass the evening on board the *Rachel*, which we accepted. To-morrow being the 22d of February, we intend to celebrate it, and in the evening have a grand illumination. Among others we invited Mrs. Potter; but she is doubtful if she will be able to accept, being quite anxious to leave. The fact is, that she has fallen on a bad dragoman, and since her departure from Cairo has been deprived of so much comfort that she is tired of Nile life. We have now had several occasions to see that our boat is the best provided of all those we have met with, and it is a satisfaction to think that, if we have paid dearer than others, our comforts and luxuries are proportionately greater.

SATURDAY, February 22.

At seven o'clock Tom was on deck, firing a national salute. The weather, as usual, is fine and warm; just enough breeze to cause our flags and banners to wave gracefully in the air. Aline and I, feeling fatigued, remained at *home*, while the gentlemen went to visit the tombs of the kings, a ride of some two hours and a half. We passed our time in writing, and in the afternoon, Mustapha Aga having come to visit us, we invited him to be present at the evening reception. Tom and Mr. Rogers returned at half-past five, very tired, and immediately sent invitations to the *Cleopatra*, *Rachel*, and *Fawn*—the latter an American dahabeeh which had arrived in the morning, having on board Mr. Beadel and two sons, from New York, whom we had already met at Assouan. In the afternoon Mohammed had anchored the boat in the midst of the stream, presenting a broadside to the port, and at half-past seven the illumination was completed, just as it had been on our first visit to Thebes. Messrs. Beadel were the first visitors, then Mustapha Aga, and while waiting for the other guests, we went with Messrs. Beadel in the yawl, to inspect the illumination. Rowing by the shore, we saw a little boat approaching, and as it neared fired a salute of thirteen guns; it was the party of the *Cleopatra,* and as we row along the river, all admired the beautiful *coup-d'œil* the dahabech presented. A few minutes after we re-entered our saloon, and soon Mrs. Potter and her two daughters made their appearance, expressing their delight. Mrs. Potter remarked that she had heard of illuminations on the Nile, but had no idea it could be done thus. "You want to revive the Arabian nights," said she.

The celebration of Washington's birthday on the *Oriental,* I am sure, will be remembered in after years by all those present, for never was a more agreeable evening passed. At half-past nine tea was served, and the table crowded with cakes, canned peaches, pears, mulberries, and several kinds of French confectionery. At eleven, champagne was offered; and as every one had their glass in hand, Mr. Ferris spoke thus:—

"Ladies and Gentlemen — Though strangers to one another a few days ago, we have met in this grand old land, where the remembrance of our common country has at once made us friends.

"Who can pass through the land of the Pharaohs, where the marvellous ruins of a long past age and evidences of a mighty race meet him at every turn, and not be struck with awe that such things have been, and are not! This, the natal day of our great hero, is a fitting occasion to compare the past of Egypt with the future of the great Republic of the Far West. The crisis is happily past, and I believe our destiny to be as great, if not greater, than ever was the condition here. Future ages will see great temples and colossal statues in our own country, and all the world doing homage, as once did all the world to this now dead land.

"Ladies and Gentlemen, permit me to give you as a toast, 'The Prosperity of the Great Republic and the Memory of Washington.'"

Then each one drank, and an impressive silence followed, which was broken by Mr. Smith, the antiquary, who spoke as follows:—"Permit me to make a few observations, ladies and gentlemen, in reference to the remarks of Mr. Ferris. In some of the ancient hieroglyphical writings of the Egyptians is written, in reference to death and a future state: '*Fear not to die, for you will again arise, and live in a great land in the West, in the United States.*'"

At midnight all was dark on board. We had met the parties of the *Cleopatra* and *Rachel* perhaps for the last time, as both boats left before morning.

SUNDAY, February 23.

We started at ten o'clock from the boat for Karnak, following a handsome road, having on both sides green fields, groves of palms, and acacias. As we proceeded, we passed through an avenue of broken colossal statues representing rams, of which I counted sixty, still in their original places. This avenue, in its perfect condition, over a mile long, consisted of six hundred of them; some holding between their paws a small statue of the king Amenophis III.

At its extremity is the most beautiful propylon we have yet seen, the two fronts being covered with sculptures and hieroglyphics. Its height is about one hundred feet; the width of the entrance, twenty feet; the thickness of its walls, twelve feet; and the depth, thirty-five feet. This triumphal arch was built by Ptolemy Evergetes, 247 years B.C. After passing beneath it, we found ourselves in a small avenue, having on our right a few broken sphinxes, and before us the remains of a temple commenced under Rameses III., and terminated by Rameses VIII., both of the XXth dynasty, between 1288 and 1200 B.C. Its columns are low and massive, and the sculptures and hieroglyphics on the walls remarkably well preserved.

We took our lunch in a shady niche on its top, having before our eyes the grand Temple of Karnak, and returned to the boat at three o'clock, where we found Mustapha Aga, who dined with us, and who in return invited us to partake at his house, to-morrow night, of an oriental dinner.

SATURDAY, February 29.

We are still in Thebes since the 23d, and have been so much occupied that I could find no time to write until to-day.

Mustapha Aga's dinner was certainly a very curious affair, but a repetition would not be desirable. His house is built on the ruins of the Temple of Luxor, which we have not yet visited. He had prepared everything in truly Eastern style; and a green arched avenue, formed of palm-leaves, through which we passed, was constructed in honor of our visit. The room which we then entered was arranged with elegant carpets and divans; on the wall at one side the American flag, and opposite the English one, were spread for the occasion, as Mustapha was expecting, among others, four English gentlemen from the *Alice*, wrecked in the cataract; Lord Ellesmere and friends. When the news of the catastrophe reached Cairo, the Viceroy gave orders that a steamer should be sent for them and placed at their disposal. We knew that they were descending the river, but they did not arrive in time to join the feast.

Having waited half an hour, which time we occupied in reading the names in the visitors' book, several gentlemen, two French and two English, who were "*doing*" the Nile in a steamer furnished by the Viceroy, made their appearance: Capt. Harvey W. Hoare, Henry Standish, Henry du Rocher, and Henry Baron de Commailles.

After introductions and salutations were exchanged, Mustapha invited us to the dining-room. Servants were in attendance, one holding an empty ewer, another warm water to wash the hands, while a third handed a napkin to each guest. A low table of white marble, round, and with a deep border, was in the centre of the room; and as many cushions as there were guests were lying on the floor about it; with a tumbler, a spoon, and a small loaf of bread for each. We sat down as well as we could "à la Turque," and commenced with the soup, each one putting his spoon into the general tureen. Fortunately, a small bowlful was placed before our party of four, and thus we did not feel quite as much disgusted as we would, had we been obliged to join the rest.

An entire lamb, stuffed with rice, came next, and was delicious; but the manner in which it was manipulated by the Governor, who with his hands tore it asunder, took much of our appetite away; while Mustapha, DOING THE HONORS, handed each a piece with his fingers. It seemed so strange to receive that greasy bit of meat from his black hand, that, for a moment, each looked at the other, and the same thought came to all, "Shall we eat or not?" But poor Mustapha had given himself so much trouble that we felt it would not be right to disappoint him, and, "*Faisant contre mauvaise fortune, bon cœur,*" conquered our scruples, and laughing more than eating, enjoyed ourselves greatly.

There were so many dishes that I can hardly remember them: stewed mutton and potatoes, stewed tomatoes, beans, cauliflower, macaroni, peas, a Turkish dish of rice rolled in little vine-leaves, a large turkey, pudding, apricots, oranges, and apples; while three kinds of wine, claret, marsala, and champagne, were freely served. This, however, was an innovation, as the *faithful* never indulge in intoxicating drinks. The gentlemen present were *gens du monde*, very witty, and helped to pass the time most agreeably.

When done with dinner, the ewer and warm water were again offered, and having washed our hands, we entered the large hall, illuminated with red, white, and blue lanterns, sent from our boat. Mustapha, for our amusement, had prepared an entertainment, which was the performance of the Ghawassee, or dancing-girls.

This was transporting us back to Ptolemaic times, when the king ordered in his maids to do honor to and confer pleasure on his guests. Thus had we often seen it delineated on the temple walls; the customs of past ages typified in their peculiar dance.

Other times, other manners! That which might have pleased the dames of the courts of Rameses and of Ptolemy was rather trying to our sense of propriety. The dance, or rather posturing, was so lascivious that we ladies retired early, leaving the gentlemen to its enjoyment. Zara, the youngest and prettiest of them, had no need to regret the occasion, for she left that night with her head-dress plentifully bespangled with little golden coins, gifts of the gentlemen present.

The manners of the ancient Egyptians, notwithstanding that thousands of years must have elapsed before they could have attained the high state of cultivation everywhere apparent, were in some instances of the most primitive order. Thus we find it rather the rule than the exception, that the kings married their own sisters, and the queens took to their beds and thrones their younger brothers, as was the case with the celebrated Cleopatra.

We do not know if this custom generally prevailed among the people. It might have been that it was confined to royalty, whose members, for reasons of state, were forced to adopt this method of concentrating power in the royal family; as at the present time the laws of England recognize no marriage contracted between royalty and a commoner,—thus hoping to avoid a repetition of the wars of the Roses, which so long convulsed that kingdom.

Whether or not this condition led to immorality is best answered by noting the career of the Egyptian Queen, who by her blandishments and beauty led Anthony to his ruin. The man who had revelled in the luxuries and dissipations of the world's capital was powerless to resist the attacks of the African beauty; sacrificed supreme power; fled while the battle was raging which had for its stake the government of a world; directed the sword-point to his breast at the false alarm of her death, rather than live bereft of her charms. This siren, who afterwards with her coquetry held spell-bound for a time the conqueror of Anthony and of Rome, felt no shame, nor did any abridgment of power or popularity among her own subjects seem to have followed, this lascivious life; but when her influence over Cæsar waned, and the cold-blooded politician determined that she should grace his triumphal entry as a captive of war, the abasement was unbearable.

There was no remorse for the former position; but the disgrace of the latter was overpowering, and death from the sting of the poisonous asp was a thousand times preferable to such terrible degradation.

TUESDAY, February 25.

We spent the day at the ruins of Karnak. Karnak was commenced under the the XIIth Diospolite dynasty, 2810 years B.C., by Ousertasen, who began the sanctuary; and for 2800 years the kings of Egypt did not cease to work for the preservation, grandeur, and embellishment of that great edifice, which was the national monument and pride of the country.

Upon our first visit we were disappointed. That immense field of ruins was not what we had expected; but the oftener you see it the more you are impressed with its grandeur and beauty. The great hall, containing one hundred and thirty-four columns, constructed by Sethi, the father of Rameses II., formed a part of the largest of all the Egyptian temples; being three hundred and twenty-five feet in width, and one hundred and sixty-five feet in depth. Twelve columns, larger than the others, form the main avenue, each being thirty two feet in circumference, and all are covered with sculpture.

These, with an obelisk ninety feet high, standing near (nineteen feet taller than the one in Paris), and covered with hieroglyphics, constitute the most perfect part of these stupendous ruins. We have been four times to Karnak, and will return once again by moonlight. Tom, as a remembrance, has taken several views.

Of Karnak, Warburton says:—

"There lay Karnak; darkening a whole horizon with its portals, pyramids, and palaces. We passed under a noble archway, and entered a long avenue of sphinxes; all their heads were broken off, but their pedestals remained unmoved since the time of Joseph. It must have been a noble sight in the palmy days of Thebes—that avenue of two hundred enormous statues, terminated by that temple. Yet this was only one of many:

at least seven others, with similar porticos and archways, led from this stupendous edifice.

"We rode through half a mile of sphinxes, and then arrived at the temple, the splendor of which no words can describe. A glorious portal opened into a vast court, crowded with a perfect forest of the most magnificent columns, thirty-six feet in circumference, covered with hieroglyphics, and surmounted by capitals, all of different patterns, and richly painted. No two persons agree on the number of these apparently countless columns; some make it amount to one hundred and thirty-four, others one hundred and sixty; the central measures sixty-six feet in height, exclusive of the pedestals and abacus.

"Endless it would be to enter into details of this marvellous pile; suffice it to say, that the temple is about one mile and three-quarters in circumference, the walls eighty feet high, and twenty-four feet thick.

"With astonishment, and almost with awe, I rode on through labyrinths of courts, cloisters, and chambers; and only dismounted where a mass of masonry had lately fallen in, owing to its pillars having been removed to build the Pacha's powder manufactory. Among the infinite variety of objects of art that crowd this temple, the obelisks are not the least interesting. Those who have only seen them at Rome, or Paris, can form no conception of their effect where all around is in keeping with them. The eye follows upwards the finely tapering shaft, till suddenly it seems not to terminate, but to melt away and lose itself in the dazzling sunshine of its native skies. For hours I wandered

7*

eagerly and anxiously on, through apparently interminable variety, every moment encountering something new, unheard of, and unthought of until then. The very walls of the outer enclosures were deeply sculptured with whole histories of great wars and triumphs, by figures that seemed to live again.

"In some places these walls were poured down like an avalanche, not fallen; no mortar had ever been needed to connect the cliff-like masses of which they were composed; at this hour the most ignorant mason might direct the replacing of every stone where it once towered, in propylon or gateway, so accurately was each fitted to the place it was destined to occupy. We rested for a long time on a fallen column, under a beautiful archway, that commands a wide view of the temple, and then slowly and lingeringly withdrew. The world contains nothing like it.

"We returned to Luxor by a different, yet similar avenue of statues to that by which we had approached. As we proceeded, we could discover other pillars and portals, far away upon the horizon, each marking where an entrance to this amazing temple once existed.

"From the desert or the river; from within or from without; by sunshine or by moonlight, however you contemplate Karnak, it appears the very aspect in which it shows to most advantage. And when this was all perfect; when its avenues opened in vistas upon the noble temples and palaces of Sesostris, upon Gournou, Medinet-Abou, and Luxor; when its courts were paced by gorgeous priestly pageants, and busy life swarmed on a river flowing between banks of palaces like those of Venice magnified a hundredfold; when all this was in its prime, no wonder that its fame spread even over the barbarian world, and found immortality in Homer's song.

"For many a day after I had seen it, and even to this hour, glimpses of Thebes mingle with my reveries, and blend themselves with my dreams; as if that vision had daguerrotyped itself upon the brain and left its impress there forever!"

Every evening of this week we have had visitors; the French gentlemen, as well as Mr. Standish, and the Messrs. Beadel, have all proved very agreeable acquaintances. Baron de Commailles and Mr. Standish expect to meet us in Paris, while probably the Beadel party will join us in our travels through Syria and Palestine. Another dahabech, the *Lincoln*, arrived day before yesterday, and Messrs. Ferris and Rogers called on the occupants. In the evening, on board the *Fawn*, two American gentlemen—General Starring and Mr. Hall, who had arrived on a steamer during the afternoon—were presented to us by Mr. Beadel. Yesterday morning Tom took two pictures of Aline and myself, mounted on camels; quite an addition to our Egyptian album.

CHAPTER XI.

STILL AT THEBES—VALLEY OF BIBAN-EL-MOLOUK—TOMBS OF THE KINGS—PETRIFIED CLAMS—GREAT SARCOPHAGUS—BELZONI'S TOMB—HARPER'S TOMB—THE PHILOSOPHER'S MISTAKE—KARNAK BY MOONLIGHT—TEMPLE OF LUXOR—DEPARTURE FROM THEBES—DENDERAH—DANCING-GIRLS OF KENNEH.

SUNDAY, March 1, 1868.

THE weather continued so warm that we dared not venture out, and while we lounged lazily with our books, Tom braved the burning rays of the sun and took two views of the Temple of Luxor.

The port does not look as animated as it did a few days past. Our French acquaintances are now on their way to the first cataract; while the *Fawn*, with the Messrs. Beadel, left this morning bound down for Cairo.

In the evening Messrs. Suydam and Stebbins, both of New York, from the dahabeeh *Lincoln*, called on us, and soon after we had a visit of General Starring.

MONDAY, March 2.

After having called upon the ladies on board the *Lincoln*, Aline and myself, attended by two servants, took a walk through the village and visited a new hotel, not yet open to the public, pleasantly situated on a hill in a garden belonging to Mustapha Aga, our consul.

In the evening we took our yawl and were rowed to General Starring's steamer, where we found a social gathering: Mrs. Clement and Miss Rutter, of New York; Messrs. Suydam and Stebbins, from the *Lincoln;* and Mr. and Mrs. Johnson, of Philadelphia, who had arrived in the *Alexander II.* that afternoon.

TUESDAY, March 3,

Has passed quietly away. A visit on board the *Alexander II.*, where we met our friends of the *Lincoln*, finished the day.

WEDNESDAY, March 4.

I was up at four o'clock, as Mr. Rogers had been kind enough to offer to accompany me to the kings' tombs; and as the excursion is the longest one around Thebes, and the weather hot, we thought it would be more pleasant to start very early; yet it was not till half-past five that we entered our yawl, the last stars having just disappeared.

We found our donkeys waiting for us, and the weather being calm and cool, we started at good speed for the valley of Biban-el-Molouk. Champollion says that the name of this valley is derived from the Arabic, and translated into English means, the doors of the kings; whereas it is a corruption of the ancient Egyptian name, Biban Ouröon, which means, the "*Hypogees of the kings.*" It was the royal necropolis, and it seems singular that they choose for their last resting-place, such an arid and desolate valley. On both sides are high precipitous rocks and hills, having frequent slits or gorges, occasioned either by the external action of the elements or internal fires; and the upper crusts are marked with large black stripes, as if they had been in part burned.

So, early in the morning, with the first rays of the sun tinting the hills, it was a glorious scene for a vivid imagination, the silence being only occasionally broken by Mr. Rogers attracting my attention to some particular point. Perhaps three or four thousand years ago that valley was green and luxuriant, the hills covered with a rich vegetation and its present condition produced by peculiar atmospheric changes. In their former visit Tom and Mr. Rogers found a large petrified clam, and a few days ago General Starring showed me some smaller ones, also found in that neighborhood. How came they there? Has the mighty sea been once the mistress of this part of earth?

We arrived at our destination, having encountered nothing but a jackal on a hill-side, who, after quietly gazing at us, slowly walked away.

We visited firstly a small tomb, known or designated as No. 2, remarkable for the immense red granite sarcophagus which has for thousands of years remained in this its original situation. It is eleven feet six inches long, by seven feet wide, upwards of nine feet high, and broken on one side. The cover had been partially shoved off, so that I was enabled, with Mr.

Rogers' assistance, to see the interior, which was entirely empty; but I observed upon it a finely sculptured crocodile. The royal mummy, that of Rameses IV., has long since been taken away.

No. 17, known as Belzoni's tomb, is the largest and most interesting of all. I had been misled by the French guide-book, which states that this is the tomb of the great Rameses or Sesostris, while Wilkinson and Champollion agree that it contained the body of King Sethi or Osirei, who was the father of Rameses the Great. This tomb is remarkable for its sculpture, and the freshness of its paintings, executed 3300 years ago.

One of the most interesting scenes, sculptured and painted, is in a square room supported by four pillars, being an allegorical representation of a procession of the four parts of the world assisting at the funeral of Sethi: the Egyptian race is painted red; the northern has light skin, blue eyes, and long beards; then comes the black race, the negroes; and then the people of the East, having also long beards, white skin, and the Jewish type of countenance, long noses and black hair, dressed in flowing robes very richly ornamented.

In a similar room adjoining, the scenes which were to adorn the walls are only designed in black; probably the king had died before they could be completed. In the last room, larger than all the others, and supported by six columns, stood formerly an oriental alabaster sarcophagus, which is now in the English museum.

No. 11, known as the Harper's tomb, which we then visited, is exceedingly interesting by reason of the subjects represented in its paintings; depicting almost all the social life of the ancient Egyptians. This was the tomb of Rameses III., chief of the XXth dynasty (toward 1260). The total length of the hypogee, which is considerably less than that of Belzoni, is one hundred and twelve, and the depth about thirty feet. We inspected very carefully all the little rooms which are on either side of the two passages. In some you see the preparation of aliments—men killing oxen, others cutting them up; others, again, baking bread, making pastry, and cooking vegetables.

In some rooms you see boats of different styles; while in others are represented the arms and instruments of war of the Egyptians, which in that time were cutlasses, straight and curved swords, poniards, lances, bows, arrows, quivers, helmets, javelins, etc. We saw drawings of chairs and beds of very elegant designs; also vases, basins, leopard-skins, which were probably used as carpets; all showing how refined the tastes of the ancient Egyptians must have been. In one of the rooms we saw a picture of the Nile overflowing, and taking its course through several channels; while men are throwing seed, and others again harvesting and garnering the grain.

In the last room are two musicians playing on the harp before the goddess Isis; and we also remarked in one of the halls the representation of the four races of the world. The paintings, being fresher than in Belzoni's tomb, gave us a more correct conception of what we had already seen.

There are many more, but the above, with that of

Memnon, are the most interesting, and give you a perfect idea of what the others are. Having finished the examination of the most important, our guide spread the cloth, and we took our breakfast at the entrance of No. 11.

From one of these tombs the mummy was taken a few years since by a distinguished philosopher and antiquary, who had it conveyed to England. He resolved that old Pharaoh should be reintroduced to the light of day with all due honors, and invited a large audience, consisting of the most distinguished literati of the times.

A learned dissertation was delivered on the grand occasion, and the different modes of embalming adopted for the two sexes were explained as he unrolled the successive cloths.

Expectation was wrought to the highest pitch to see how the "old fellow" would strip. Presto, change, and lo! the king of trumps became the queen of spades! "He" had been a woman.

Going back by the Ramesium, we stopped at tomb No. 35, which is by far the most curious of all the private ones in Thebes, since it throws more light on the manners and customs of the Egyptians; but we should have seen it before visiting the Harper's, which is far superior in the beauty and vividness of its coloring.

It was twelve o'clock when we regained our boat.

In the evening we went to see Karnak by moonlight, which, illuminated by the queen of night, whose rays—playing between the innumerable columns and majestic obelisks—here bringing into prominence some jutting cornice or capital, there hiding in the dense shade unseen beauties, produce effects rarely to be equalled.

Soon our party was joined by Mrs. Amory and Mr. Stebbins, and afterwards by the Johnson family. At half-past eight we were on our return, and upon reaching the bank found our dahabeeh in the stream, illuminated as on former occasions. The deck, in the afternoon, had been tastefully arranged by Mohammed, and astonished all our visitors by its luxurious and comfortable appearance. The *Lincolns*, the *Alexanders*, and the *Orientals* passed the remainder of the evening pleasantly together, listening to each other's relations of their experiences during their various excursions. Mr. Stebbins declared that the high wind, during his visit to Medinet-Abou, the day previous, had so filled his eyes with sand that he felt an inexpressible relief when again on board his dahabeeh, and able to obtain a good ablution. He affirmed, in all seriousness, that he washed a scarabee out of one eye, while from the other he extracted a small crocodile. Whether true or not, we could, one and all, appreciate his vivid description, having equally suffered with him the inconvenience caused by the high winds, which carries through the air the impalpable sand from the desert.

Thursday, March 5.

After breakfast we called on Mr. Smith, inspected his collection of antiquities, and, leaving the gentlemen with him, went to bid the Consul Mustapha Aga adieu, who introduced us to his wife and daughter. Our afternoon was passed quietly on board, reading, sleeping, and writing, until five o'clock, at which hour we were joined by Mr. Smith, whom we had invited to dine with us. This gentleman is from New York, has been living here the past ten years, is a man of good education, has a vast knowledge of the country; and after dinner we went with him to visit the Temple of Luxor.

We could but partially inspect it, and even then only in detail, on account of the village built on an artificial mound, formed of rubbish of the ancient city; and though the ruins of the temple predominate, their inferior parts are half buried amid mud and brick habitations.

But we were much pleased with the *coup-d'œil* we had before us. The moon was fuller and clearer than on the preceding night, and silvered brightly the long colonnade of the temple. This was the work of two illustrious and powerful princes, Amenophis III. of the XVIIIth dynasty, and Rhamses II. or Sesostris the Great of the XIXth dynasty. Amenophis, in 1290 B.C., had the sanctuary and the principal part of the temple erected; and one hundred and seventy years later Rhamses added to it the pylones on the north, and also erected in front of them two beautiful obelisks, of which only one remains; the other having been taken to Paris.

A little behind the obelisks are two statues of red granite of Syene, each cut from a single block, which are now, except the head and bust, buried in the ground, while the parts exposed are much mutilated. This is all we saw of the temple of Luxor—enough, however, to keep in our memory a grand idea of its past magnificence.

We returned to the vessel, and soon after received the final visit of Mustapha Aga, who had come to wish us "Good-by." At half-past eight, our boat being illuminated, we rowed into the stream and commenced floating down the river, the men singing and playing on their drums and tambourines, while Tom and Abousaid fired a parting salute of sixty guns.

The night was calm and beautiful, not a breath of air, and thus the lights were reflected in the pure and limpid water. Our guns were answered by all the dahabeehs and steamers in port, and not only answered but repeated again and again, until we slowly turned the first point of the river; while the occasional boom from the consul's cannon awoke the echoes, which my imagination readily converted into the voices of the spirits of the old kings.

This illumination, while leaving Thebes, was an idea of Tom's, which could not have taken place had it been at all windy; but as it happened, the effect produced was extraordinary and magnificent. And our men—how well I remember the happy smiles illuminating their dusky countenances—manifesting hope and eagerness to reach Cairo again, for two months and a half have elapsed since they parted with families and friends.

Shouting and singing, they get still more excited by Mohammed keeping the measure with his head, hands, and feet. And now Thebes is almost out of sight; a few minutes more, and—all is a vision of the past.

FRIDAY, March 6.

We had been compelled to stop in the night, the

wind blowing strongly against us, and this morning early were again under way; but at about nine o'clock it increased to such violence, and the boat rolled so unpleasantly that Aline, Mr. Rogers, and I were obliged to lie down. It was the first time we had encountered such weather on the Nile. Mohammed moored to the shore at noon, to let us take our lunch quietly, and at one the men attempted rowing again, but they found it impossible to make headway. We stopped, therefore, all the afternoon at El Bales, a very pretty spot, with handsome gardens, having groves of lemon-trees in full blossom, cedars, acacias, and palm-trees.

Aline, Mr. Rogers, and myself sat down under the shade of the lemon-trees, while Tom amused himself gunning. At six o'clock, the wind having in great part died out, we got under way and arrived at Kenneh, on the Denderah side, at midnight.

SATURDAY, March 7.

At nine o'clock we started for Denderah, which, a few years ago, was almost buried in the sand. This temple dates from the last of the Ptolemies, and was only finished under Nero. We thought the portico beautiful, although the sculptures and hieroglyphics are considered inferior to those of other temples. It has twenty-four columns, and the chapiters are handsomer than any we had yet seen; for, instead of the lotus flower, on each of its four sides were represented faces of Egyptian women; alas! all mutilated with one or two exceptions.

The interior of the temple is in a very good state of preservation. To the portico succeed three rooms of unequal size, the first only with columns; the two others having lateral chambers. We afterward visited the building north of the great temple, known by the name of Typhonium; also the little temple of Isis, behind the grand temple.

We took our lunch in the handsome portico, and, having remained several hours, returned to our boat at four o'clock. Soon after the *Alexander II.* arrived, and moored beside us; Mr. Johnson paid us a visit, and then started with his party for Denderah.

In the evening the gentlemen, duly armed with a bottle of champagne, and provided with candles, which Mohammed said was quite necessary, the former to impart vigor to the animals, and the latter to add brilliancy to the scene, went to Kenneh to see the dancing-girls, which are here reported to be the finest in Egypt; while we ladies remained *at home* and received a visit from Mrs. Johnson, her son, and two daughters.

SUNDAY, March 8.

Both boats left Kenneh last evening at 10 o'clock.

We have floated all day together, and passed an agreeable evening on the *Alexander.*

MONDAY, March 9.

Mohammed is decidedly unfortunate with the wind, and certainly will not be back in Cairo within his contract time. This morning at half-past eight we were again obliged to tie up, and still the boat rolled so much that as soon as we had finished breakfast we went ashore; but the wind blew so violently, and the dust was so unpleasant, that we were glad to regain our dahabeeh. The *Alexander* was moored a short distance from us; both boats remained thus all day, and only commenced to move at sunset, at which time the wind died out, and we arrived in Bellianeh at nine o'clock P.M.

CHAPTER XII.

ABYDOS—THE CLIFFS OF GEBEL*-SHEICK-HEREDEE—ORANGE AND LEMON GROVES—A LONG PULL—SIOUT—STABL-ANTAR—AMERICAN CONSUL—GEBEL-ABOOFAYDA—RHODA—THE PALACE—TOMBS OF BENI-HASSAN—MINIEH—DEPARTURE OF MR. R.—BENESOEF—FLOATING DOWN—AGROUND—MEMPHIS—TOMBS OF THE APPIS—SERAPIUM.

TUESDAY, March 10, 1868.

WE were surprised this morning to learn that the *Alexander* had left at midnight, as Mr. Johnson had manifested a great desire to see the temple of Abydos, which, he stated, was described as handsomer than that of Denderah; but Mohammed said that his dragoman told him he could not get donkeys.

At half-past eight we started for Abydos, two hours' distance from Bellanieh, and enjoyed a refreshing ride through a richly cultivated country, covered with groves of acacias and palm-trees, and the Lybian chain forming a picturesque background.

The ruins of Abydos are of considerable antiquity, dating from the time of Sethi, or Osirei I., and his son the great Rameses. They consist of two large edifices; the palace of Memnon, and the famous temple of Osiris,

* Gebel—Arabic for hill.

who, it is said, is buried here. We only visited the Memnonium, which, from its peculiar construction, is particularly interesting, and consists of two halls, supported by columns, communicating with each other by a door at one end of each of its avenues or colonnades, while in the centre are several vaulted rooms covered with hieroglyphics, and sculptures beautifully colored; but the columns are low and roughly done, having none of the grandeur of those in the portico at Denderah.

Several staircases lead to the top of the building, and although from here the temple does not appear to advantage, yet you can see what an immense work it must have been to disengage it of its mantle of earth, by the enormous mounds of rubbish piled on every side.

As we were taking lunch, we were surprised by the arrival of Mr. Johnson and his children. As Mohammed had told us, they could not find donkeys at Bellanich, and had to go to Girgeh, which is a ride of three hours and a half from Abydos. We were back on our boat at half-past four, very tired, and under way at five.

WEDNESDAY, March 11.

We overtook the *Alexander* during the night; both boats remained together all day, and in the evening Mr. and Mrs. Johnson came to play cards with us, and only retired at half-past ten.

THURSDAY, March 12.

The weather was so delightful this morning, and the scenery so grand, that Tom had the dahabeeh moored to the shore, under the cliff of Gebel-Sheick-Heredee, where he took a view.

While Aline remained seated beneath the shade of some palms, Mr. Rogers and I inspected the locality, and visited a few sheiks' tombs. We tarried here the greater part of the day, only leaving at sunset.

FRIDAY, March 13.

I was quite surprised this morning to see the *Alexander* abreast of us; but heard afterwards that she had been aground, and just as she was again afloat we had arrived, only to get aground also. They sent ten of their men to help our crew, and after four hours of hard labor succeeded in freeing us.

We have floated all day together, and are nearing Siout. The shores looked so green and inviting that Tom proposed to take a walk, which proposition was acceded to by all the party. Taking the yawl, with two stout rowers, and leaving the dahabeeh to float down stream, we were soon roaming through a garden full of orange and lemon trees.

As we were thinking of regaining the dahabeeh, the sun being very hot, Tom, who had remained behind, called us back, and led us to a green and fresh oasis which he had just discovered. It was a delicious spot, a truly Egyptian paradise, with a rich carpet of verdure for the feet, and luxuriant groves of palms, acacias, and lemon-trees in blossom; while the whispering breezes rustling through the foliage was sweet music to the ear, and, lulled by its harmony as we lay on the grass, we soon fell asleep.

At half-past four we awoke; the dahabeeh was miles away from us; a long pull was before us; but our men with strong arms and willing hearts, soon sped the way, and we regained the boat just before she arrived at Siout.

After dinner we went to spend the evening with the *Alexanders*, and were surprised to hear, that after a short ride through the bazars, they were going to leave as soon as the moon should rise. Siout is the third city in Egypt, and although we had stopped twenty-four hours on our previous visit, we now intend to remain long enough to see it more in detail. We parted with the Johnsons this evening, and probably will not see them again until our arrival at Cairo.

SATURDAY, March 14.

After breakfast we received a visit from the American consul, a very intelligent and agreeable Egyptian, who brought us letters.

At ten o'clock we mounted our donkeys, and a delightful ride of forty minutes through the picturesque city of Siout, and a richly cultivated country, brought us to the foot of the Libyan hills, where, a short distance above, is the grotto of Stabl-Antar, an ancient tomb cut in the solid rock.

Arab traditionary legend affirms that it was the stable of a renowned hero named Antar, whose extraordinary exploits are related in Egyptian lore, occupying the space of three volumes. Here we had a view seldom surpassed in loveliness in Europe or America; and while Tom and Mr. Rogers went to examine various tombs, which are in great numbers on this side of the hill, Aline and I remained for more than two hours admiring it.

On our return we stopped at the consul's, who lives in a fine house, elegantly furnished—better certainly than some of the vice-royal residences that we have visited. He received us most courteously, and introduced us to his two sons and a nephew, who are well educated and dress in European style; the eldest speaking French and the two others English. Having conversed for some time, inspected the visitors' book which he keeps, and partaken of refreshment, we left; each one taking an Egyptian fly-brush, with which we had been presented.

In the afternoon these gentlemen and the governor of the place called on us, and two hours were passed with them most agreeably. At five o'clock Aline, Mr. Rogers, and myself took a walk in the pacha's garden, and along the banks of the Nile, admiring on our return a golden sunset.

SUNDAY, March 15.

This morning early we moored before the cliffs of Gebel-Aboofayda, of which Tom took a splendid view. We left at eleven o'clock, and floated slowly down the shining river, while the thermometer marked eighty-five degrees in the shade.

At three o'clock we got aground, and, notwithstanding the efforts of the crew, three hours passed before we were afloat again, and then had to be very careful, the river being shallow at this part, and for better security stopped at midnight, arriving at Rhoda at seven o'clock on the following morning.

MONDAY, March 16.

Rhoda is a delightful place, of which I gave a description two months ago, when we passed it going up the river.

This morning we visited the palace that the Viceroy has built here, and which is entirely finished, though not yet furnished. It is a splendid habitation, the apartments large and spacious, some beautifully arranged in Oriental style; a marble fountain in the centre of the room throwing jets of sparkling perfumed water, cooling and purifying the atmosphere; whilst divans ranged around the walls invite to revery and repose. On every side of the house are marble balconies with balustrades, having views of different parts of the river and the garden, the latter being full of flowers and tropical plants.

Tom took a very good *view* of it, and also of Rhoda from another point. We left about noon, and arrived in Beni-Hassan at eight at night.

TUESDAY, March 17.

As we were getting ready this morning to visit the tombs, the American dahabeeh *Lincoln*, which we had left at Thebes, arrived and moored near us; and as we were leaving our boat we met their party, and all proceeded together.

We regretted that we had not stopped at Beni-Hassan

on the ascent, for then we probably would have found the tombs more interesting; but having seen the grand ones of the kings in Biban-el-Molouk, and others up the river, these appear very inferior. Yet they are remarkable on account of their antiquity, dating from the time of Ositasen I., and the condition of the paintings on the wall, which are very fresh and distinct. Processions, wrestling, music, fishing, boating, glass-blowers, sculptors, goldsmiths, farming, and hunting are among the various scenes depicted.

In one of the northerly tombs I observed upon the wall a picture of a dahabeeh transporting a mummy, and at once you come to the conclusion that the ancient city, of whose dead these caverns were the burial-places, was situated on the opposite side of the river, although not a vestige remains at any point in the vicinity to mark its site. This, however, is easily accounted for, when we remember that the Nile is constantly changing its course; and the accumulated soil of one age is carried away in the next, and probably all that is left of ancient Nus is buried thirty feet below the present level.

We left Beni-Hassan at half-past two P.M., and arrived in Minich at half-past eight. We passed the evening playing cards, and at ten o'clock separated for the night, bidding good-by to Mr. Rogers, who will start to-morrow morning at five o'clock, by rail, for Cairo, from which place he intends going to Suez, to visit the canal, and to rejoin us, upon our arrival at Cairo, for the tour through Syria and Palestine.

WEDNESDAY, March 18.

As Minich does not offer anything worthy of notice we left at eleven o'clock, and continued floating all day and night.

THURSDAY, March 19.

Head-wind, and the boat making slow progress down the river. Tom, observing an old broken wall and Roman ruin on the bank, ordered the boat to be tied up, and, while I was busy sketching, took a very good photographic view of it. After stopping here five hours and a half, we got under way and continued our course down the river.

FRIDAY, March 20.

Came to anchor early this morning, on account of heavy head-wind, and upon rising found that we had overhauled the *Lincoln*, which had continued sailing the night we stopped at Minich, and a French boat we had left at Thebes, which had passed down the river in tow of a steamer while we were tied up at Beni-Hassan. We got under way about nine A.M., and at eleven observed a shower to the westward over the desert. It gradually approached, the wind soon changed, and we had lightning and thunder, but scarcely enough rain to sprinkle the decks. However, it was a novelty, as being the only rain we have had for nearly three months.

While the clouds obscured the sun, Tom ordered the boat to stop, that he might take a view of our deck, and one hour after we were under way again, and arrived at four P.M. at Benesoef, a large modern town, but uninteresting to the voyager.

SATURDAY, March 21.

Yesterday, after the shower, and during the evening, we found it exceedingly warm, but this morning the weather is cloudy and cool. As we approached a village called Zowyah, the trees and palm groves looked so inviting, and there being a strong head-wind, causing much motion of the boat and Aline and myself a sensation of sea-sickness, that Tom ordered the small boat, and we went on shore.

After walking through the village, and a short distance beyond, we stopped at a place protected by shade-trees; and while Aline amused herself sewing, I took a sketch, and Tom a *fusin*, employing thus the greatest part of the day.

At one P. M. the boat had arrived, and tied up opposite to us, and as the wind continued blowing very strong we remained here until morning.

SUNDAY, March 22.

At three A.M. the wind lulled; we got under way; and when we arose saw, a long distance ahead, the French boat, and another which we at the time took for the *Lincoln;* but as we gained upon her discovered her to be the *Alexander II.*, that we had supposed already at Cairo.

The wind again rose, and both boats having been compelled to tie up, we went ashore, and, after a walk of about a mile, came to the *Alexander*. We accepted

Mr. Johnson's invitation to come on board, and soon after the boats again got under way. We remained until five P.M., when Mohammed sent the yawl, and we returned to the *Oriental* for dinner.

MONDAY, March 23.

Continued floating and rowing during the night until two A.M., when we were awoke by a grating noise, and then a jerk. We were hard and fast on a sand-bank.

Our sailors jumped into the water, pushed and yelled, but all to no purpose, as mother Earth held us with a firm grip. After one hour's hard labor they gave it up and took some sleep. At daylight they were again at work, and at seven the *Alexander*, that had anchored above during the night on account of shallow water, passed us on her way to Bedryshayn, the stopping-place for Memphis. Her little boat was pushed off, and soon came alongside with five men to assist our crew. It was no easy job; and with all the men's united strength, two hours passed before we were afloat again, and we only moored near Memphis in the afternoon.

As it was too late that day to visit the ruins, we remained at "home," and in the evening received the parting visit of Mr. Johnson, who is exceedingly well pleased with the tombs of the Appis. They left at eight o'clock for Gizeh, as they intend to visit the pyramids to-morrow.

TUESDAY, March 24.

MEMPHIS! This our last visit to temples and tombs

has proved one of the most interesting, and we have returned delighted with what we have seen.

The weather was warm, windy, and oppressive; but the forest which covers what once was Memphis is dark with thick foliage, the road smooth, and the luxuriant grass (a very rare thing in Egypt) covered with flowers —descendants probably of those which grew in the gardens where Moses wandered with Pharaoh's daughter. We had ridden a mile when Tom perceived he had forgotten his photographic instrument, and while, with his servant, he went back to the boat, we pursued our route until we arrived at the fallen statue of Rameses the Great, which lies near the site of the temple of Vulcan, of which we could yet find some traces.

This statue, whose height, without the pedestal, is forty-two feet, has a beautiful face perfectly preserved. From his neck is suspended an amulet, in which is the royal prenomen. In the centre and at the side of his girdle is his name: Amun-men-Rameses. At his side are some remains of the statue of his daughter; her shoulder reaching a little above the level of his knee. We sat down on grass-covered mounds, which must conceal some parts of the temple, and, while waiting for Tom, fell into a fit of musing. Our thoughts carried us back five thousand years ago, when Memphis, as Thebes, was in the prime of all its glory; and as a climax to my philosophical reflection, I arose, went near the great Sesostris, and kneeling down, took out of his ear some running vines for the collection in my album.

A great many antiquities were shown us, remains of other statues, but to me they were uninteresting compared with that of the great fallen warrior; and as the weather was threatening rain—yes, rain—we galloped our donkeys at full speed and hurried to the tombs of the Appis.

They lie to the westward of the pyramid of Abouseer, to the north of the great pyramid of Sakkara, and were discovered by Mr. Mariette, together with the Serapium, with which they communicate.

They consist of long underground passages hewn in the rock, on both sides of which are deep recesses, each containing an enormous sarcophagus of granite, measuring twelve feet five inches by seven feet six and a half inches, and seven feet high, or, to the top of the lid, eleven feet. They are unsculptured, with the exception of two or three which are of a later period, just before and after the Persian conquest. The recesses and passages have been compared to immense wine-vaults.

At the visit of the Prince of Wales torches had been placed at regular distances, and the tombs lighted up for the benefit of his Highness; but poor we had only a few candles to guide us in our observations.

We were greatly pleased with the Serapium, a handsome little temple, which, having been for centuries buried by the accumulated sand of the Sakkara desert, when opened by Mr. Mariette, presented to the admiration of the present age walls decorated with a profusion of sculptures in very slight relief, and paintings of most excellent design and workmanship. The colors, too, are most vivid; the figures admirably drawn, and with no little spirit. Birds and animals of various kinds, and all manner of trades, are here depicted—among them carpenters at work.

Here we lunched, and then turned our donkeys homeward, glad when we re-entered the thick forest and left the dreary desert behind.

We were soon again on deck, enjoying one of our last sunsets on the Nile, and bidding adieu to the place where Memphis lay buried with all its wonders; and as we glided on the water the distant minarets and citadels of Cairo were seen faintly sketched against the sky, while on our left a long succession of pyramids towered over the dark belt of forest that led along the river. Night had driven out the day as we approached brilliantly lighted Roda, and moored in the stream opposite its palace.

CHAPTER XIII.

ISLAND OF RODA—THE "NILOMETER"—FATIMA—WOMAN'S RIGHTS—GOOD-BY TO OUR CREW—IN CAIRO AGAIN—DEPARTURE FROM ALEXANDRIA—PORT SAID—SUEZ CANAL—JAFFA—THE CONVENT—THE CAMP—HOUSE OF SIMON THE TANNER—SELECTION OF HORSES—"THE SACRED SOIL."

WEDNESDAY, March 25, 1868.

THE night has been quite stormy; we have had rain, lightning, and thunder, and when we arose this morning the heavens were still overcast; but at nine o'clock the clouds gave way to the sun, and Tom was able to take a photographic view of the "Nilometer," on the island of Roda.

While returning to the boat he was hailed by Mr. Rogers, who, with the Messrs. Beadel, were coming to see us, having heard through Mr. Johnson's dragoman that we were moored opposite Old Cairo.

We all sat down to lunch, when Mr. Beadel stated that they had employed a first-class dragoman, one Joseph Carem, for the tour in Syria and Palestine, and having awaited our arrival until the last moment, had concluded a contract with him, leaving a clause whereby it was optional with us to join or not. He had the highest recommendations, and they did not think we could find a better one. His price, compared to that which we had paid Mohammed for the Nile trip, seemed moderate, and as everything was ready we could take the steamer of the 28th and thus lose no time in Cairo.

After Tom had consulted with Aline, it was decided that we should join their party, and as we had no time to lose, after lunch we all went to visit the "Nilometer," which consists of a square well or chamber, having in the centre a graduated pillar for the purpose of ascertaining the daily rise of the Nile. This is proclaimed every morning in the streets of the capital, during the inundation, by four criers, to each of whom a portion of the city is assigned.

The island of Roda, on which it is situated, is very pretty; the gardens which surround the palace are crowded with orange and lemon trees in full blossom, as well as various other tropical plants, and quantities of flowers. We were not allowed to go too near the palace, and particularly the part containing the harem; and looking at the windows, whilst smelling the perfume of a bouquet given me by the gardener, I saw in vision the Fatima of whom Warburton has made such a charming chapter.

"Poor Fatima! shrined as she was in the palace of a tyrant, the fame of her beauty stole abroad through Cairo. She was one amongst a hundred in the harem of Abbas Pacha, a man stained with every foul and loathsome vice; and who can wonder, though many may condemn, if she listened to a daring young Albanian, who risked his life to obtain but a sight of her!

Whether she did listen or not, none can ever know; but the eunuchs saw the glitter of the Arnaut's arms, as he leaped from the terrace into the Nile, and vanished in the darkness. . . . .

"The following night a merry English party dined together on board Lord Exmouth's boat, as it lay moored off the Isle of Rhoda; conversation had sunk into silence as the calm night came on; a faint breeze floated perfumes from the gardens over the star-lit Nile, and scarcely moved the clouds that rose from the chibouques; a dreamy languor seemed to pervade all nature, and even the city lay hushed in deep repose, when suddenly a boat, crowded with dark figures, among which arms gleamed, shot out from one of the arches of the palace; it paused under the opposite bank, where the water rushed deep and gloomily along, and for a moment a white figure glimmered among the boat's dark crew; there was a slight movement and a faint splash;— and then—the river flowed on as merrily as if poor Fatima still sang her Georgian song to the murmur of its waters!" . . . . .

Oh! shades of Joan of Arc and the Maid of Saragossa, inspire with increased fervor your modern heroines, and female champions, Miss Anthony, Anna Dickinson, and Mrs. Mary Walker—Egypt is the place to "*exercise*" your abilities and "*exorcise*" that inhuman monster, "*man.*" Cairo is your stamping-ground, wherein to establish a "*Woman's Rights Convention,*" with ramifications and branches throughout the length and *narrowness* of the land. The Egyptian woman has no soul; she cannot even quietly die and go to heaven;

she simply is annihilated. To all intents and purposes she is a chattel, belonging bodily to the man who calls himself her husband.

In all the villages on the Nile you see these poor victims at work as busily as bees, tilling the land, or drawing water for domestic purposes, while the lazy husbands sit or loll in the shade, dreaming over their chibouques, or listlessly sipping their coffee-grounds. I never saw them do it, but I imagine they get up sometimes to rest.

These brutes never even take care of the babies—nor do the most strong-minded of the women ever dream of "*voting*."

On returning to the dahabeeh we gave orders to float down to Embabeh, the port of Cairo, and passed the afternoon packing, so as to be able to leave the boat early the following morning. It was five o'clock when we moored in the stream, near the other dahabeehs, among which were the *Rachel*, *Cleopatra*, and *Lincoln*. Tom went immediately to the banker, Abcarius, and the evening was passed reading letters from home. Poor Mohammed felt very sad at the thought of our leaving him, and gave us some useful advice about our Syrian trip.

Our final night on board!—let us take a look at our sailors, who, seated together, smoking, seem also to be affected by the approaching separation.

Good-night to all, and may God bless you!—a last gaze at the starry heavens—and then to bed.

THURSDAY, March 26.

At ten o'clock, everything being in readiness, and the

carriage waiting for us, a backsheesh of fifty dollars was distributed to our faithful sailors, who did not know how to thank us; and then good-by to all; once more let us shake hands, good-by, good-by! But it was not enough,—until the last moment they must have a glimpse of us, and when we were seated in the carriage they all approached, and, one after another, kissed our hands, and poured forth their best wishes for our welfare.

It was a sad parting, and the tears were ready to fall; but—speed away, good driver! on and away to Sheppard's Hotel. Here we found all our friends—the Johnsons, Beadels, and Mr. Rogers—and soon after made the acquaintance of Joseph Carem, our new dragoman.

His appearance is far from being, like that of Mohammed, mild and inoffensive. His immense black eyes are rather protruding, yet he appears quick and smart. We will see how he fulfils all the promises he makes. He is to start to-day for Alexandria, so as to have everything in readiness for the steamer. Our afternoon was employed shopping, and our evening very agreeably passed with Mrs. Johnson, who related some incidents of her journey in Greece and Turkey.

FRIDAY, March 27.

In the morning we went to Desiré, the photographer, where Tom had all his bottles refilled, for use in Syria and Palestine; and as we entered into conversation with him, heard that Edmond About (the celebrated French writer), after visiting the canal at Suez, had left ten days since, to go up the Nile, on a steamer furnished him by the Pasha; also that Jerome, the artist, with a party of friends, had been to Sinai, and must be now in Jerusalem; perhaps we may meet him there. Mohammed came to give us his last farewell, and soon we were in the cars, ready to start for Alexandria. While at the depot we encountered Henry du Rocher, Baron de Commailles, Henry Standish, and Captain Hoare, the gentlemen who dined with us at Mustapha Aga's house at Thebes.

We found Joseph waiting at the station in Alexandria, who took us to the hotel Abbatt, where rooms had been prepared.

SATURDAY, March 28.

The morning was passed making purchases, and looking at a city that perhaps we will never see again; and at two o'clock we went aboard the steamer *Alexander II.*, a new and magnificent Russian vessel. The state-rooms are the handsomest and largest we had ever seen, and to add to all this comfort, the commander is exceedingly amiable and obliging.

M. de Commailles, who will return hence to Paris, came on board to bid adieu to his friends Mr. Standish and Captain Hoare. He remained until the last moment, and when taking leave again assured us of the great pleasure it would afford him to meet us in Paris. At three o'clock the anchor was raised, and though we fought as well as we could against sea-sickness, were obliged at last to give way to it, and all retired early.

SUNDAY, March 29.

This morning the sea is smooth, permitting us to listen with pleasure to the very interesting account Mr. Standish gave us of his visit to St. Petersburg the winter previous; also that of Capt. Hoare to Sackara and Memphis. The captain relates well, and we all wished that we had had the good fortune which he encountered when he went to visit the ruins. Their steamer ran on a sand-bank, and, after several hours of fruitless efforts, they were told that it would require one or two hundred men to get the boat afloat again; so they determined to hire donkeys and make their way back to Cairo. Messrs. Standish, Du Rocher, and De Commailles arrived very late in the night, but the captain decided not to hurry, and when near Memphis thought that it would be a pity to pass that celebrated place without visiting its ruins, and so resolved to stop for the night in an adjacent hut.

While there he heard that Mr. Mariette, the director of the French Museum at Cairo, had just arrived on a steamer, and upon sending his card was most cordially and graciously received by that gentleman, who gave him a room on board his boat.

Nor was this all. Mr. Mariette was with very good company, having, among others, two distinguished surgeons from Prussia; and in the morning the whole party (with assistants amounting to twenty) went to visit the tombs of the Appis. Every subterraneous passage was lighted up as at the visit of the Prince of Wales; and after having taken lunch in the great sarcophagus, which was large enough to contain them all, three mummies were unrolled, and a very animated discussion commenced between the doctors as to the manner of embalming by the ancient Egyptians.

It was eleven o'clock before we arrived at Port-Said; and as soon as breakfast was over, took a boat and went to inspect the immense manufactured stones which are to be used for the new pier; and then to examine the great dredging machines, without which invention it would have been impossible to have completed the great work of excavation. The port is exceedingly animated, and crowded with foreign vessels, whilst the city itself is very gay; the houses and bazars cleanly, and the market, with its crowd of merchants, camels, and dogs, a sight in itself.

Before returning to the steamer we took a row on the Suez canal, whence we returned to the ship, and at four o'clock were pursuing our route towards Jaffa. The sea continued smooth, and permitted us to dine comfortably.

MONDAY, March 30.

At nine o'clock A.M. we came in view of Jaffa, and soon the steamer stopped to allow the passengers to land.

The anxiety which we all had experienced was now relieved, for as the so-called port is nothing more than a narrow and shallow inlet, with an unprotected roadstead outside, it is impossible to effect a landing except in calm weather, and then only with the aid of small boats.

The steamer anchored about a mile from shore, and

was soon surrounded by dirty little boats, manned by Arabs, who were far from possessing the meek looks of our good Egyptian sailors. For an hour intense excitement and hubbub prevailed on board, and the dragomen had a great deal to do getting all their furniture together. Bedding, tents, hardware, carpets, kitchen utensils, chairs, tables, trunks—everything had to be raised from the hold, and lay scattered about the decks in indescribable confusion, and a hard time we had to prevent the Arabs of the port laying hands on some of our property and getting ashore with it.

The wind was fresh, the waves quite high, causing the steamer to roll so much that it was very difficult to keep steady; the captain therefore advised us ladies to land as soon as possible and leave the gentlemen to attend to the baggage. So with his kind assistance we managed to jump from the companion-ladder into a little boat, and accompanied by Mr. C. Beadel and Mrs. Henrietta, a lady passenger, made for the shore.

I looked at the city we were slowly approaching. "High above the rugged rocks and whitening surge," says Dixon, "stands a cone of houses, a town having a low-lying beach, dark walls, and on either side of these walls a clump of wood." Yes, thus it is, and very picturesque did it appear to us, lighted by the morning sun.

As we approached the outer reef or wall of rocks, upon which the waves break with their foamy crests, through which it is necessary to pass by an opening only about twelve feet in width, our rowers wished to impress upon our minds the idea of the danger should we by chance miss the opening and strike upon the rocks; but we laughed at the thought, and the boat went rolling and surging through, reminding us somewhat of the passage of the first cataract on the Nile.

Soon we were landed among a great crowd of natives assembled to see the strangers. We left Charles Beadel paying our men, and followed Mrs. Henrietta to the Latin Convent, where we were received by the priests, who overwhelmed us with kind attentions, and while waiting for the rest of our party amused ourselves looking over the visitors' book, and there noticed that the Marchioness of Ely, with her son, had passed through Jaffa two days previous.

Soon Messrs. Standish and Hoare joined us, and we all stepped out on the terrace to enjoy the fresh air. After a few minutes we saw our gentlemen coming in a little boat, while farther off lay the steamer rolling majestically on the waves. We shouted a salute, and dinner being announced, proceeded to the dining-room, where two priests were in attendance. Soup, fresh fish, and potatoes, with oranges from the groves near by, composed our repast, which, being offered with good grace was equally well received.

Messrs. Standish and Hoare's dragoman soon came to inform them that he was ready to start at any moment they pleased; so they shook hands all around, hoping to meet us soon in Jerusalem. After remunerating the priests for their kindness we left the convent, proceeding towards the Jerusalem gate, near which, flanked by the orange groves beyond, we were to find our tents, that we had ordered to be in readiness for us, as we did not intend to leave for Jerusalem until the following morning.

Here we found them, five in number, with the American flag waving overhead. There are two of fourteen ropes, two of twelve ropes, and one of ten ropes, which will be the kitchen. One of the fourteen, with a curtain dividing it in two parts, is to be our bed-room—Aline, Tom, and I—for forty days; the other fourteen is to be occupied by Messrs. Beadel, Sr., and Rogers. One of the twelve ropes will be our dining saloon, and the other similar one is for Henry Beadel and his brother Charles. These tents are all new, with double roofs, and I will describe the interior arrangement of ours, so as to give my friends an idea of our airy "home."

Two rugs of Turkey carpet are spread on the ground; the three bedsteads occupy each a side of the tent; in the centre is a table with a fancy cover, and a vase containing flowers. A table near the doorway is to be our wash-stand, having upon it all that is required for one's toilet. These, with our valises and three folding-chairs, compose our furniture. Joseph, our dragoman, soon came to inform us that lunch was ready, and repairing to the saloon tent we sat down at table, enjoying the novelty of the scene.

But muleteers with horses are outside, at least fifty of the latter; so, leaving Tom and Henry to make selections therefrom, Aline, Mr. Beadel, Sr., Charles Beadel, Mr. Rogers, and myself went to visit the house of Simon the tanner.

We again entered the city by the Jerusalem gate, and near it stopped to admire the beautiful Saracenic fountain, called Abon-Nabbout, with jets of water flowing into marble troughs, and over which a pious verse from the Koran is printed in golden type. It is the rendezvous of all the unoccupied people of the town, and there are always many such to be found in the East. The streets of Jaffa are exceedingly narrow and dirty; so narrow that you have to range yourself every now and then against the houses to avoid troops of horses and camels; but after passing under arches, and going up and down steps, we arrived at the "*house*," said to be the one in which Simon the tanner had lived, and soon were seated under the shade of a fig-tree on the terrace, where the angel appeared to the prophet Eli.

The weather was very warm; the walk had fatigued us, and while my eyes were resting on the calm sea spread before us, and admiring its silvery surface, which in the far distance seemed mingling with the blue sky, I tried to recall all that is said of Jaffa, the ancient Joppa of the Scriptures, spoken of by Pliny as being an antediluvian city. It was here, according to tradition, that Andromeda was tied to the rock and exposed to the marine monster; here that Noah constructed the ark; here that the cedars of Lebanon were brought by order of King Solomon to serve for the construction of the temple; here that the prophet Jonah embarked, 862 years B. C.; here that Tabitha was resuscitated by St. Peter. The city was fortified by St. Louis, in the time of the crusaders, and in 1799 it was taken by Bonaparte, and by his order all the Turkish prisoners were massacred.

Surprised, after waiting an hour, not to see Tom and

Henry Beadel coming to join us, we returned to our encampment and found both still among horses and muleteers, and heard that among fifty or sixty horses only two had been chosen by Tom as passable; and he proposed that we should try those he had selected. Aline was easily satisfied, being a good "Amazone;" but as my equestrian tuition had never advanced beyond riding an Egyptian donkey, I felt quite nervous, and it was with dread that I anticipated our next morning's departure.

Our first dinner in the tent proved to be excellent; we were in fine spirits, chatted a great deal about the journey we had before us, and all felt happy to tread at last that earth where such divine feet had trodden before us. Yes, we were in the Holy Land, and when I wished all good-night, and stepped out of our dining saloon into the open air, how could I express the sensations and emotions that took possession of my heart and spirit at the novel, strange, and sublime scene I had before me. Our five white tents, almost lustrous in the bright moonlight, formed a circle around me, looking weird-like and fantastic; the kitchen fire was still glowing, and lying around it were our men, muleteers, servants, and dragomen, some of them smoking, others talking; the mules with their tinkling bells, walking to and fro, were making a new and sweet music; the air was impregnated with the perfume of the lemon and orange trees; before me I could see the city spread out on the hill, and to my right the desert of Gaza; my feet were treading on a carpet of flowers; far, far off, I heard the roaring of the waves on the beach, and above, the stars were looking down from the blue heavens. Here I had none of the antique monuments of Egypt to admire, and yet my heart was filled with sweeter emotions than ever it had felt in all the grand scenes of Thebes and Karnak; in that moment I felt purer and better; and it seemed as if treading on this *"sacred soil"* had been enough to wash out the sins of the past. I could only repeat to myself, again and again, "The Holy Land, the Holy Land!" and with thanks to God I entered my tent and laid me down to sleep.

CHAPTER XIV.

OUR CARAVAN—PLAIN OF SHARON—LYDDA—BIRTHPLACE OF ST. GEORGE—AN ACCIDENT—RAMLEH—MOUNTAINS OF JUDEA—ABOU-GOCH—DAVID AND GOLIAH—MOUNT OF OLIVES—BAD WATER—JERUSALEM.

TUESDAY, March 31, 1868.

THE order was to be in the saddle at eight o'clock, so as to "*do*" half the route between Jaffa and Jerusalem that day; but though we breakfasted very early, it was ten o'clock before we started.

It took at least two hours for the men to fold the tents, pack up the furniture, put the baggage on the mules, etc., etc. Joseph said it would not be thus every day; that they had to get accustomed to arrange the loads, and learn exactly what should go on each mule. Seated on chairs in the shade of some trees, we watched the performance; for the animals were not always docile, and some would try to shake their burdens off.

At last all was ready; Mrs. Henrietta, attired in a tight-fitting velvet suit, a little hat trimmed with cherry, with a white turban wound around, and high-buttoned Louis XVth boots, who had asked as a favor to join our caravan as far as Jerusalem, whither she was going on a pilgrimage to visit the tomb of her mother and sister, who had both died of cholera twelve years ago in the holy city, arrived, mounted on a little white horse, and followed by a servant. During the first half hour of our journey I was too much occupied with my horse to notice anything around me. This lasted only for a time. I soon gained confidence, and then, like everybody else, admired the prospect. We had just passed a fountain (Ain-Dalab) shaded by sycamores and palms, and on both sides of the road extended a varied forest of all the fruit-trees and flowering shrubs of the Orient. It is almost impossible to describe the richness and beauty of this vegetation. For a mile or two we followed, on both sides, hedges of myrtle, jasmine, cactus, and pomegranate-trees; while the fine grass, covered with wild flowers, caused me to regret that I was not versed in botany. I could admire, but not know the names of the beautiful plants I saw passing through Syria and Palestine. In the latter country they are not so plentiful, but Syria possesses thousands of varieties, painting the landscape with their varied and brilliant hues.

Our party of seven, Mrs. Henrietta, a German who joined us and placed himself under our protection *nolens volens*, the dragoman, eight muleteers, and two servants—twenty persons in all—with twenty-six horses and mules, constituted quite an imposing caravan; and we knew there was no danger, with such numbers, of an attack from the Bedouins of the desert. We had seen some at Jaffa, mounted on fine horses, wrapped in white and black striped camels' hair burnouses; equipped in war costume, guns on their shoulders and pistols in their belts. They looked far nobler than the Arabs of Egypt, but we felt no fear of them, for we had heard in Jaffa that if there was a woman in the caravan there was no danger of their attacking it. They have a profound respect for courage, and it surprises them to see European ladies travelling through the country unapprehensive of danger.

After passing an avenue of olive-trees, which marks the place of a farm built by order of Colbert, and under the trees of which it is said Bonaparte encamped during his expedition, we passed Beit-Dedjan, once Beth-Dagon —House of Dagon—the ancient fish-god of the Philistines, who elevated in his honor a magnificent temple at Gaza.

Travelling through the beautiful plain of Sharon, we arrived after a three hours' ride at Lydda, and selected a charming spot in the outskirts of the town for our luncheon. For an hour clouds had been gathering overhead, and a light shower admonished us that it would be advisable to remain here over night, more especially as the dragoman said the ruins of the church of St. George were worth visiting.

Quietly seated outside our tents, which stood in a magnificent orchard of olive-trees, the grass under our feet being thicker and softer than the softest carpet ever trodden on, we soon had a bouquet of wild flowers on our table, taken from the carpet itself, and amused ourselves reading the story of Lydda, the town of so many names.

It is spoken of in the Scriptures as one of the possessions of the Benjamites (1 Chron. viii. 12). It was given to Jonathan Maccabees by Demetrius Soter, and Josephus tells us that Cassius, the Roman governor of Judea, reduced its inhabitants to slavery, and later it was rebuilt under the name of Diospolis. In the fourth century it was erected into a bishopric dependent upon Jerusalem, and the crusaders had it rebuilt under the name of St. George, who was born and is buried in the place. It is also in Lydda that the New Testament places the cure of the paralytic by St. Peter (Acts ix. 32, 39).

The church of St. George, which we visited late in the afternoon, is a handsome ruin, bearing a great similarity to an old English abbey; which would confirm the tradition that after having been destroyed by Saladin, when he was retreating before Richard Cœur de Lion, it was rebuilt by this prince, who passed some time in Lydda and in the neighboring town of Ramleh. We were sorry Tom was not ready to take photographic views, for certainly the ruins of this church would have been one of the handsomest of the collection, and a view of the city itself, situated on a hill in the midst of the plain of Sharon, surrounded by olive, fig, pomegranate, orange, and lemon trees, would have helped to keep the remembrance of it more vivid. In all our pilgrimage through Syria we have not found a second Lydda.

WEDNESDAY, April 1.

As we had a long day's work before us, we were up early, and at half-past seven in the saddle. Mr. Rogers,

Mr. Beadel, Sr., and I were behind, and wishing to rejoin the rest of our party, put our horses to the trot, when my saddle turned, and I was thrown to the ground, luckily more frightened than hurt, my wrist only being bruised; but I did not recover from the nervousness created by the accident for several days.

After an hour's ride we passed Ramleh, a Mussulman city, which the Arab Abou-el-Feda affirms was established in A.D. 716 by the Caliph Suleiman, son of Abd-el-Melik. The first traveller who mentions Ramleh is a priest named Bernard, who visited Palestine in the year 870. Taken by the crusaders in 1099, it fell into the hands of Saladin in 1187, and became afterwards the general head-quarters of Richard Cœur de Lion. In 1266, by the conquest of Sultan Bibars, it fell again under the Mussulman domination. To-day it is a small town inhabited by two thousand Mussulmans, and about one thousand Christians, almost all of the Greek rite. The Latin Convent, where travellers generally stop, was founded in 1240 by Philip le Bon, Duke of Burgundy, and later restored by the liberality of Louis XIV.

We alighted for lunch at the end of the plain of Ramleh, near a fountain cut in a rock, called throughout the country Jacob's Well. It was about one o'clock, the sun very hot, and all somewhat tired; so while Joseph and the servants were preparing the meal, we threw ourselves full length on the grass, under the shade of olive-trees, our eyes resting on the mountains of Judea.

"Joseph, at what time shall we arrive at Jerusalem?"

"You have yet three hours' ride, sir."

" Well, it is now two o'clock ; let us start so as to arrive early."

In approaching the mountains a rough and narrow path leads by a rapid ascent through a dark ravine to a green valley named Wady-Aly, the natives of which in former times had a very bad reputation.

Valleys and mountains succeed each other; on a hill-side we admired the picturesque effect of the village of Abou-Goch, so named from a celebrated robber chief, who, twenty-five years ago, spread terror all around. The real name of the place is Kariet-el-Enab (Grape Village), and is said to be the ancient Kiryat-Jearim, where for twenty years the ark was deposited. It overlooks a green valley covered with fig, olive, lemon, and orange trees, and at the entrance of the village we passed the Gothic church of St. Jeremy, converted to-day into a stable. At sunset we are at the top of a mountain pass, admiring the glorious hues reflected on all the surrounding scenery. What the names of all these mountains are I do not know, but this dark and black valley at our feet must be Elah or Terebinthe, where David with his sling killed the Philistine giant.

" Joseph, when will we see the Mount of Olives ? "

"Very soon, sir; after you have passed those mountains that you see yonder."

Up and down we go again, pass the mountains pointed out by Joseph, but there is no sign of Jerusalem. Night has succeeded day; and Tom, Aline, Charles Beadel, Mr. Rogers, and the German gentleman, with one of the muleteers, who followed with our shawls, commenced to gallop their horses. Mr. Beadel, Sr., Mrs. Henrietta, as much fatigued as myself, and I, were incapable of so doing, while Henry kindly remained with us.

On they went: Joseph assuring us all the time that we would soon arrive. The moon rose, and at seven o'clock we saw some tents pitched in a valley near us, and soon passed the Russian Convent and then the Jaffa gate.

The road, now skirting around the walls of the city, became so stony and dangerous, though Joseph endeavored to assure us it was not so, that we dismounted and walked down regular steps of stone that led to Gethsemane; we then remounted, and riding across the Valley of Jehoshaphat, ascended the Mount of Olives. The higher we rose, the more we felt the cold and violence of the wind. At last we reached the camp, heard welcome voices, saw bright fires burning; and, while waiting for dinner, were glad to rest our weary limbs, after being in the saddle twelve hours and a half.

The others had arrived an hour before, and every one was dissatisfied with Joseph, who had so badly divided his journeys.

Dinner was announced; but our extreme weariness and the cold westerly breeze forbade the enjoyment of our meal, and soon all retired. The wind increased to such violence that the men were obliged to watch the tents during the night; and from time to time we were awakened by the noise of hammering the pins in the ground.

Thursday, April 2.

This morning we made the discovery that the drinking-water was very impure—filled in fact with lively red animals.

The dragoman was called, who informed us that nearly all the water in and about Jerusalem was rain caught in cisterns, and this was as pure as any. We however ordered him to obtain some from another cistern, and found a decided change—*i. e.*, the little animals were now all white. Fearing that this would produce sickness, Tom made a filter with charcoal, and thenceforth our water was clear and sweet.

Having risen late,—it was twelve o'clock by the time we had finished breakfast,—we went to visit the chapel of the Ascension, where it is said Christ appeared to His disciples after the crucifixion and thence ascended to heaven. We were even shown His footprint in the stones. This chapel belongs to the Mussulmans, and the Catholics have only permission to perform mass on Ascension-day. From the top of the minaret of the mosque we had a splendid view of the Valley of Jehoshaphat, of the dry bed of the Kedron, and, as far as the eye could reach with a lorgnette, we could see, shining amid a blue chain of mountains, the Dead Sea.

But how well repaid we were for all our fatigue of the previous day when we saw Jerusalem at our feet! It was a glorious sight, of which Tom had taken a view before we ladies had arisen. But I do not think any description could bring it more vividly to the memory than that given by Lamartine:—

"The Mount of Olives, on the top of which I am seated, sinks by a rough and rapid declivity to the profound abyss which separates it from Jerusalem, and which is called the Valley of Jehoshaphat. From the bottom of that dark and narrow ravine, whose naked sides are spotted or speckled with white and black stones,—funereal stones of death,—rises an immense and wide hill, whose rapid declivity resembles a high, tumbled rampart; no tree can grow there, no moss even can be seen; the inclination is so steep that earth and stones are constantly rolling down, and it only presents to the eye a surface of dried dust, looking like some mountain of ashes thrown from the top of the city. Towards the centre of this hill or natural rampart, high and strong walls of large stones, uncut on their exterior faces, begin, hiding their Roman and Hebraic foundations under those same ashes that cover their feet, and rising hence from fifty to a hundred feet above that base of earth.

"Three city gates are cut in these walls; two are blocked up, and the open one looks as empty and deserted as if it only gave entry to an uninhabited city. [When Lamartine wrote this, in 1832, the pest was raging in the Holy City.] The walls are still higher than these gates, and sustain a large and wide platform, extending two-thirds the length of Jerusalem on the eastern side.

"This platform may be one thousand feet in length and five to six hundred in width; it is nearly level, except in the centre, where it inclines imperceptibly, as if to call back to the eye the valley that formerly separated the Hill of Zion from Mount Moriah.

"This beautiful platform, without doubt formed by nature, but evidently enlarged by the hand of man, was the sublime pedestal on which stood the temple of Solomon. To-day two Turkish mosques have taken its place: one is that of Omar, in the centre of the platform; the other El-Axa, at the south-eastern extremity touching the wall of the city. The Mosque of Omar, an admirable edifice of Byzantine architecture, octagon in form, of stone and marble, is of immense dimensions; with eight faces, each ornamented with seven arcades terminated by pointed arches, and above this first order of architecture is a terraced roof, from which project some narrower arcades, capped by a graceful dome, covered with copper, formerly gilt. The walls are incrusted with blue enamel, and to the right and left extend wide partitions, terminated by light Moorish colonnades corresponding to the eight doors of the mosque.

"Beyond these disengaged arches the platform continues and terminates,—one extremity at the northern part of the enclosure, the other at the walls of the southerly side.

"Very high cypresses scattered about, some olive-trees, and green and graceful shrubs growing here and there between the mosques, set off their elegant architecture, and the bright colors of the walls, by their pyramidal forms, and the dark foliage which overshadows the façades of the temples and the bright domes of the city.

"Beyond the two mosques, and the site of the temple, all Jerusalem extends before us, without permitting the eye to lose a roof or a stone, like the plan of a city in relief that an artist would spread upon a table. This city is not, as it had been represented to us, a confused mass of ruins and ashes, on which are thrown some Arab huts, or some Bedouin tents. No; it is a city bright with light and color, presenting to the eye of the stranger its untouched and embattled walls; its blue mosque with its white colonnade; its thousands of glittering domes on which the light of a sunny autumnal day falls and remounts in dazzling vapor; the façades of its houses tinted by age with the golden and yellow color that distinguishes the edifices of Pæstum or Rome; its old towers, keepers of its walls, of which not a stone, not a loop-hole, not a battlement is missing.

"And then in the midst of that ocean of houses, and that multitude of little domes that cover them, one, black and larger than the others, presents itself overcapped by another white one. They are the St. Sepulchre and Calvary, which commingle: and drowned as it were in the immense labyrinth of domes, edifices, and streets which surround them, it is difficult to form an idea of their sites, which should be on an isolated hill, outside the walls, and not in the midst of Jerusalem. The city, narrowed on the side of Zion, has without doubt enlarged on the northern side, to encompass within its enclosure the two locations which make its shame and glory: that of the torture of the Just; that of the resurrection of the Man-God! Thus appears the city from the top of the Mount of Olives; it has no horizon behind it, either on the side of the west or the north. The line of its walls and towers, the spires of its numerous minarets, the arcs of its dazzling domes, are cut out firmly on a blue oriental sky, and the city, thus presented on her wide and elevated platform, seems still to be lighted up with all the antique splendor of its prophecies, only to await a '*word*' to come forth, all dazzling, from its seventeen successive ruins, and become that Jerusalem which sprang from the bosom of the desert brilliant with light."

The weather all day has continued very windy, and at four o'clock in the afternoon we resolved to take a walk in the city before the closing of the gates, which is at six o'clock. Aline and the gentlemen took their horses, except Henry Beadel, who remained with me, as I preferred walking, feeling acutely that I had had too much horseback riding the day before.

In going down the steep path that leads to the base of the mount, we passed before some ruins where tradition places some of the last scenes of the life of our Saviour—where He taught "*Our Father who art in heaven,*" where He predicted the ruin of Jerusalem, etc., etc. As the horses descended slowly, we arrived first; and crossing the Valley of Jehoshaphat, entered by the St. Stephen gate, and walked through the French and Mussulman part of the city, which is far from looking as inviting as we had anticipated from the top of the mount. The streets are very narrow, irregular, and badly paved; occasionally we passed through dark, vaulted bazars, with little openings above to permit light to penetrate; while the walls of the low arched doors of many of the houses were covered with green vines, giving them the aspect of old ruins.

CHAPTER XV.

GARDEN OF GETHSEMANE—GROTTO OF AGONY—TOMB OF THE VIRGIN—HOUSE OF MARY'S PARENTS—PROCESSION FOR MECCA—VIA DOLOROSA—HOUSE OF PILATE—ECCE HOMO—HOUSES OF VERONICA AND THE WANDERING JEW—CHURCH OF THE HOLY SEPULCHRE—THE TOMB—CHAPEL OF THE TRUE CROSS—CALVARY—PALM SUNDAY—ON THE WALLS—LEPERS.

FRIDAY, April 3, 1868.

ALTERNATELY cloudy and clear this morning, like April weather in America.

Before descending the mount we gave orders to have our tents removed to a place less exposed to the wind and cold, and Joseph promised to meet us in the city, and take us to our new abode.

At ten o'clock we entered the Garden of Gethsemane, which contains eight of the oldest olive-trees of the mount; they are surrounded by a wall, and the ground about them has been formed in flower-plots, cultivated by the Roman Catholic priests, who have possession of the garden and grotto near by. An old monk pointed out the tree where Christ prayed to His Father. We all sat down around it, and received some flowers that he culled, and olive leaves picked from its sacred branches; and when the gentlemen had left us, to wander about the place, Aline and I gave vent to the religious feelings that had taken possession of us, and both prayed fervently. Upon leaving the Garden the monk showed us the place where Christ told His disciples to "watch and pray;" and afterwards the Grotto of Agony, where Christ passed several hours before His arrest.

We could almost imagine that only a short time had elapsed since the agony of the Divine Son; since it is in its natural state, except that a chapel has been erected, and paintings of the disciples, and of Christ, are hung about the walls.

Leaving the Grotto, we passed before the Tomb of the Virgin, which was formerly part of a church and convent erected by Godfrey de Bouillon. The convent was destroyed in 1187 by Saladin, but the church was spared, on account of the veneration the Mussulmans profess for the blessed Virgin. It belongs now to the Greeks and Armenians, and is only open a short time every morning. Entering the city, the guide showed us what is called the "Baths of Mary;" also where the house stood, according to tradition, occupied by Mary's parents, and where she was born.

In going to Jerusalem you must prepare your mind to listen to all the stories that dragomen, guides, and priests have for so many years invented for the traveller; and in remembering how many times Jerusalem has been destroyed and rebuilt, one is convinced of the uncertainty that must exist as to the exact position of sacred places. There is no doubt about the localities of Mount Zion, the Valley of Jehoshaphat, Mount Moriah, and Gethsemane; but for the rest, let us be thankful to be permitted to tread "*the sacred soil.*"

As the gates of Jerusalem are closed during the midday hour of prayer, and as that time was approaching, our guide advised us to repass the portals that we might see a procession about departing for Mecca. Adjoining the walls of the city the ground is covered with sepulchral enclosures, and we entered one of these to screen ourselves from the keen wind, and soon forgot the weather in looking at the strange spectacle before us. All the hillocks around were covered with hundreds of persons, dressed in their holiday garments; the women wrapt in long white veils and their faces masked; the men and children in various bright costumes. As we are approaching the Holy-week, the place is crowded with Europeans, and all around we could see French, English, and Americans; and here we had the pleasure of again meeting General Darling, and also Mr. Standish and Captain Hoare, accompanied by the Marchioness of Ely. After viewing the procession, which comprised only the devotees, escorted by two regiments of soldiers with a few flags, we re-entered the city to follow the Via Dolorosa—divided into fourteen stations, commencing near the St. Stephen gate and ending at Calvary—where tradition locates the last acts of the life of Christ.

The guide called our attention to a sculptured door, that opened on the palace of Pontius Pilate, near some remains of the tower of Antonia. Passing before the convent of the Flagéllation, we entered into the chapel where Christ was crowned with thorns, and as it was raining, we leisurely examined the sacred paintings which represent the stations. Thence we visited the arch of "*Ecce Homo*" (Behold the man !). At the extremity of the street, a broken column marks the first fall of our Lord, and a few steps farther on are the ruins of a Gothic chapel where the Virgin fainted. We were shown also the house of Veronica, and opposite, that of the Wandering Jew; also the place where Simon the Cyrenian took charge of the cross; and farther a gray stone column that marks the place of the second fall. Still fifty steps farther, another place where He spake these words: "Daughters of Jerusalem, weep not for me, but weep for yourselves, and for your children" (St. Luke xxiii. 28). Lastly, after stopping a moment before the two columns that indicate the place of the third fall, a narrow street led us directly to the Church of the Holy Sepulchre.

We entered the building, passing before a guard of Turkish soldiers seated on divans at the entrance, who ask a small backsheesh from each visitor, and followed the crowd of pilgrims, who had come from all parts of the world to assist in the devotions appertaining to Holy-week.

Near the door, and almost on a level with the floor, a large red rectangular marble slab, which the devotees were kneeling before and kissing, marks the spot where the body of Christ was deposited after his death, and washed with perfumes by the holy women. It belongs jointly to the Latins, Greeks, and Armenians. Onward a few more steps is the place where the Virgin stood during the embalming of her son; and thence we penetrated into the Rotunda or St. Sepulchre.

Here we had to await our turn to enter the Tomb, as it is only large enough to hold about three persons at a time. Before it is a vestibule, called the Chapel of the Angel, because, according to tradition, it was here that the angel announced the resurrection to the holy women. The Chapel of the Tomb is only about six feet square, entirely inlaid with marble, and ornamented with two pictures, and forty-two lamps of gold and silver. A priest is constantly in attendance, burning perfumes, lighting tapers, and receiving alms from travellers.

There were so many waiting their turn, that Aline, Mr. Rogers, and myself, who entered at the same time, could not remain so long as we wished; we ladies there-fore promised ourselves to return soon, and get permission from the Greek Patriarch to enter alone. Directly facing the sepulchre is the Greek church or chapel, occupying the great nave of the edifice, in the middle of which is a small column, indicating the centre of the surface of the earth, and whence *the clay was taken to form the first man.*

After visiting various chapels, of which the most interesting was perhaps that of St. Helena, where tradition says she found the remains of the true cross, and which is excavated within the rock beneath the building, we repaired to Calvary, a platform of about fifteen yards square, whose base is the solid rock. It is divided into two chapels: that of the Crucifixion, belong-ing to the Greeks, and that of the Elevation of the Cross, to the Latins. A split in the rock, which, accord-ing to tradition, opened when Christ expired, is covered by a silver trellis.

Before leaving the church we visited the tomb of Joseph of Arimathea,—situated in the wall west of the

Rotunda,—as well as the sepulchre of Nicodemus, dug within the rock.

It was quite late when we arrived at our encampment, located in a valley near the Damascus gate, surrounded by tents bearing flags of different nations, and on a hill behind us we saw those of Mr. Standish and the Marchioness of Ely.

SATURDAY, April 4.

The weather has been bad through the night; it rained, and the wind blew with such violence that Mr. Beadel's tent was partially thrown down, and at seven o'clock ours collapsed on the side occupied by Aline and Tom. Rain continued all day, and obliged us to stay at *home;* but the novelty of such a life made us take our present discomforts quite gayly. A brasier filled with live coals was placed in each tent to keep us warm, and the day passed in reading, sleeping, and chatting.

In the afternoon we heard near by, a fresh arrival of mules, and soon there was a new encampment, displaying the American flag. While we were conjecturing who were the occupants one of the party, Mr. Dow, our old Nile acquaintance of the *Cleopatra,* made his appearance. He had just returned with his wife, Mr. Briggs, and Mrs. Sherer from a tour to the Jordan and Dead Sea. Two hours passed most agreeably, speaking of by-gone days upon the Nile, and a good dinner and game of whist completed the day.

SUNDAY, April 6.

The weather is more pleasant this morning, though the sky is overcast. At ten o'clock we re-entered the

Church of the Holy Sepulchre, and attended the mass of the Copts and Greek Catholics.

It being Palm-Sunday, the crowd was dense, and almost every one carried in his hand a branch of palm. One of the Turkish guard cleared the way for us, and took us behind the priests, who were in procession, stopping at all the holy places on their way to the Sepulchre. They gave us each a palm-branch and some *giroflées* from a basket of blessed flowers which they carried. Latin, Greek, Armenian, Catholic, each rite had its turn; as soon as one was ended the Turkish guard would make room for another.

To-day, Aline and I were permitted to again enter the Holy Sepulchre; the door was closed behind us, and we stood once more before the tomb of our Saviour. Our hearts were full, and overflowed in prayer. We kissed the marble stone, permitted the priest in attendance to burn perfumes and light tapers for the welfare of our Catholic friends far away, and then slowly withdrew to make room for the rest of our party.

While occupied looking at the multitude, a sight always interesting to a stranger who never tires of the variety of costume, we were accosted by the two Misses Potter, accompanied by Mrs. Sherer, their governess, and the courier, and with them again visited different chapels; but, as the crowd was so great, and the mass of pilgrims in such a filthy condition as made their close proximity very unpleasant, we made for the door, found our horses and attendants awaiting us, returned to our camp, and all participated in a good lunch.

In the afternoon we took a long and interesting walk

upon the walls, thus getting a better view of all parts of the city, though occasionally some of us felt quite giddy. Under one part where we passed were a colony of lepers—miserable descendants of Gehazi, the unfaithful servant of Elisha, who was cursed with the leprosy of Naaman "to cleave unto him and his seed forever," and who overwhelmed us with their lamentations and prayers for backsheesh. The sight was extremely distressing, and we hurried to get past, although we had already seen some outside the city gates, where numbers are constantly lying in the sun, stretching out their hands to the traveller for alms.

Near the mosque of Omar we had to deviate from our route, as it is strictly forbidden for the *giaour* to look inside, except at stated times, and then only under guard. Mr. Rogers would not listen to the guide, but continued on: soon, however, he returned, informing us that he had been assailed with stones.

After returning to our camp, Charles and Henry Beadel accompanied Aline for a ride in the country; Mr. Beadel, Sr., and Mr. Rogers remained together; Tom went to take a nap, while I seated myself outside the tent and arranged some flowers for our albums. The weather was becoming settled; the sun shone brightly on our olive-trees; birds were singing among their branches, the mules and horses resting in the shade; the cook was preparing dinner, while the two servants and some muleteers were seated in a group, talking and smoking; the sound of church bells announcing vespers would come quite distinct to the ear, and often I would stop working, rest my head on my hand,

and gaze upon the picture spread before me, so that, when back in my quiet home, I could close my eyes and again see it as it then was. May it also bring back the sweet emotions felt in that quiet hour!

When again together, we received a visit from Mr. Standish, who came to wish us "good-by," as he and his friend proposed to start the day after for Hebron, Mar-Saba, the Dead Sea, and Jordan, desiring to be back for Easter Sunday.

CHAPTER XVI.

TOMB OF THE VIRGIN—TOMBS OF THE PROPHETS—SILOAM—FOUNTAIN OF THE VIRGIN—POOL OF SILOAM—MOUNT ZION—TOMB OF DAVID—WAILING-PLACE OF THE JEWS—QUARRIES—JOAB'S WELL—PALESTINE EXPLORATIONS—THE SPRING OF THE ARCH—TYROPŒAN VALLEY—ANCIENT HALLS AND AQUEDUCTS.

MONDAY, April 6, 1868.

AT eight o'clock we were off to visit the Tomb of the Virgin, and as it was the first time since our arrival that the weather was really fine, and the skies without a cloud, we enjoyed our walk exceedingly.

Why did I feel so happy, why so light, so full of life, that it seemed as if my feet scarcely touched the ground, as I walked quietly near my companions? Are Jerusalem and its surroundings so grand, so beautiful? As I have already said, the city itself is far from being handsome; the streets are narrow, irregular, badly paved, and the part where the Jews live is so dirty, nay, more than dirty,—filthy,—and the odor so abominable, that when passing through we would even accelerate the gait of our horses.

The surroundings I can describe in a few words:—hills without shade, valleys without water, a stony earth with here and there a patch of green, a clump of olive-trees, throwing a little shade on the steep hillside, and,—that is all: all for the traveller who looks unimpassioned on these things; but for one like myself, possessing an enthusiastic temperament, there was much poetry in all I beheld. The walls of Jerusalem that we were following are very picturesque, and along the roadside are many Mussulman cemeteries, strewn with bright wild-flowers, bathed with the morning dew and sparkling in the sunshine, where we could see veiled women, dressed in white, engaged in prayer and talking with the spirits of their dead; men sitting on tombs, surrounded by women and children, were singing some pious verses; then suddenly a cavalcade would start up before us, going on their pilgrimage to the Dead Sea and Jordan; and in approaching Gethsemane we saw the hillocks crowded with the inhabitants of Jerusalem, who had come to witness a procession, starting for the Tomb of Moses. As the sun lightens all this, observe the deep blue sky above; enjoy the light breeze which flutters the ends of our white turbans, and say, was it not more than delightful; was it not grand and glorious?

We found so great a crowd of pilgrims at the Virgin's Tomb, that it was with much trouble we could force an entrance. Soon I lost sight of all my companions except Henry Beadel, whose arm I had taken, and we advanced only, it seemed to us, by inches. A wide staircase of an hundred steps leads to the church below, but the difficulty was to force a way through the dense and suffocating crowd. For a few moments our eyesight failed us, as we had not yet become accustomed to the sudden transition from bright daylight to the deep gloom of this subterranean hall; but soon our eyes grew familiar with it, and the spectacle that greeted the view was indeed strange and grand. Beneath us were thousands of people, and away on the altar, far below, hundreds of lights, making a scene fit for the pencil of Rembrandt.

It took us more than an hour to go down, and in fact we were about giving it up, when we saw Mr. Rogers returning, who assisted in clearing the way for us. We followed him closely, and soon stood before the tomb, where a priest offered what appeared to me to be a Bible, to kiss: a book which *he said* was from the time of Christ. We visited also two other chapels, said to contain the tombs of the Virgin's parents, St. Joachim and St. Anne, and thence forced our way from the sacred cavern through the filthiest crowd that it was ever my lot to form part of.

Having enjoyed a substantial meal, we took horses and went again on the Mount of Olives; then visited some sepulchres called the Tombs of the Prophets, and going down to the Valley of Jehoshaphat, stopped before the so-called tombs of Absalom, Jehoshaphat, and Zachariah, which are cut in the hill-side, near Siloam, and are certainly antique.

The bed of the torrent Kedron, on our left, is entirely dry; and all the ground, as far as the village of Siloam, is but a large Jewish cemetery, covering the side of the valley. Siloam is picturesquely situated, being a mass of houses built in terraces on the sides and peak of

ABSALOM'S TOMB.—*See page* 218.

a rock, and under which are large caves, formerly tombs, but which have been converted into storehouses and habitations.

Opposite Siloam is the Fountain of the Virgin, so named from a tradition which says that here she came to wash the linen of her Divine Son. The fountain is an excavation cut in a rock, with a descent by a stairway of thirty steps, divided into two parts by a vaulted room. The interior grotto has a depth of about eight yards; the water runs into a basin five yards in length by two in width, and of the same depth, and disappears into a subterranean canal which carries it to the Pool of Siloam, not far distant.

Thither we then repaired, and did not leave without tasting its waters; for here it was that Christ made the blind man to see; and since then the popular tradition has always caused a belief in its marvellous effects in the cure of ophthalmia.

Leaving the pool we gradually ascended Mount Zion, where the palace of King David once was; where his tomb now is. But the religious fanaticism of its guardians is such that Christians are not allowed to enter, and we had to content ourselves with visiting parts of the basilica which covers it. Built in the ninth century, under Adrian, destroyed by the Sultan El-Haken, it was in ruins at the end of the eleventh century, but rebuilt under the Crusaders, and at last the Mussulmans took and have kept possession of it. The guide showed us a room where, according to tradition, the Last Supper took place; another where the washing of His feet was performed by the Magdalen; a column where Christ was tied and flagellated; a room where the Virgin died, etc., etc., all of which was so much more than doubtful that it was with pleasure we returned to our tents, where we found dinner awaiting us.

TUESDAY, April 7

To-day we visited the Tombs of the Kings, the Tombs of the Judges, and the Wailing-place of the Jews. This ceremony of wailing is a sight that would be ridiculous, if the comedy was not drowned in their sincere devotion. Standing without the walls of the enclosure of the temple, the men on one side, while the women are on the other, a rabbi, with book in hand, was praying and reading; imploring God to drive out the infidel and permit His chosen people to reoccupy the sacred mount; and soon became so excited that he commenced to cry and sob, and then all his followers joined therein. They are so much in earnest that you cannot help pitying them, and wish that a Divine pardon might permit them to re-enter the temple whence they expelled the Master.

Upon leaving this place, we went to look at the remaining part of an arch, belonging to the viaduct which crossed the valley between Mounts Moriah and Zion, connecting the king's palace and the temple area. This is known as the "Spring of Robinson's Arch," of which I shall have occasion to speak more hereafter.

WEDNESDAY, April 8.

Every one of the party, except Tom, being dissatisfied with the horses which we had obtained at Jaffa, Joseph was ordered to furnish a fresh supply. Accordingly a number were brought into camp, and from them we ladies had the choice.

Tom selected for Aline a beautiful sorrel mare, a most graceful creature, with fine limbs and glossy hide; and for me a small, lively, dark gray horse, so quick that at first I was afraid of him, and the splendid animal seemed to know it, for instead of mastering him he mastered me; and though Tom tells me to use the whip, and make him obey, I have commenced to love and cannot bear the idea of punishing him.

We have already passed nine days in Jerusalem—a longer time than the generality of travellers occupy; for after giving six days to the Holy City, it is usual to start on the trip to the Dead Sea and the Jordan; returning thence to tarry a few days more before going north.

We have seen very little of our dragoman lately, and are not pleased to hear that within a few days he has gambled away one hundred and twenty napoleons, part of the money which we have advanced to him; and we are told that it will be impossible for him to fulfil his contract.

This morning we visited the quarries, which are very extensive, reaching for miles under the city; immense rooms, supported by natural columns, have in their partitions openings which lead into other rooms as large; while in various places confused masses of heaped up rocks, a chaos of enormous calcareous boulders, rolled pell-mell together, meet your eye. Other blocks hang perpendicularly from the ceiling, and the measure of the empty places left by the stones taken away, coincide with the enormous masses in the wall of the temple court. Having taken a walk within of nearly half a mile, we returned to the light of heaven, mounted our horses, rode past the Pool of Siloam, and visited farther on, located in the valley between the Mounts of Scandel and of Bad Advice, Joab's Well—Bir-Eyoub—the ancient En-Rogel, called by some Nehemiah's Well, because tradition says that this prophet found therein the sacred fire which had been hidden during the Babylonian captivity.

En-Rogel marked the dividing line of the tribes of Judah and Benjamin. It is mentioned in the history of Absalom, and when Adonijah, son of David, aspired to supplant Solomon, it was there he assembled his partisans. This well is beneath a square building, open on its eastern face, and on the right is a square basin, partially filled with stagnant water. It has a depth of one hundred and twenty-three feet, and its masonry shows stones of very large dimensions, which appear to be very ancient. Medjr-el-Din says that at the bottom is a lateral cave whence the water issues, and when the winter has been very wet the water of this well springs out in the beginning of January, and this sign of a good harvest is celebrated by a feast of several days around Bir-Eyoub, and the Kedron then becomes a real torrent.

On our way back the guide pointed out to us, on a hill-side, the tree whereon *Judas hanged himself.*

As soon as we had taken our lunch we started for

the Mediterranean Hotel, having an appointment with Lieut. Warren of the Royal Engineers to visit the excavations.

In the year 1865, by the liberality of Miss Burdett Coutts, a fund was placed at the disposal of Captain Wilson, R. E., for the purpose of explorations in and about Palestine, in order to satisfactorily locate various places mentioned in the Scriptures, thereby arriving at a more intimate knowledge of the customs of the times and the habits of the people, making plain many passages hitherto ambiguous, and clearing away the doubts of ages upon many disputed points and subjects.

A matter of such vast importance to the historian, the geologist, the architect, the antiquarian, the sculptor, the engineer, and the theologian, soon excited the attention of numbers, who, if not members of either of the above enumerated callings, still were attracted by that something implanted in the minds of all, a curiosity to know correctly men and things existing in the earlier ages of the world; a desire that might satisfy the skeptical and confirm the believer.

A society for this purpose was accordingly formed, known as the "Palestine Exploration Fund," under the auspices of the Archbishop of York, the Dukes of Argyle, Devonshire, and others, and under the patronage of her Majesty the Queen of Great Britain. The work commenced by Miss Coutts was therefore continued in various parts of the Holy Land, bringing to light many remarkable relics; but the most interesting exhumations have been those in and about the city of Jerusalem, and more particularly in the vicinity of the Harem area, or site of the Temple of Solomon, and in the Tyropœon valley, separating Mount Moriah from the king's palace on Mount Zion.

On the exterior surface of the Harem wall, and facing Zion, a slight projection or bulging out had frequently attracted the attention of the savants, and was supposed to have been caused at some remote period by an earthquake.

Robinson, however, contrary to the received opinion, at once pronounced it to be the spring of an arch. "Dig down," said he, "fifty feet from this wall, and you will find a pier which supported the other portion." This theory, derided by all, has proved correct; for the pier has been found within six inches of the position designated, and it is now generally believed that a succession of these arches spanned the Tyropœon valley, supporting a viaduct over which Solomon escorted the Queen of Sheba when he showed to her the riches and wonders of his capital and the magnificence of the Temple.

This was one of the first results obtained, since which other excavations have disclosed large chambers, passages, aqueducts, and granaries, whose uses are still shrouded in mystery: but as the work progresses these riddles will be solved; the earthy pall, from fifty to one hundred feet in depth removed, and the skeleton exposed, which the genius of the engineer and architect will rehabilitate, giving us a perfect idea of edifices as they existed in all their glory thousands of years before our era.

As Aline thought the task too arduous, she remained

at the camp, and Messrs. Henry Beadel, Sr. and Jr., Mr. Rogers, Mr. Ferris, and I, met Lieut. Warren (who has succeeded Captain Wilson) according to appointment, and with several workmen proceeded to the vicinity of the Wailing-place of the Jews, near the southwestern corner of the Temple area, where the most interesting works are now in progress.

Each one being provided with a candle, we entered a passage-way cut in the hill-side, and soon passed down a rough ladder and into a good-sized hall, thence through various passages where the workmen had cut through massive walls—sometimes crawling on hands and knees through mud emitting a most disagreeable odor, composed as it was of the drippings and sewerage of the city above.

At one place a succession of arches denoted the position of a causeway, and it would appear as though it had become too narrow for its uses and had been widened; but the new part was carried on arches of a smaller radius than the older, and of course the piers were nearer together. The reason for this incongruity is yet to be explained.

At another place we traced for some distance an aqueduct, probably intended and used to conduct water from the Pools of Solomon to the Temple; but why, then, was another one, running parallel with the former, but at a level some three or four feet lower?

Having wandered through these wonderful subterranean ruins for a couple of hours—at one time being held by the arms and dropped down a black pit, whose (to me) unknown depth fortunately proved but slight; at another time tied in a chair and lowered some forty feet, by means of a crank and rope—we were glad at last to regain and once more freely breathe the pure air of heaven.

Having made our exit by the shaft which we had previously descended, the seat unslung, and all about to depart, we were astonished to hear a sepulchral voice from the bottom of the pit: "Are you not going to send down the chair?" Startling as was its effect, we almost instantly recognized the voice as that of Mr. Rogers, who was quietly waiting his turn to be hauled up, but whom by some inadvertence we had supposed to be already on the surface. Reversing the crank again, and unwinding the rope, we requested the *speaker* to take the *chair*, and soon received his *resignation*, as he said he preferred to be *a member at large*. But a few minutes more and he would have had the doubtful gratification of passing the night in company with the shades of the kings and patriarchs of yore.

Having subscribed to the "Fund," and thanked the Lieutenant for his urbanity, we returned to our tents, where our first care was to get a thorough cleaning, much needed by all the party, after which Tom and I went to the French bazars shopping, and on our way home met Lord and Lady Conyngham, who had just returned from Petra.

CHAPTER XVII.

MOSQUE OF OMAR—MOSQUE OF EL-AXA—SOLOMON'S TEMPLE—GREEK FIRE—RACHEL'S TOMB—HEBRON—CAVE OF MACHPELAH—TOMB OF ABRAHAM AND SARAH—ABRAHAM'S OAK—POOLS OF SOLOMON—BETHLEHEM—CHURCH OF THE NATIVITY—BIRTH OF CHRIST.

THURSDAY, April 9, 1868.

NOTHER pleasant day, and we accompanied Tom to the Tomb of the Virgin, the Garden of Gethsemane, and the Tomb of Absalom, of which he took views.

We remained a long time in the Garden, for, being Holy Thursday, it was crowded with a procession of pilgrims, coming to pray before the Tree of Our Saviour, and receive from the hand of the guardian some olive-leaves and flowers. Our old friend the priest appeared delighted to see us again, and still more so when we told him we wanted him to stand with us for the picture Tom wished to take. We roamed for one hour through the grounds, praying, dreaming, chatting; and then, the doors having been locked, to permit Mr. Ferris to take his view, we grouped around the Holy Tree, recommending our old friend to remain quiet, which he promised to do. "One, two, three!" said Tom, and every one took a statue-like appearance; but we could hardly keep serious when we saw the old priest moving his head, while turning his beads with one hand and crossing himself with the other. "I am sure this view is spoiled," said Tom; but when developed, to our astonishment, though a little dim, the face of our priest was perfectly visible, which made him feel both proud and happy.

Having rewarded him with a good backsheesh, we left for Absalom's Tomb, and at five o'clock returned to our encampment.

FRIDAY, April 10.

We have now become so well acquainted with Jerusalem that to-day Aline and myself chose to remain in camp, writing letters for home, while the gentlemen went out; and remembering that a great many of our friends were not as fortunate as ourselves, sent them olive-leaves and flowers.

In the afternoon we received a visit from the American Consul, Mr. Johnson, a very agreeable gentleman, who advised us to try and keep our dragoman, who continued to give us much annoyance, and offered us a letter to his brother, who is Consul in Beyrout, so that if any further trouble should arise during our journey we could refer the matter to him.

SATURDAY, April 11.

This morning we went to visit our friend and companion Charles Beadel, who, not feeling well, had removed some days since to the Mediterranean Hotel: he is not yet entirely recovered, although improving.

We there met Lord and Lady Conyngham, Mr. Hale our Consul-General at Alexandria, of whom I have spoken during our stay in Cairo, and Mr. Messenger and family, whom we had lost sight of after their visit on our boat before we left for the Nile. To-day they accompanied us in our visit to the Mosque of Omar and of El-Axa—a permit for which is necessary, while a fee of ten francs each is expected, in fact must be given.

In order to give a good description of the two mosques a better inspection and more time than our guide allowed us would have been necessary. Certainly two days would not have been too much, while we had hardly as many hours;—the dislike of the Mussulmans to see Christians in their holy places is so great that they hurry you through, hardly permitting you to take a look at each notable object, interesting either by historical association or tradition; yet the remembrance, in my imagination, is that of a beautiful dream.

A few words, however, as to the location. Passing through a gateway we found ourselves in a great square, or rather a parallelogram surrounded by huge walls; and this is the site of the Temple, this the Temple court! Here, on the summit of Moriah, was Abraham about to offer up as a sacrifice his son Isaac; the ages roll on, and here again is David led by divine instinct, to purchase the threshing-floor of Ornan the Jebusite, whereon to erect an altar to the Most High. The lifetime of the great shepherd king is spent in garnering up riches wherewith to build such a temple as the eyes of man had not seen before; but finding the years creeping upon him, and his energies failing, he bequeathes the sacred task to his wise son, and soon is gathered to his fathers, and sleeps the sleep that knows no waking in the cave on Mount Zion, nearly adjoining the royal palace.

And now the glorious task begins for which such vast preparations have been made. Having associated with him Hiram king of Tyre, from whose subjects came the hewers of wood, as well as artisans and artists of various degrees of merit, and Hiram the widow's son as the chief architect, with perfect system and regularity the Temple rises, and soon is consecrated to the worship of the great, the living God!

How the wise and mighty king degenerated in his old age, how the Temple was destroyed and afterwards rebuilt, are but matters of history.

Here, at the porch, is the pool of Bethesda, where Christ bade the cripple "*Take up thy bed and walk*" (St. John ch. v. 2, 8); here did He dispute with the doctors; from this holy enclosure did He drive forth the money-changers. Of all the places on the face of this fair earth, is there a spot more holy than this of Mount Moriah? Strange that the weak Turk should guard with special awe and reverence that which the strong Christian scarce thinks worth the holding!

In the afternoon the gentlemen went to the Church of the Holy Sepulchre, to assist at one of the strangest ceremonies that takes place during the year, called the reception of the Sacred Fire. Having gone early, and found places in the upper gallery, they could without danger observe the curious spectacle. Thousands of Greek Catholics crush themselves around the tomb, and wait with a feverish impatience the arrival of their bishop, who enters the Chapel of the Angel, and the doors are closed upon him.

Soon an angel coming down from heaven brings to the bishop the holy fire, which he passes through an orifice cut in the wall of the chapel, by means of a sponge dipped in alcohol attached to the end of a rod.

It is the solemn moment: the crowd, crazy with enthusiasm, rushes to light candles from this celestial fire, and the cries, the swaying of this agitated multitude, the glare of thousands of torches, the songs and the dances which accompany this profane ceremony, give it an indescribable character. Very often the Turkish militia is not strong enough to prevent accidents, and often loss of life is the price of these odious saturnalias. In 1834 over four hundred bodies covered the pavement of the Holy Sepulchre at the end of one of these "*festivities.*"

EASTER SUNDAY, April 12.

It will seem strange to hear that we did not wish to assist at the service this morning in the Church of the Holy Sepulchre. The fact is, every time we have been there, the crowd of pilgrims has been so great, and by such close association we brought *home* so much more than we bargained for, that we have become utterly disgusted, and decided to visit it no more.

In the afternoon Aline and Tom went to return the call of Lord and Lady Conyngham, who had left cards the day previous, and met Mr. Johnson and family in the city, who had arrived the day before.

In the evening we called to say good-by to Captain

Hoare and Mr. Standish, who had returned from the Dead Sea and were again encamped near us. The latter was dining with the Catholic bishop, but we met the English Vice-Consul and Lord Ely, with whom we passed a pleasant evening. Joseph says he is all ready, and that to-morrow we will start for Hebron.

Monday, April 13.

A few miles south of Jerusalem, on the road-side, stands a small plain white edifice, perhaps twenty feet square and as many high, and which the traveller would pass by without giving it a second thought. This building, erected and kept in preservation by the despised Mussulman, would probably soon be in ruins if left to the care of the enlightened Christian.

Beneath this modest roof rest the mortal remains of the gentle mother of Israel.

"And they journeyed from Beth-el; and there was but a little way to come to Ephrath: and Rachel travailed, and she had hard labor.

"And it came to pass when she was in hard labor, that the midwife said unto her, Fear not; thou shalt have this son also.

"And it came to pass as her soul was in departing (for she died), that she called his name Ben-oni: but his father called him Benjamin.

"And Rachel died, and was buried in the way to Ephrath, which is Beth-lehem.

"And Jacob set a pillar upon her grave: *that is the pillar of Rachel's grave unto this day.*"—Gen. xxxv. 16.

"And as for me, when I came from Padan, Rachel died by me in the land of Canaan, in the way, when yet there was but a little way to come unto Ephrath: and I buried her there in the way of Ephrath, the same is Beth-lehem."—Gen. xlviii. 7.

Tarrying a short time before the mausoleum, and again at mid-day for lunch, we arrived in view of Hebron, where our tents were pitched, near the quarantine, at five o'clock P.M.

The weather had been excessively warm all day; the bad roads, winding through masses of rock, and the dreary prospect had fatigued us all; so we were glad to finish dinner and retire early.

TUESDAY, April 14.

The magic touch of refreshing sleep took away the fatigues of the preceding day, and all being up early, enjoyed the picturesque sight. Behind us we had the quarantine building, backed by green hills intersected with gray rocks, and covered with tombs: on both sides luxuriant terraces, covered with olive-trees, grass, and flowers, and before us the city spread on a hill, the houses seeming one above another around an imposing mosque, which covers the grotto of Machpelah.

After breakfast our tents were struck, and sent in advance for the Pools of Solomon, while we walked through this most ancient city of the world. It has much the same appearance as all oriental towns, very narrow streets, arched bazars, which, as the weather was warm, felt cool and comfortable.

We desired to visit the tomb of Abraham, but the

entrance is forbidden to strangers; and when Aline and myself advanced towards the door, a Mussulman guardian made signs to us to pursue our way. The authenticity of this place where the patriarchs are buried is incontestable; and we went all around it, so as to engrave it well on our memory. The exterior enclosure is of great antiquity. It is a parallelogram, sixty-one yards by thirty-five, built of large blocks, some of which measure nearly eight yards in length. The walls, sixteen yards in height, are ornamented with pilasters without chapiters, supporting a high relief cornice; and in the interior of this first enclosure is the mosque which covers the grotto of Machpelah, having a dome and four minarets. After having rested and gathered some flowers for our albums, Tom took a good view of it, with all of us standing near.

It was then noon, and the weather so warm that we questioned whether we should rest and lunch at Hebron or go on and take it under the shade of Abraham's Oak in the woods of Mamre, said to be the spot where that patriarch, after separating from his nephew Lot, pitched his tent and built an altar unto the Lord. (Gen. xiii. 18.)

We decided for the latter place, and mounting our horses were soon seated under the shade of the celebrated oak; the trunk measuring seven yards in circumference, while some of its branches are fifteen yards long. There we spent two hours; and Tom attempted a picture of our lunch scene, which, unfortunately, did not succeed; so, leaving him there with Henry Beadel— for he said he would not leave without at least having a view of the tree—we proceeded towards Solomon's Pools, and had not been *en route* half an hour when we were rejoined by the two gentlemen.

The road was far more pleasant than the day before; although the hills were rocky, barren, and desolate, the valleys, with their green velvet carpet, and darker shades of bushes beyond, formed an agreeable contrast. The air being cooler, we enjoyed our ride; sometimes, when the road permitted it, galloping at full speed. During one hour before arriving at the reservoirs we had to give all our attention to our horses; for while passing through the Wadi-Ortas we were between two walls of rocks, sometimes filled up with fallen blocks, so that we were delighted when we reached our encampment, and it being six o'clock, we at once prepared for dinner.

After dinner Henry Beadel and myself went to view the reservoirs, which were three large basins walled up and cemented in the interior. - They are placed on a declivity: the most elevated pours its water into the second, from whence it runs into the third, which is the largest of all, and, according to Robinson, one hundred and seventy-seven yards in length by eighty-three yards at one extremity and forty-five at the other, having a depth of fifteen yards. The intermediate reservoir is forty-five yards distant from the former, and measures one hundred and twenty-nine yards in length by seventy in width and twelve in depth. The upper reservoir, which is also at a distance of forty-five yards from the second, is one hundred and sixteen yards long, seventy in width, and eight in depth. This last is fed by a fountain situated one hundred and fifty steps farther off, in the neighborhood of a little fort, Kala'l-el-Borak, and which is occupied by the guardian of the waters. This spring, over which a vault has been built, has a circular opening like that of a well, and is generally covered with a large stone. After lifting the stone you can go down a depth of four yards to a room fifteen steps long by eight wide; adjoining which is another small chamber.

The water comes out by four openings; it is first gathered in one basin, and then flows by a subterranean conduit towards the north-western angle of the superior reservoir. There a portion falls into this basin, while the aqueduct continues parallel with the reservoir to the second and third, which it supplies in the same manner, and then continues parallel with another aqueduct from the lower basin to Bethlehem and Jerusalem. This complicated system was evidently so arranged in order to bring to the Temple the pure water of the fountain, while accumulating the surplus in the reservoirs, and these fed the city by the brick aqueduct, that is still seen near the inferior one.

WEDNESDAY, April 15.

At eleven we were in the saddle, and our first stopping-place was Bethlehem.

The road from the pools to this place is short, occupying about one hour and a half, and very undulating. The day was fine, and we had read the evening before, in the "Holy Land," by Dixon, all the touching episodes that took place in this blessed among the blessed cities; the pastorals of Rachel, of Ruth, and of David, and, above all, the most sacred story of the birth of "Our Saviour." It is charmingly situated on the summit of a high hill, which inclines by a series of terraces covered with vines, olives, and oak-trees, to the deep valley which surrounds it on three sides.

A fine panorama spread before us as we approached it: on our right was a peak crowned by an old fort, which dates from the time of the Crusaders, and thence is called "the Mountain of the Franks;" on the left we saw the domes and minarets of Jerusalem; and opposite, towards the east, a blue chain of hills—the mountains of Moab.

To reach the Church of the Nativity, covering the holy stable, we had to pass through the village, which had a cheery aspect as the sun shone on its white stone houses surrounded by gardens. As soon as we were in sight of the edifice we were surrounded by a number of chaplet and relic venders, and it was with some trouble that we could get rid of them and enter the building, which is surrounded by the high walls and gardens of three convents—Latin, Greek, and Armenian.

The present structure was commenced by Helena and terminated by Constantine, between the years 327 and 333. We took only a cursory view, and then passed down the circular staircase which conducts to the grotto of the Nativity, covering the stable and the manger, and is about twelve yards long by five wide and three high. The surface of the rock is entirely covered with marble, as well as the pavement of the grotto; and the place which is pointed out as the birthplace of Christ is on the eastern side, marked by a silver star, around which you read: *Hic de Virgine Mariâ Jésus Christus natus est.* 1717.

Now Cæsar Augustus laid a tax on all the world, and each man must go unto his own city, there to pay it. Joseph, who lived with his young wife at Nazareth, belonged to the royal house of David, and the city of David was Bethlehem.

Thither then did Joseph journey with Mary, big with child, mounted on an ass, as it was and still is the method of journeying in Syria, stopping by the wayside as convenience and pleasure suited.

But lo! when they had arrived at Bethlehem, the rude building which affords shelter to the wayfarer in this country, called a khan, was filled to overflowing with others who, like themselves, were come up to pay their taxes.

Near by the khan was a sort of cave, cut in the rock, and used as a stable, and thither did Joseph drive the ass; and as no lodgings were attainable, here Mary was compelled to remain.

During the night travail came upon her, and thus it happened that the Redeemer was born in this place, and here laid in the manger; and a few steps further on you are shown the place where it stood. It has been transported to Rome, and is now in the Church of St. Marie Majeure. Twenty-one silver lamps and two pictures ornament this sanctuary.

The identification of this place is undeniable; but we all thought and felt that it was a pity the holy stable had been thus transformed. Why not have left it in its original condition? What had gold, and marble, and precious stones to do with the birth of the Holy Child? We had come from far, far off, to worship in that humble place, the witness of such a marvellous event, and while we knelt and prayed, the gawd and glitter of worldly wealth added naught to our reverence.

We took our lunch in a valley at the foot of Bethlehem, and then proceeded on our way to Mar-Saba. The country soon assumed again its peculiar character—naked and dreary mountains, without a tree or brook; for water is exceedingly scarce throughout Palestine, and notwithstanding the heat, our horses could only get to drink morning and night.

CHAPTER XVIII.

CONVENT OF MAR-SABA — SHAWAAL — ARAB HORSEMAN-SHIP — DEAD SEA — JORDAN — PILGRIM'S PASS — JERICHO — FOUNTAIN OF ELISHA — RETURN TO JERUSALEM.

AS we arrived at Mar-Saba early in the afternoon, Aline and Mr. Rogers went to see the convent, the entrance to which is interdicted to ladies; and even gentlemen can obtain admittance only by a written permit, signed by the Greek patriarch at Jerusalem, with which talisman we were duly armed.

When near the entrance they met a party among whom was a lady (whose name we afterwards ascertained to be the Countess Rapp), provided with a special order from the Grand Duke Constantine of Russia, and who supposed, with such authority, denial would be impossible: yet even she was only admitted to the outer court.

The Countess invited Aline to enter with her, which was gratefully accepted, as the heat of the sun was very oppressive, and the ladies remained seated in the shade, in the court-yard, while the gentlemen were conducted through the various parts of the building.

THURSDAY, April 16.

We determined to pass the day in this place, remarkable for its strange, wild scenery, and make an early start on the morrow for the Dead Sea and Jordan; and as Tom wished to take a view, orders were given for the camp to be moved near to the convent.

The gentlemen had gone, leaving Aline and I to follow, guarded by Shawaal, the Bedouin chief of our escort, a young man of about twenty-five years of age, with a very characteristic face, regular features, piercing black eyes, black, silky, curly hair and light brown complexion, polite, obliging, and attentive. As on the preceding afternoon I had found the road to our tents exceedingly bad for the horses, being almost the entire way composed of large, flat, slippery stones, I preferred to walk. Aline, however, mounted, and, helped by Shawaal, we proceeded towards the convent, stopping from time to time to take a look at the immense ravine, one edge of which the road skirted, while on the other side were naked sand-hills, with here and there a red flower, remarkable for the richness and beauty of its color, a few of which I gathered for our albums.

The Convent of Mar-Saba, which is to-day one of the richest of all Palestine, stands in the midst of a wilderness on the brink of a profound gorge, and was originally founded by St. Saba, in the year 483; and when the gentlemen visited it they were shown the grotto where the saint, after having driven out the lion who had made there his lair, devoted his life of sixty years to meditation and prayer.

We passed in that place a quiet but uncomfortable day, for, not having a tree to shade us, the heat in our tents was almost insupportable, and the monotony was only broken by the novelty of having our Bedouins about us, and the spectacle of caravans arriving, or others passing behind our encampment.

FRIDAY, April 17.

At half-past five we were in the saddle, on our way to the Dead Sea, which we were in hopes of reaching before the greatest heat of the day came on.

It is impossible to travel in this part of Palestine unaccompanied by the wild Bedouin inhabitants as escort. Our sheick, Shawaal, formed the head of the cortége, while the rest of the guard remained behind with the mules, men, and baggage.

Until ten o'clock the heat was tolerable, and as we travelled the greater part of the time along the side of precipices, or up and down mountain passes, where our horses were unable to go faster than a walk, were wrapt in astonishment and admiration at the wild and desolate state of nature surrounding us.

The hills are completely without vegetation : rocks, sand which the wind sweeps about, and a tint of black earth, cover like a funeral pall all that land. From time to time the mountains look as if broken, and disappear in narrow and profound abysses where no path leads, and where the eye only sees the eternal repetition of the scenes which surround it. All has a volcanic appearance; the stones piled up on every side look like blocks of lava hardened and cracked by centuries; and when you are on the summit of a hill, and the horizon opens for an instant to your view, as far as the eye can reach you only see a black chain of truncated cones, heaped up one upon another, detaching themselves from the deep blue of the firmament. It is an entanglement without limit of avenues of mountains of all forms—torn, broken, split in gigantic pieces, and bound one to the other by similar chains of hills. Profound ravines, whence in Switzerland you would hear the roaring of a torrent, here seem spell-bound in mystic silence. It is the ideal chaos; not a tree—not a flower—the ebullition of an earth on fire, of which the petrified bubbles have formed these waves of scoria, sand, and stones.

At nine o'clock we could see distinctly the Dead Sea, which appeared like a beautiful sheet of blue water, and we expected soon to reach its shore; but on, on we continue our route, and frequently it appears and disappears as we mount and descend the hilly slopes. Our spirits were impressed by the wildness of the scene, and the silence was only broken by the hoofs of our horses clattering on the stony ground.

Aline and I remained close to our chief, Shawaal, for it was easy to understand what a secure hiding-place these mountains and valleys afforded to the tribes of wild Bedouins. Occasionally an Arab, wrapped in his camel-hair cloak, with gun on his shoulder, would appear on the top of a mound; a few words would be exchanged, between our chief and the stranger, and we would continue our route.

This is the district given by tradition to the forty days.

The heat was now becoming unbearable, and all were fatigued when at last we gained the plain. Shawaal assured us we would soon arrive, and as the road was good, exhibited the docility and swiftness of his Arab horse. He fired his gun near his car, and the noble animal, understanding the signal, flies away at full speed—the chief meanwhile dismounted and remounted, and finally at a word stopped the horse, which instantly became as quiet as one of ours. Many daring things he did with him; but while admiring his feats Aline and I had to be careful of our own steeds, who, recognizing a brother in that animal of the desert, wished to follow him. Mine once did so, and being unable to stop him, I was nearly thrown by my Saladin jumping a ditch when I did not expect it. Oh! how thoroughly Shawaal seemed to be in his element in that wild region; how smiling and happy he looked; his face so expressive that I could not tire observing him.

We have now passed the site near where, so many centuries ago, stood Sodom and Gomorrah—the plain, full of short bushes, covered with little pink flowers, which Shawaal says is "the apple of Sodom,"—and have dismounted on the little peninsula which forms the north-west angle of the Dead Sea, twelve hundred feet below the level of the Mediterranean.

We had heard so much of that sea, and of its water, so calm as to resemble liquid oil, that we were surprised to find there the ripple about the same as on any other lake on an ordinarily calm day; while to the east and west well-defined mountains throw their shades on its shores. Here are the Heights of Abraham, the crests of Gilead, the mountain of the Temptation; on our right are the burnt cities of Lot; on our left the ruins of Gilgal and Jericho; in front the long flat plain of sand and ashes, the green fringe of the sacred stream, and the great ford over which Joshua passed, and on which Jesus was baptized by John.

While the gentlemen went to bathe, Aline and I stretched ourselves on the sand, tired by our six and a half hours' ride, and endeavored to rest; but the time seemed uncommonly long, exposed as we were to the burning rays of the sun. Tom took a view of the Dead Sea with the gentlemen bathing, but it was very difficult for them to keep quiet.

The water is of a most peculiar character. A strong taste of salt, bitumen, and sulphur pervades it, while a dry bitterness remains a long time upon the tongue. Perhaps no water is so strongly impregnated with salt as this, rendering it so heavy that the human body cannot sink below the arm-pits, and when attempting to swim the feet are thrown quite into the air. The effect upon the eyes is to produce a powerful burning sensation, lasting the remainder of the day; while the person, after bathing, felt incrusted with a coating of salt, notwithstanding a vigorous application of the towel, only removed by another bath, a couple of hours after, in the cool and fresh water of the Jordan. The difference of temperature between the waters of the sea and river was very great, probably as much as twenty degrees, although we had no means of measuring it exactly. Appearances are often deceitful, is an old proverb, never better exemplified than here. The waters of this salt and bitter lake were beautifully clear and transparent, while the sweet waters of the Jordan are as yellow and muddy as the current of our own Mississippi. I am now speaking of the Jordan near its mouth, between the Dead Sea and the Sea of Galilee, for we afterwards found the river a hundred miles north of this (near ancient Dan) as clear and babbling a brook as ever watered the fairest land of America, fringed with trees and bushes, grass growing near its banks, bold wooded hills near its margin, the type of the Happy Valley of Rasselas.

Two hours passed at the sea, and it was with a sigh of relief that we remounted our horses, and rode for an hour and a half across the plain of the Jordan. Hot though it was, we galloped most of the way, and arrived at half-past two at the Pilgrim's Pass, said to be exactly the spot where our Saviour was baptized.

After that wilting ride it was delicious to sit beneath the shade of the willows, acacias, and tamarisks which bordered the shore, covered with reeds and bushes, wherein the Arab marauders sometimes hide themselves. It is generally prudent to keep together, but to-day there was no danger, as there were several parties, and the escorts combined made quite an imposing show.

We drank of the water of the Jordan, which, as I have said, is here rather muddy, but having filtered it found it cool and agreeable to the taste. How vividly I remember the strangeness and novelty of the scene! It seemed like a dream to think that I was reclining on the shore of the Jordan, that holy and sacred stream. Yes, here it was running at my feet—not pure and limpid, as I had anticipated, but a narrow, yellow river; for even at this place, its widest part, the width is only from twenty-five to thirty yards. The blue sky, the fiery heat of the sun, our Arabs smoking at some distance off, the neighing of the horses, anxious to get to the river-side, the laughter of our friends, happy in the enjoyment of their delicious bath—all this—Helloa! it is lunch-time. "*Joseph, spread the cloth!*"

But it was time to be in the saddle, as our place of encampment for the night was at the Fountain of Elisha, on the site of ancient Jericho; and the long and arid plain which separates us from Rihha, the Jericho of to-day, is quite monotonous. This little mount that we see at a short distance on our left is Gilgal, or Galgala; it is here that the Israelites encamped after having crossed the Jordan; here Joshua, after his fight against the Canaanites, established his headquarters; and on the same spot the Israelites celebrated their first Easter in the Promised Land. (Jos. iv. 19, 20; v. 9–11.) It was also here that Samuel proclaimed the royalty of Saul; and the miracles of Elisha illuminated that hill, to-day deserted and almost forgotten. After one hour and three-quarters we passed Rihha, the Jericho of the time of Herod, that Christ visited when He cured the blind. (St. Luke xviii. 34–43.) It is now only a group of poor houses, and the citadel, a square building half in ruins, is said to be on the place where the house of the rich Zaccheus stood. (St. Luke xviii. 35–43.)

It was five o'clock when we came in view of our tents, this time delightfully pitched beside the spring called the "Fountain of Elisha," because it is said that the prophet, touched by the prayers of the inhabitants of Jericho, took away the bitterness of its water. It is the source of a beautiful brook, which runs for some distance before discharging into the Jordan, the shores of which are covered with various kinds of trees, and forming a pretty little wood, where I accompanied Mr. Rogers soon after our arrival. How refreshing and delicious this little oasis felt after the hot and fatiguing labor of the day! We met there one of the wild Arabs, a young man who was making bread, and we watched him until he put it in an oven built of stones and mud. After dinner we retired to our tents, for we were all fatigued; but there being many encampments, the Arab escorts came before each tent, singing, dancing, and playing rude music, until we had to send them away with a backsheesh.

Long after being in bed we could hear their joyous and merry laughter, and by those sounds and the tinkling of the bells of our mules were lulled to sleep.

SATURDAY, April 18.

We were up very early, and after breakfast, while the horses were being fed and saddled, took a walk along the brook of Elisha, and by the shapeless ruins. Fragments of broken pottery are still seen on its shores, as well as on the banks of a large reservoir which extends south-west from the foot of the mountain. And this is all that remains of that Jericho built by Hiel the Bethelite, which the Hebrews, under the leadership of Joshua, besieged fifteen and a half centuries before the Christian era.

But already some of the other encampments had moved, and as we wished to reach Jerusalem this day, took the road, passing the Mount of the Quarantine, which rises to the west above the ruins of Jericho, and is so named from the tradition which identifies it as the place where Christ fasted during forty days.

The sun was already very powerful, and though our path was now constantly rising, and we were leaving behind us the level of the Dead Sea, which could from time to time be perceived through the openings of the hills, we suffered greatly from the heat, and thought it was even warmer than it had been the day previous. The return road to Jerusalem bears a great similarity to that from Mar-Saba, but the more we advanced the better it became, and we could now and then put our horses to the gallop.

Shawaal had already tried his gun twice, and both times missed his aim; as we all laughed at him his pride was evidently touched, and he felt quite mortified. Seeing some birds in the valley near, swift as lightning horse and rider were going with frightful rapidity down the steep hill, and, as we pursued our route, lost sight of him, thinking he would soon return. Two hours elapsed, however, and I began to think that we had seen the last of our sheick, when we perceived him coming up behind us, having succeeded during his absence in shooting one quail. I judged from this that the Arabs are but poor marksmen, which I afterwards heard was actually the case.

I felt glad when he had returned, for we were without escort, the other men being far back with the baggage, the country wild and savage in the extreme, and that day we met many Arabs, all of them armed.

Oh! how delighted we were when, after several hours' ride through a scorching sun, we alighted before

11*

the fountain Ain-el-Haoud, which in the time of Joshua marked one of the borders of Judea. So cool and refreshing was the limpid element that we could not quit the place. It was near an old khan, and our horses as well as ourselves were in the shade, while the poor beasts had even more need of water than ourselves. We had been there half an hour when Mr. Beadel, Sr., arrived with one of the mooks, or muleteers, and wishing to make room for him, in getting away from the fountain I jumped on a stone, which moved beneath my weight, my foot turned, and I sprained my ankle. Happily, as we were near the water, I immediately placed it beneath the stream, notwithstanding which it swelled a great deal and was very painful. Good Shawaal, how kind he was! I could not ride quickly after that, and he remained constantly by my side, asking from time to time how I felt.

In Bethany, where we took our lunch, I had to remain quiet, while the others went to look at Lazarus' tomb. The village itself is unimportant except from its religious reminiscences; it is composed of some twenty or thirty houses, surrounded by plantations of fig and olive trees.

Leaving Bethany we could soon see the summits of Mount Zion, Mount Moriah, and the walls of the temple, and at four o'clock arrived at about the same time as our mules and baggage; and as soon as our tent was ready I had to lie down on my bed, while the rest of the party went to Jerusalem to see our sick friend Charles, and make some purchases. Soon I received a visit from Shawaal, accompanied by Mohammed as his interpreter.

He had come to wish me good-by, as his intention was to return this evening to his people. He expressed his sorrow at the manner in which I thus ended my journey, and hoped I would soon be better, etc., etc. I then asked him if his tribe was a powerful one, and he said that he and his brothers were at the head of three thousand men; that they did not live very far from the wilderness of Mar-Saba, and that he was sorry while we remained one day idle we had not gone to visit them. Nothing would have pleased me more than to have seen the internal economy of such an encampment, for I knew that under the protection of the chief there was nothing to fear. I wrote down the name of Shawaal, and promised that if ever I returned to this part of the world I would inquire for him, and would certainly visit him at his home.

Aline and the gentlemen, accompanied by Charles Beadel, who was much better, returned for dinner, but it was with the greatest difficulty that I could walk to the dining saloon. While at our meal we received a visit from Mr. and Mrs. Amory, who were camping not far from us. They had also made the trip to Jordan and the Dead Sea, and would be ready to start on their way to Damascus and Beyrout the following Monday.

CHAPTER XIX.

BETHEL—JACOB'S DREAM—SHILOH—NAPLOUSE—SICHEM—SYCHAR—THE WOMAN OF SAMARIA—MOUNTS EBAL AND GERIZIM — SEBASTIA— SAMARIA—JEZEBEL — SEPULCHRE OF ST. JOHN THE BAPTIST—DOTHAN—DJENIN—THE MARSEILLAISE—A STORM—" SIR, YOUR REVOLVER, THE BEDOUINS !"

SUNDAY, April 19.

WE had wished to leave Jerusalem at an early hour, but as Joseph said he could not be ready, we ordered him to be prompt at noon. One o'clock came but no Joseph, and the mooks informed us that he has not paid them.

Messrs. Beadel and Mr. Rogers determined to submit to his impositions no longer, but leave the camp and refer the matter to the American Consul. Shortly after their departure, Joseph who had heard of it, and had succeeded in effecting a loan, came to say he was ready; and through the intercession of Mr. Ferris the others were finally persuaded to return, and we eventually left at three P.M. It soon after commenced to rain, and we stopped for the night at El-Birah, half an hour's journey from Bethel, and encamped near a picturesque Arab fountain.

Monday, April 20.

At seven this morning we passed Bethel, situated on a steep rock, to-day an insignificant village, only interesting to the traveller by its religious associations. Here it was that Abraham pastured his flock, and here that Jacob's dream took place. "And he called the name of that place Beth-el: but the name of that city was called Luz at the first." As we had a long way before us, we were not sorry to see the sky overcast, and rode bravely on, remarking with pleasure that the more we advanced towards Samaria the pleasanter and richer was the country. We passed several small villages, surrounded by the Mounts of Ephraim, in ancient times celebrated for their vineyards; to-day arid and naked, except that from place to place we could see a few vines and olive-trees. Passing through Ain-el-Haramych (spring of the forty robbers), a green and inviting valley, with water running in its midst, Joseph told us to keep close together, as it deserves its bad reputation; and one hour and a half after we stopped for lunch before the ruins of Shiloh.

The grapes were ripe, the vintage at its full, and the fair maidens of Shiloh rested from their labors of gathering the luscious fruit.

As was their custom at this season, a feast was held, and praise given unto the Lord for all His goodness. The girls had come forth to dance upon the green, keeping time to the cymbals and the reeds. The skies were clear, the air balsamic, and the gentle breeze only ruffled the shivering leaves. The gleesome laugh, and shout of merry voices from happy hearts told of contentment in the present and hope in the future.

But hark! What noise is that coming from the vineyards near by? The dance is suddenly interrupted; armed men by the score hastily appear; the maidens scream, running hither and thither in their alarm. Haste, men of Shiloh, haste if you would save your dearest and best—possessions more precious to you than house and land. Too late, too late! each sturdy pair of arms clasps a light form, and the stifled cry can give no notice to fathers, brothers, friends.

A hasty wooing, faith, and none of the quietest; but the daughters of Shiloh made for the sons of Benjamin exemplary wives, and for their children faithful mothers.

Here was the tabernacle deposited after the conquest of the country, and here the partition of the territory between the twelve tribes took place.

It was in Shiloh that young Samuel was brought to Eli ("And they slew a bullock, and brought the child to Eli"); and here also that the great high priest died suddenly, after having learned the defeat of his sons, and the taking of the ark by the Philistines; after which event Shiloh commenced to lose its importance.

The day was now getting darker and darker, and when we passed before Joseph's Tomb and Jacob's Well it was raining hard, and we hurried to our encampment, which was pitched just outside the walls of Naplouse. This ancient city, the Sichem of the Bible, is delightfully situated on a slope at the foot of Mount Gerizim, amid rushing waters, olive orchards, and palm-trees. Having passed through the whole town by a series of narrow and crooked streets, often covered with vaulting, badly paved, and made so slippery with the rain that it was with the greatest difficulty our horses could retain their footing, it was a relief for us to dismount, and, while waiting for dinner, rest our weary limbs.

The rain ceased early in the evening, one by one the stars made their appearance in the heavens, and every sign indicated a bright day for our visit to Mount Gerizim, Joseph's Tomb, and Jacob's Well, on the morrow.

TUESDAY, April 21.

From the long ride of yesterday my sprained foot was so sore, it was thought prudent that I should remain *at home* during the morning, and start with the servants and mules for the next place of encampment, Sebastia, the ancient Samaria.

It was not without regret that I gave up the idea of resting at the same place where Jesus, tired, had sat, while His disciples went to Sychar to get bread, and where He had asked of the astonished Samaritan woman a drink of water. The weather was warm and delightful; and while the servants were folding the tents I sat under the shade of a large tree facing the village, flanked on either side by the Mounts Ebal and Gerizim, and recalled to mind all the historic associations of Sichem.

It was here that Abraham pitched his tent; here that Jacob bought a field, and made his servants dig the famous well; here that Simeon and Levi massacred all the men of Sichem, to avenge their sister Dinah, and four centuries later it was at this same place that the tribes, under conduct of Joshua, assembled, and built on Mount Ebal an altar where were inscribed the words of the law. It was on Mount Gerizim that Jotham, after the massacre of the seventy sons of Gideon by Abimelech, repeated his celebrated fable, the most ancient in the world (Judges ix. 8–16), 1236 years B.C. It was after the death of Solomon that Rehoboam went to Ephraim to be named king; but his great pride caused the Israelites to revolt. From that time the empire of David was divided into two separate kingdoms, and they raised to a separate throne one of their own tribe, Jeroboam, chief of Ephraim and of Manasses, who had been the soul of the revolution. After the return from captivity in Babylon, the men of Samaria sent a deputation to Jerusalem to ask permission to contribute their part to the work and expense of the reconstruction of the Temple and the walls; but they were disdainfully refused, and the Jews would not even admit their claims to be descendants of Abraham. From thence dated the hatred which always existed between the two peoples; so much more profound, being both political and religious. Then it was that a temple, in all parts similar to that of Jerusalem, was built on the top of Mount Gerizim.

But the time for our departure was approaching; the mules were nearly ready; the muleteers, as is generally the case, were making a great noise, while about fifty of the inhabitants were looking on. Mohammed, who was to be my guide, came to tell me that it would be better for us to start and be in advance of the mules; so mounting our horses, with the cook as a rear-guard, we left Naplouse.

Our two hours' ride was very pleasant, though sometimes the path, leading up a desolate, stony, and arid mountain, would be very difficult, and then so steep in descending that I was forced to dismount and walk, leaning on Mohammed's arm.

The richness of the country in approaching Sebastia was enchanting. I could not feast my eyes enough on the well-cultivated fields, the forests of olive-trees, and the various flowers which crowned, as a garland, the edges of the road. At one o'clock we stopped for lunch in a delightful spot, and Mohammed made me understand that we had to wait here for the mules to pass us, as we were only ten minutes' ride from the place where we were to encamp that night. We let the horses loose, and I extended myself full length on the grass, while Mohammed spread a cloth and prepared my lunch; then going to a respectful distance, he sat on the ground and commenced to eat his black bread. Calling the faithful servant, I gave him some of my cold chicken, eggs, and oranges; and though he accepted with some hesitation, it was a pleasure to see with what a smile of delight he enjoyed his meal. I still had a piece of bread left for Saladin, who at the sight approached and ate it; and then I gave way to the sweet revery that fell upon me. The valley was full of wild flowers, of which Mohammed was making a collection for me; behind was an orchard of apple-trees, loaded with fruit; at my feet a rivulet was running; and the hills opposite were covered with olive-trees in full blossom.

Soon we saw our baggage approaching; but we did not leave our resting-place until we thought our tents were pitched and in readiness; and it was three o'clock when we arrived at the camp near the village of Sebastia, through which we passed, composed of about sixty houses, solidly built with the fragments of old ruins, which we met at every step. It is situated on a platform, a little below the summit of Mount Summer. The ancient city Samaria was founded 925 years B.C. by Omri (1 Kings xvi. 24), and became the capital of the kingdom of Israel. It then extended over the entire hill. But few traces now remain, as almost all the ruins, as I have already stated, have been utilized for the construction of the houses of the village, and the numerous terraces which sustain the gardens on the hill-side.

Our encampment was on the site where the temples of Baal and Augustus were elevated; the former erected by Ahab the son of Omri, who did evil in the sight of the Lord above all that were before him, and who married the daughter of Ethbaal, king of the Zidonians,— that Jezebel who procured the death of Naboth, so that she might obtain for the king her husband his vineyard at Jezreel, near the palace, and which the king wanted for a garden. For this wickedness Elijah prophesied that the blood of Ahab and all belonging to him should be licked up by dogs, as was the blood of Naboth.

In the fine house at Jezreel, built in the gardens which

had been the vineyard of Naboth, dwelt Jezebel when Jehu came as conqueror to Samaria. Why should she not captivate the new king? So she caused her servants to paint her face, dress her hair, and then sat herself at the open window.

But these blandishments were lost on the warrior, who caused the eunuchs to cast her down, and her body was trodden under foot by his horses. Having entered and refreshed himself, he bethought him to order the body to be buried; but the skull, feet, and palms of the hands was all that the fierce dogs had left of the once proud and powerful queen.

We found many columns still standing, and the view we had was magnificent; all the mountains of Ephraim, and a part of the beautiful plain of Sharon, to the Mediterranean, was before us. When Aline and the gentlemen arrived they said the view they had had from the top of Mount Gerizim was somewhat similar, but certainly not handsomer. This was a consolation for having been unable to accompany them; and the flowers they brought me from Joseph's Tomb and Jacob's Well went the same evening to enrich my album.

WEDNESDAY, April 23.

This morning we were up at sunrise, and the changing colors of hills and valleys, as they were successively illuminated by the orb of day, lent an additional charm to the prospect.

As soon as we had breakfasted, some of the party went to visit a handsome ruin occupying a conspicuous place in the village. It was the ancient Church of St. John, to-day a mosque, built by the Crusaders in 1150 and 1180, on the site of an old basilica which was said to cover the sepulchre of St. John the Baptist. But as it was too difficult, with my lame foot, to dismount, I had to be content with a view of the exterior; and as Aline and Tom had visited it the day previous, leaving the others, we started in advance, headed by the dragoman. They soon rejoined us, and we commenced a really hard day's journey, for Joseph repeatedly lost the road, which kept us in the saddle for nearly ten hours. But while my companions all felt more or less fatigue from their excursion of the preceding day, I was in high spirits, enjoying my ride exceedingly, as the scenery the whole way was very fine. We passed several large villages of little importance in ancient times.

A short time before arriving at Djeba, near El-Fandekoumich, and while on top of the mountain, a grand panorama was spread before us. All the heights were towards the west, and the luxuriant green valleys were sloping towards the Mediterranean, whose azure blended with the heavens at the horizon. We stopped for lunch on a mountain covered with various beautiful trees; the heat was intense, and Mr. Ferris, not feeling well, after resting for an hour decided to go with Mrs. Ferris directly to Djenin, while we proposed to visit Dothan or Dothain (the two pits), where Joseph was placed when sold by his brethren.

The descent from the mountain into Kabalych was very difficult. Imagine a steep declivity, with no path to guide you, constantly encountering large, slippery flat stones, on which the horses would slide as on ice. Being now accustomed to Saladin—I knew he was very sure-footed—I had therefore no fear, and we arrived safely at the village, which has a bad reputation, and passed without appearing to be noticed by the inhabitants. A guide was then taken by Joseph, and one hour's ride brought us to a verdant hill called to-day Arabe, and in ancient times Dothan.

We were shown two dry pits. Are these the true ones? Have faith! Let us be content to believe it.

And now it is time we should return to camp. It is yet a two hours' ride; the sun is setting, the atmosphere is becoming cooler; clouds are gathering in the sky, and Joseph, who does not know the road, leads us across field after field. At last we are on the right path, and far, far in the distance, the snowy peak of Hermon is visible.

At six o'clock we arrived very tired at Djenin, and dismounted before our tents. Djenin, as well as the surrounding country, has a very bad reputation, and all travellers going either to Nazareth or Naplouse encamp near the same spot, so as to be a protection to each other. At least fifty tents were pitched in the valley, the greater number bearing the American flag. Our caravan arrived late, and the best locations having been chosen, our mooks selected for the camp a bit of low-lying meadow-land, which Tom observed upon our arrival, and remarked that in case of rain we would be submerged.

In the evening Aline and Mr. Rogers went to visit the Johnson and Amory parties, whom we found here, and, more fortunate than ourselves, were encamped on a hillock near. When they returned we had all retired, and rain had commenced to fall.

THURSDAY, April 24.

The rain in Syria does not fall—it pours; and as it did not cease all night, we were awoke in the morning by the voices of Charles and Henry Beadel calling lustily to have their tent removed, for on awakening they found it flooded, and even their beds were wet. We were fortunate enough to escape such a mishap, and while taking breakfast in our tent, where a brasier filled with live coals was placed, were occasionally saluted with "Are you dry yet?"

The day passed wearily away talking, reading, eating (each one of us being carried to the dining saloon by servants). In the afternoon Mr. Rogers went with Mr. Beadel, Sr., through the mud to the village, and returned with a glowing description of the beautiful country, and brought us roses and orange-flowers from the gardens he had so admired. There is a merry French party near, who evidently enjoy themselves, and at dinner became so lively that until late in the evening song after song resounded from their tents; and as they knew not that under that American flag hard by were two French ladies who could hear and understand every word they uttered, were gay without affectation; and to them we were thankful for the few pleasant hours passed that day, and fell asleep listening to their songs of "*Margot la Belle*" and the "*Marseillaise*."

FRIDAY, April 25.

The rain did not abate through the night, and it was only at half-past ten A.M. that the clouds broke and the first rays of the sun came to apprise us of approaching good weather. It was amusing to witness with what rapidity the tents were folded, the baggage was loaded on the mules, and camp after camp left the place.

As we knew it would be impossible to reach Kaïfa, at the foot of Mount Carmel, that night, it being a ride of fourteen to fifteen hours, we did not hurry, and it was half-past eleven when we mounted our horses. We were *en route* but half an hour when a heavy shower surprised us, the rain and hail lasting at least fifteen minutes; our waterproofs proving but poor coverings, while our horses, half blinded, stopped short, turning their backs to the storm. The roads being very wet, and the ground soft and muddy, we could advance but slowly; and after four hours' ride, having twice forded the Kishon, we chose our place of encampment in a green valley not far from the road, and there took lunch while the tents were being pitched.

Soon we saw the Amory party pass, who encamped a short distance beyond us. While dinner was being prepared every one retired to their tents to take a nap. We were in the land of dreams, and night was approaching, when the sound of a gun suddenly awoke us; we heard the raised voices of the muleteers, the mules and horses running to and fro, and Joseph rushed into the tent, exclaiming: "Sir, your revolver, the Bedouins!" Half dreaming and half awake, this announcement sounded terrifically in our ears, and while Tom rushed to the scene of danger we supplicated Henry Beadel, who was following him, to remain with us, for we were really frightened. Until then we had believed but little in attacks of Bedouins; we had even jested about them, wishing to have the luck of an encounter; but at the approach of danger all the stories we had heard came back to our minds, and for my part I already fancied I was carried off by an Arab chief, tied behind him on his horse, riding at a fearful rate over mounts and valleys to the place of his abode.

How quickly our imagination travels! Bang! bang! three, four, five shots were heard, then all was silent again; and a few minutes after Tom entered the tent with his pistol smoking, and told us there was nothing to fear; that when they arrived on the road, though it was already dark, they saw some Bedouins ride rapidly past; that one turned around and fired; our people returned it, but as it was too dark to aim well, they did not think they had wounded any, as they did not slacken the speed of their horses. It was, then, but a bloodless skirmish, which made a subject for conversation during our dinner, and it was only the next morning that we heard that the rascally marauders had stolen two fine horses from the Amory camp.

Our animals were tethered between the tents; our muleteers kept guard part of the night, and Mohammed, our servant, lay down across our door-way, so as to be aroused by the least noise; but when Tom got up in the night, and went out to reconnoitre, he found every one asleep, and passed and repassed over Mohammed's body without awaking him. But the assurance that he would keep guard procured us a profound and refreshing slumber.

CHAPTER XX.

PROVINCE OF GALILEE—PLAIN OF ESDRAELON—MOUNT CARMEL—THE DESERTERS—"THE TURKEY ATE IT, SIR"—NAZARETH—CHURCH OF THE ANNUNCIATION—JOSEPH'S WORKSHOP—FOUNTAIN OF THE VIRGIN—RHAPSODY AND FACTS—CANA—PLAIN OF HATTIN—TIBERIADE—SEA OF GALILEE.

SATURDAY, April 26, 1868.

"THE province of Galilee," says Dixon, "has always been considered the garden of Syria. Everything grows on its soil, from the Caspian walnut to the Egyptian palm. While the hills of Judea are stern and barren, and the meadows of Sharon burnt and dry, these wadies of Galilee are almost everywhere laughing with herbs and flowers.

"A forest of oak clothes the side of Mount Carmel; cedar clumps nestle in the clefts of Mount Hermon; myrtles enlarge into trees, and myriads of orange blossoms throw their scent into the air. Every hill is a vineyard, every bottom a corn-field.

"The Delta of the Nile is not more sunny; the Vega of Granada is not more picturesque; the Ghota of Damascus is not more green and bright. For here the fierce sun and the refreshing rain come together, and water flows through Galilee not in tanks and pools, but poured out royally towards the sea in streams."

Such indeed was the character of the country we travelled through that day, and though we had a fatiguing ride of nine hours, for the rain had changed the many rivulets we had to cross into as many little streams, and often our horses would sink into marshy and muddy ground to their chests, no one complained; and our lunch was taken under the shade of the oaks of Carmel, overlooking the lovely plain of Esdraelon, the battle-field of Israel.

How charming was the approach to Kaïfa! How gorgeous looked the setting sun beyond the blue Mediterranean, just then calm as a lake, while we could see St. Jean d'Acre on the opposite side of the bay. We postponed our ascent of Mount Carmel until the following morning, and after dinner took a stroll on the beach, amusing ourselves gathering shells.

Sunday, April 27.

To horse at eight, and leaving our beautiful camping ground by the shore, embowered in trees, and hedged in by cacti, we take our way along the plain where the husbandmen are busy at their labors, pass through an orchard of olive-trees skirting the base of the mountain, and soon commence the ascent of the steep, rough staircase, cut in the rock, about half a mile in length, which leads to the eyrie of "Our Lady of Carmel."

The ascent over these shelves and banks is a dangerous pilgrimage, not to be undertaken too late in the afternoon: you want the full daylight to lead your horse up and over the slippery white stones edging a precipice where a single false step, or a sudden start of the animal might precipitate you into the abyss.

But the noble beast knows the way; he mounts rapidly, stopping by the way-side neither at cross nor chapel, which at intervals invite the pilgrim to rest and pray; and soon we have before us the pharos, a beacon to the storm-tossed mariner—a guide to the worldling in the plain below.

Suddenly turning a sharp angle of the rock to the left, we find ourselves before the convent door, and our arrival announced by the furious barking of two enormous black dogs. We are welcomed by Father Pedro, a merry-looking little Italian priest, who, after silencing the faithful guardians, invited us to dismount, and escorted us into the refectory, where we were served with lemonade, syrup, and spiced wine.

While entering our names in the visitors' book, the chant of the monks at mass in the chapel below came floating to us by the open window.

Father Pedro led the way, and soon we were kneeling, with others who had come up from Kaïfa, before the altar of "Our Lady," while the perfume of the incense lingered above the shrine.

High, high up on this mount, where the soul seems nearer its heaven, sectarianism disappears: Roman and Protestant worship together, feeling only the presence of the one living God. Never had these offerings, these prayers, these songs of the priests, found a devouter audience. No hum of a busy city, no outer sound, save the warbling of the birds, to disturb the solemn stillness, as our prayers found their way to the Almighty throne.

And then Father Pedro took us through the many neatly furnished rooms reserved for the use of travellers desiring to remain for a few days at the convent; and we were surprised to find that several were double-bedded.

Although the marriage tie is eschewed by these worthy anchorites, they consider it no myth, but have provided appropriately for those *more or less* fortunate than themselves—non-believers in celibacy.

But this was our limit. The entrance to the cloisters is forbidden to the softer sex; and the extended view which greeted the eyes of our male companions was lost to us—nay, only lost in part, for we were six hundred feet above the Mediterranean, and then we thought that all this loveliness, extending far, far around, had been gazed upon not only by the prophet Elijah, but by our Saviour Christ.

From the Convent of Carmel, on this bold headland jutting into the sea from the mountain range, and overlooking the rich plain, the indented shore, and shallow bay, the eye stretches over the immense expanse of waters, the crests of whose billows sparkle in the noonday sun. At our feet, and on a line with the shingly fringe of the sea, nestle the white walls of the Arab town of Kaïfa, in contiguity with our own snowy tents. Beyond and around the circle of the open bay, those bristling ramparts and tall minarets mark where stands Acre, coveted and conquered by the Crusaders, as the *point d'appui* for their future conquests; held and defended by the English when besieged by Napoleon, whose early idea was the founding of a mighty empire in those countries once so rich in worldly wealth, commanding, as they did, the commerce of *"further Ind"* and of the world.

Beyond Acre see you yon promontory, the apparent duplicate to that on which you stand? Near that point of Capo Blanco must have been the dividing-line between the realms of King Solomon and those of Hiram.

His magnificent capital close by the sea-side, once so proud, is now so debased that the poor hind who tills the soil knows not that he is delving in imperial dust. Even the Tyrian dye, once so famous that its use was an exclusive privilege of royalty, is lost forever. The Lebanon hills, receding from the coast, still have living timber which was young, too young to cut, when king Hiram furnished the cedars for the building of the Temple; but kings and kingdoms, palaces and cities, ay, even the Temple itself, dedicated to the ever-living God, is gone, and naught is left but those frail young saplings.

Beyond and farther off we plainly see the high peaks of Hermon, eternal winter crowning its top with a diadem of icicles. Farther to the right, over beyond Kaïfa, and anent that valley where you see flowing the gentle Kishon, coming from out the fertile plains of Esdraelon, the battle-field of Israel,—fertile with the black blood and bleached bones of thousands of victims of ambitious rulers,—lie the woody, park-like hills of smiling Galilee, the pleasantest land of all the East, where from infancy to manhood the Redeemer lived and taught.

But Father Pedro, who has probably had this picture

"*spread*" before him an hundred, or it may be a thousand times, gently insinuates that there is a "*spread*" in the refectory more substantial, and therefore more suited to his taste.

Taking another hasty glance afar, and noticing near that the only ground cultivated by the monks was a small garden, and the only trees grown a few olives; that walls, bolts to doors, and bars to windows were in favor; the conclusion is irresistibly forced on the mind that bold marauders, and thieves who prowl by night, were not far distant from this "*sacred soil.*"

Following the pleasant little monk, we were soon seated at the homely board, partaking of a plain though hospitable lunch.

The origin of this convent is very remote, for the priests date their order from the time of the prophet Elisha, who received from the high-priest Eli possession of his grotto, on which in later years a monastery was built.

In 1185 it was in ruins, but in 1209 it was repaired, and belonged to the order of the Carmelites. But it appears that both convent and church were several times destroyed and rebuilt. In 1821 it was demolished by order of Abdallah Pacha, the governor of St. Jean d'Acre; and afterwards a simple priest named John Baptist, having by the intercession of the French ambassador obtained a firman of reconstruction, travelled over Europe during fourteen years to collect pious donations for the construction of the present building, occupying the platform at the north-western extremity of the Cape.

The Mediterranean is not always as calm as it then appeared, and its shores have witnessed many a shipwreck. On such occasions the good priests have distinguished themselves by their courage in trying to save some unfortunate voyagers, and many memorials are recorded in the visitors' book by the wrecked, showing the tender care and kind hospitality which they have here found.

Depositing an alms for the benefit of the institution, and with benedictions from the monks, we made our adieux.

Before leaving the mount, Tom conducted us to the plateau at the rear of the buildings, where he obtained a good view; we then descended in safety the rough roadway cut in the side of the beetling crag, and galloped across orchard and plain back to our pleasant tent *home* on the beach, over towards the sea.

Charles Beadel has not been feeling well since a few days, and as his father and Mr. Rogers are tired of the dragoman and their horses, and a steamer is expected to leave to-morrow for Beyrout, they have decided to take passage in it, and promise to meet us at Damascus.

MONDAY, April 28.

At ten o'clock we were on the beach parting with three of our companions. As the westerly land breeze caught the bellying sail, their little craft sped lightly on, and with " *au revoir* " to the deserters, we followed with our eyes the silvery line she left behind.

Tom and Henry Beadel accompanied them to St.

Jean d'Acre, whence they embarked; and it was late in the afternoon before they returned.

"Joseph," said Mr. Ferris, calling the dragoman while at dinner, "why do you not give us salad, which I see is plentiful in Kaïfa and St. Jean?" (Mohammed had previously informed us that Joseph had not bought any.) "Salad, sir, why I got some this very morning. Why have they not placed it on the table?" Then calling the second waiter—"Hercule, what did you do with the salad?" Then followed a few words in Arabic, and Hercule promptly answered: "The turkey got loose and ate it, sir." The lie was too good. Joseph retired triumphant, while our tent resounded for a long time with merry laughter.

TUESDAY, April 29.

We had intended to start at six o'clock this morning, but owing to some difficulty with our dragoman, we only got into our saddles at half-past seven; the weather was fine, the road good, the scenery beautiful, and Tom intended to make us gallop a good part of the way.

On then through Kaïfa's gates and walls of bleached stones; across the valley of the sparkling Kishon, fresh from the peaks of snow-bound Hermon; near a camp of Turkish cavalry; up and through the groves and hills of Galilee; taking our lunch and noontide siesta under the shade of their enormous oaks; gathering the bright wild flowers that carpeted our path as we loitered by the way-side; on to those vine-covered hills encircling Nazareth, surrounded by gardens, fig and olive trees, and hedges of enormous cactus, with scarlet flowers in full bloom.

As we were far in advance of our mules, we dismounted at the door of the Latin Convent and Church of the Annunciation, built on the site where once stood the house of the Holy Family. The original church dates from the time of the Empress Helena, which was destroyed and rebuilt in 1620, and enlarged towards the middle of the eighteenth century. It is of medium size, remarkable for its fine proportions, possessing several clever paintings, and in the choir, which is built above the crypt, is a figure of the Virgin, well executed in wax, holding her Divine Son.

Under the great altar is the chapel where the Annunciation took place. A fine picture represents it, surrounded by silver lamps and natural flowers, while on the granite tablet which forms the pavement you read these words: "Verbum caro his factum est." Descending a few steps we were shown a small room cut in the rock, which is said to be the Virgin's kitchen; and in returning met one of the priests, who had just brought a bouquet of fresh flowers for the altar, and kindly gave me some, which I added to my album.

We passed a few hours in the garden which belonged to the Holy Family; it is very carefully kept, and filled with flowers, sacred to the pilgrim and the traveller, grown on the place where He passed thirty years of His life! We visited the workshop of Joseph, and passed through the village to the Fountain of the Virgin, where the fair-haired girl would come morning and evening with her jar to get water for the household. Young damsels clad in loose white trousers and flowing blue robes thrown carelessly and gracefully about their forms and over their heads, partially concealing their features, were going to and fro, as they were wont to do eighteen hundred years ago; but none so fair as She, none with the ideal beauty of the Christ-mother.

WEDNESDAY, April 30.

"What is all this you have been writing yesterday?" said Tom; "you seem to have mounted your Pegasus and flown away to the dreamy land of romance. Did you not promise me to write facts, things as you see them, and not let your imagination feed on fancy fare? You have been looking through the wrong end of my lorgnette. Ah, yes! A pleasant peep of pretty petticoats in perspective, and dainty dimity in the distance, lending '*enchantment to the view.*' Now turn the glass and let me take a peep. Bah! I see a number of half-clad, bare-footed, dirty women; slaves of the water jar, the plough, almost beasts of burden; there are no *damsels* amongst them, unless you mean to designate children by that euphonious title. Each of these females is taken as a wife by the time she attains the age of thirteen or fourteen, by some filthy Mussulman boor, adding one more to his perhaps already overstocked household, or rather huthold. Well, never mind, we will call them damsels, and won't syllable the word. It will not do to examine things too closely; we might find fleas and other parasites. You are right to admire the painting, and not inquire of what pigments the artist has composed his brilliant colors."

Tom and Henry were up very early, in order to take a view of the village, and at half-past seven we left

Nazareth for Tiberiade, on the Sea of Genesareth or Galilee. We continue to be favored with good weather; our horses are docile and obey the least command; every step brings to remembrance an act in the life of the Son of God! My heart is full of pious thoughts and thankfulness, and I cannot respire enough of the fresh, perfumed morning air.

Here is Cana, a pretty village surrounded by hills covered with oaks and olives; and on a large open space surrounded by fig-trees a spring, where at least twenty women were busy washing or getting water. Saladin asked no permission, but trotted into the midst of them to quench his thirst, while the women pleasantly smiled at me. Having rejoined my companions, we visited the house containing the so-called miraculous vases in which the water was turned to wine; but soon mounted again that we might arrive early at Tiberiade. We passed a large village, El-Loubich, on the summit of a little hill covered with gardens, protected by hedges of enormous cacti, and having Mount Tabor occasionally in sight; crossed the plain of Hattin, which in 1187 was the theatre of a terrible battle, where the Christian army, under Guy of Lusignan, was completely defeated by Saladin, and where the true cross found by Helena was forever lost.

And now the country assumes a similar aspect to the volcanic country of the Dead Sea. Up and down rocky, dreary mountains, meeting only a few Bedouins, who stare at us as we pass; but how magnificent is the view we get from the summit of a mountain in approaching Tiberiade. There is the Sea of Galilee, a limpid lake, with the mountains of Safed to the north; the great Hermon, with the sun shining on its white and dazzling summit, to the north-east, while far away to the southwest is the bald peak of Mount Tabor.

It was half-past one when we arrived, quite exhausted, at the city of Tiberiade, for this was one of the hottest days we had experienced in Palestine, and when we sought a shady place there were only a few scattered and sickly trees, under which were some horses that we had to drive away before taking possession. Carpets were spread on the ground, lunch was served, and we tried to repose for an hour, but it was impossible—the heat was too intense.

Tiberiade, so rich in the time of Christ, is now but a poor town, nearly in ruins, having been visited and almost destroyed by an earthquake in 1837. It occupies a narrow parallelogram: on the easterly side the houses are built quite down to the shore; on the other three sides is a massive wall, strengthened by towers, built of heavy basaltic blocks, the citadel being at the north-west angle; but the earthquake injured it more than a fearful siege would have done. Everywhere are immense crevices; parts of walls fallen down or threatening to do so; large breaches affording numerous entrances besides the only entire gate, which opens on a mosque, also in ruins. The population, which does not exceed two thousand souls, is composed for the most part of Jews, who have come from all parts of the world to pass their last days on the shore of *this* sea, and to be buried in *this* country.

Our tents were pitched by the lake, near those of the

Amory party, who had arrived before us; and here we rested for several hours in the midst of a stillness only broken by the wavelets fretting on the strand at our feet. We could not but be impressed by the solemn scene, and yet it imparted a feeling of sadness, for everything around was dead:—ruin and desolation everywhere. That sea on which He had so often been; whence had been drawn the miraculous draught of fishes; where He had calmed the tempest, and on which He had walked; on these shores where He had chosen His disciples, and which had been witness of His miracles; all was now silent and deserted—not a sail upon its waters. The surrounding hills, in His time so luxuriantly green and beautiful, were now arid and naked!

There is but one boat in the town, and some Jews came to us and proposed an excursion; but the heat was too great, and we were too much fatigued. In the evening we had a visit from Mesdames Amory and Suydam, and all retired early.

CHAPTER XXI.

CAPERNAUM—HOSPITALITY—SAFED—KEDESH—UPPER JORDAN—DAN—BANIAS—A COLD DAY ON HERMON—KEFR-HAOUR—TOMB OF NIMROD—DAMASCUS—THE ABANA AND THE PHARPAR—NAAMAN THE LEPER—OLD ACQUAINTANCES—THE CROOKED STREET CALLED STRAIGHT—MASSACRE OF DRUSES AND MARONITES.

THURSDAY, May 1, 1868.

TO-DAY we travelled from Tiberiade to Safed or Saphat. For a long time we followed the lake shore, which, after leaving Tiberiade, is covered with laurels, now in full bloom; and passing through large reeds, and thick bushes which cover the plains of Genesareth, while our eyes were resting on the smooth surface of the lake, or on the variegated tints of the mountains, we arrived at Capernaum, where Christ sojourned after being expelled by his townsmen from Nazareth; rested in the shade of its sacred hills, and drank from its fountain near Khan-Minyeh.

Hospitality is a sacred word in the East. The weary, foot-sore wanderer, dragging his exhausted limbs through the scorched sands, descries in advance the black tents of a wandering tribe.

Turn not aside; advance boldly; there is no danger if you come as a friend, asking hospitality; you are clothed in a mantle of mail, and each wild son of Ismail would sooner lose his life than that you should suffer the slightest injury.

You shall share his black crust, partake his scanty supply of camel's milk, occupy as your couch the best nook of his tent, and be sent forth on the morrow with refreshed frame and renovated blood.

But be on guard through the day, for the chances are more than even, if you have anything worth losing, that he will rob you before another sunset.

We stopped to-day and spread our carpet for lunch on the shady side of the wall of an old khan. Our horses were browsing near, our mooks stretched on the ground or smoking, when a miserable and filthy-looking old fellow came by, and, *sans cérémonie*, seized our leathern water-bottle, glued his mouth to the nozzle, and commenced to drink. This was too much for our equanimity, and we could hardly admit that we were very sorry when our dragoman grasped the bottle with one hand, and with the other sent our unbidden guest spinning several yards off. He was, without doubt, considerably astonished, and slunk away, muttering curses deep if not loud on the inhospitable Christians. Joseph was reproved "*mildly*."

FRIDAY, May 2.

This morning we started at the same time as the Amory party, which had been encamped near us, and stopped for lunch at the ruins of Kedes, the antique Kedesh-Naphthali, conquered by Joshua from the ancient kings of Canaan. (Josh. xii. 22; xix. 37.)

The hill and the plain are strewn with fragments of columns, an edifice in ruins, and several remarkable sarcophagi, in ancient times enriched with sculptures, to-day unrecognizable.

Historians differ as to the ruin. Robinson concluded it must have been a synagogue, while others think it a Roman construction.

Strange that differences of opinion should exist on a subject so simple when carefully examined. Messrs. Ferris and Beadel, Jr., were much interested in this building, consisting of a groined or double arch, resting at the four corners on a square platform, having an opening in the centre. This opening was filled with huge blocks which had fallen from the roof; but by crawling down among them, forcing aside bushes and brambles that choked the way, they discovered four niches on each side, sixteen in all, about seven feet deep, two feet high, and as many wide, intended, without doubt, for the reception of human bodies. This then was not a Roman edifice, as they burned their dead; neither was it a synagogue, but simply an immense Jewish tomb. We slept at Meis-el Djebel, a large village inhabited by hospitable Arabs.

SATURDAY, May 3.

From Meis to Banias, visiting during the morning the old citadel of Hounin, which dates from the time of the Phœnicians; and stopping for our lunch on the shore of the upper Jordan, in a shady spot with forests of pink laurel, near the antique Dan, we arrived about four o'clock at Banias, the ancient Cæsarea Paneas, or Cæsarea of Philip. We found our tents pitched in a grove opposite the ruins of the old citadel, the castle of Sobaibeh perched on the edge of a precipice three hundred yards above the valley, the torrent Wadi-Zalarch running at our feet; the country around us covered with bouquets of trees, green fields, and flowers, while the grand Hermon reared his white crest in the distant background; and had it not been that Messrs. Beadel and Rogers were waiting for us at Damascus, we would have passed a few days in Banias, the most picturesque place we had seen in Syria.

Crossing a bridge thrown over Wadi-Zalarch, we visited the great fountain, one of the principal sources of the Jordan.

It comes forth at the foot of a high wall of calcareous rocks, where are to be seen several rooms with sculptures defaced by time, and a large natural cave, whose entrance is obstructed by immense fallen rocks and remains of antique construction. It is believed to be the grotto consecrated to Pan, near which Herod the Great had a beautiful temple erected in honor of Cæsar Augustus.

Banias was visited by Jesus Christ and His apostles, and it was here He said to His disciple: "And I say also unto thee, That thou art Peter, and upon this rock I will build my church: and the gates of hell shall not prevail against it." (Matth. xvi. 18.)

SUNDAY, May 4.

We left Banias by its ancient bridge, went up the Wadi-Zalarch, passed near the mountain which bears the castle of Banias, or Es-Sobaibeh, and then—Joseph lost his way. Instead of the easy road we had expected, and the view of Lake Phiale which we were anticipating, he had led us by frightful and precipitous ways, occasionally passing a miserable hamlet, whose inhabitants might be seen making desperate efforts at husbandry. Tom insisted that they were attempting to cultivate fields of stones, only interfered with by occasional patches of earth—the thin, meagre covering of wheat, broken by black boulders, looking like a mendicant's mantle covered with unsightly and badly patched rents. A few specimens of dwarfed cows told whence came no small supply of consumption, without whose milk and cheese life would go badly with these mountaineers.

Following almost all the way the chain of Hermon, mounting nearly to its summit, the wind blowing violently, and the cold from the neighboring snow causing us intense suffering, the only pleasant remembrance I have of this day's ride were beautiful wild tulips that Tom gathered on the heights for our albums.

We slept that night at Kefr-Haour, at the foot of Mount Hermon, a large village, half Druse half Mussulman, near which tradition places the tomb of Nimrod.

MONDAY, May 5.

A ride of four hours this morning brought us in sight of Damascus, whose appearance from afar is perfectly enchanting, and well deserves its name of "Ancient Paradise." From whatever side you may approach it, the same surroundings of beautiful plantations of olive, walnut, and fig trees are to be seen, while its meadows and gardens are watered by the many streams coming from the two celebrated rivers, the Abana and the Pharpar.

Naaman was a mighty man in Damascus, and captain of the king's host; few warriors were his equal, and by him the Lord had given deliverance unto Syria.

In the wars that had lately raged between the Syrians and Israel a prisoner had been taken and brought here—a wee little maid, scarce worthy of notice, and who was a servant in the house of Naaman, the possessor of wealth and power, but who was a leper.

"Mistress," said the child, "would God my lord were with the prophet that is in Samaria, for he would recover him of his leprosy!"

As the drowning man catches at a straw, so did Naaman listen to the words of the girl, and with talents of silver, pieces of gold, changes of raiment, with horses and with chariot, repaired to the house of Elisha and stood before the door.

Then sent Elisha word by messenger: "Go and wash in Jordan seven times, and thy flesh shall again come to thee, and thou shalt be clean."

But the proud man was wroth, and answered: "Are not Abana and Pharpar, rivers of Damascus, better than all the waters of Israel?"

But by the intercession of his servants he went and bathed as directed, and "his flesh came again like unto the flesh of a little child, and he was clean."

Certainly few cities in the world present a more fairy-like aspect than Damascus, with its cupolas and innumerable minarets; its large white mosque, overtopping the confused mass of its houses; its terraces and its gardens. The green girdle which surrounds it contrasts marvellously with the reddish tints of the desert all around, while the chain of Anti-Lebanon and great Hermon are constantly in view. But as soon as one enters the gates commences the disillusion; for, though so ancient in the world's history (Josephus dates its foundation from a son of Shem), it is but an ordinary Oriental city, far inferior to Cairo. The streets are narrow, badly paved, irregular, disappointing the more from contrast with the gardens which surround it.

We dismounted at the Dimitri Hotel, where we obtained rooms with difficulty, as it was crowded with the various parties we had constantly met during our entire trip; and at dinner it was amusing to see so many familiar faces. Here was Captain Hoare and Mr. Standish; at the head of the table sat Lady Ely and her son; near me was the Rev. Mr. Wight, who had witnessed the passage of our dahabeeh through the first cataract on the Nile; at the opposite end of the table was the party of French gentlemen who had helped to make the rainy time pass pleasantly at Djenin; the Johnson family had also arrived a few days previous; and lastly, Messrs. Rogers and Beadel, Sr., of our own encampment. They reported Charles as better, but he had remained in Beyrout. He, however, unexpectedly *put in an appearance* the following day.

Feeling fatigued by so much time passed in the tent and on the saddle, I was far from being as enthusiastic as I had felt when first beholding Cairo.

TUESDAY, May 6.

Damascus is the capital of Syria, and the most important city of Turkey in Asia. It has considerable commerce with the Arabs of the desert, and serves as an entrepôt for all the products of Persia and India, which arrive by the caravans from Bagdad. Its population is about one hundred and fifty thousand, composed of Mussulmans, Druses, Greeks, Syrians, Armenians, Maronites, Latins, and Jews; few Europeans are seen within its walls; in fact, at the commencement of the present century one could not go to Damascus clothed as an European; and until the Egyptian occupation by Mohammed Ali, strangers had to submit to humiliating formalities.

Before passing its gates it was necessary to dismount, and to deposit all arms. Now you can go about in security, without fear of insult, although it is well to be prudent, and remember that the people are far more fanatical than at Cairo or Constantinople. Damascus was the head-quarters of the conspiracy formed a few years since among the Mussulmans, having for its object the extermination of the Maronites and other Christians throughout Syria.

A second St. Bartholomew was the result of this terrible fanaticism. Through all the towns of Northern Syria, on an appointed night, began the massacre. The neighbor who had been born and lived in the same place with his unconscious victim from infancy to manhood, suddenly appeared as his executioner, and struck down, without remorse or pity, men, women, and children. This horrible carnage continued for some days, until the astonished authorities could collect their forces; and to the honor of the government be it said, used every means to suppress the strife.

The number killed will never be known. Those who could escape fled to the forests and the mountains; but so far from the affair accomplishing the desired object of its projectors, it would seem that in Damascus alone, where it is estimated five thousand lost their lives, there are to-day more of the hated faith than there were before.

The "*crooked street called Straight,*" mentioned in the Acts of the Apostles (ix. 11), was in the time of Christ ornamented with colonnades; and parts of Corinthian columns, still in place, are often discovered in digging foundations. It was about a mile long, and nearly two hundred feet wide.

O tempora, O mores! It is now a tortuous and narrow passage, perhaps fifteen feet wide, with dirty bazars on either side, covered over, the greater part of the way, with matting and boards, to keep out the heat of the noon-day sun.

Apart from its peculiarly oriental character there is little or nothing to be seen in Damascus at the present day. Hemmed in, as it were, by wooden houses are the remains of a triumphal arch, by whom or when built is unknown, of which a considerable portion still remains; but it is only by ascending to the roof of one of these edifices that you can observe it.

The Grand Mosque occupies the site of an ancient temple, as is evinced by the remains of a magnificent colonnade partially surrounding the court. Entrance is entirely prohibited to strangers, but you are permitted to tarry at the portal, whence you can view the interior.

One of the curiosities of the modern city is a huge plane-tree, whose trunk measures seventy-three feet in circumference. It is hale and thrifty, and seems destined yet to survive a thousand years.

THURSDAY, May 8.

We left Damascus for Balbek at four o'clock in the morning, in a good carriage, with strong and vigorous horses, and arrived at Stoura, at the foot of Anti-Lebanon, at noon, where Messrs. Rogers and Beadel, having preceded us a day, had ordered dinner and good horses for us. After having refreshed ourselves, our guide (the proprietor of the house where we had found such good cheer) desired us to mount, as the ride from Stoura to Balbek was from six to seven hours' duration. Having passed Zahles, a large village with well-cultivated surroundings, we arrived at Nebi-Nouhh, where the guide made us visit the "*Tomb of Noah*," a square edifice, measuring sixty-three feet on each side.

We entered the large plain of Beka'a, and travelled thereon for several hours, passing, at intervals, small villages, while on our right was the chain of Anti-Lebanon, and on our left that of Lebanon. We travelled but slowly, for only we ladies had English saddles (the gentlemen being compelled to use Arab ones), so that Charles, but more especially Henry Beadel, would fall behind, and we had to stop from time to time to wait for the laggards.

The road generally was good, though sometimes it was difficult for the horses to pass marshy ground, caused by the melting of the snows of Lebanon; but inasmuch as the fatigue did not overcome me, I thoroughly appreciated the beauties of the route.

The thousand hues of the two sublime mountain chains on my right and left, imperceptibly changing with the declining sun, caused a regret that I had not with me a copy of "Lamartine's Travels in the East;" for I had always retained a vivid remembrance of his description of the two ranges, and of the ruins of Balbek; and when the fire-king retreated behind Lebanon I gave full scope to my enthusiasm. No scenery in the Alps had ever impressed me thus: the broad, deep-green plain extended to the north and south beyond the line of vision, bounded on the east by Anti-Lebanon, still lighted by the reflection of departing day, the dark base of whose empurpled sides formed a pleasing and delicate contrast with the shade of its summit; and Lebanon on the west, black and gloomy in its majesty, sharply defined against the evening sky.

Over Anti-Lebanon the first star appeared, and night came on apace; Charles had rejoined us, but Henry was far back with Mr. Andrews, our host, and we had only a serving-man as guide; but as his horse carried the provision and crockery-ware for our usage, he could only go on a walk.

Anon the full moon "*came peeping o'er the hills,*" reversing the twilight shade left by the setting sun; bringing new beauties from out the sides of Lebanon; shimmering on the fretful stream; tinging with silvery touch the facing shrubs; imparting her borrowed light to the wide plain walled in by black Anti-Lebanon.

But ah! how intimately connected are the spiritual and bodily sensations. Our seventeen hours' travelling had so "*used up*" us ladies, long before we arrived at our destination, that all the beauty of the moonlight playing on the ruins as we passed them failed to revive us; and we dismounted before the house where we were to pass the night at ten P.M., with hardly the necessary strength left to undress and go to bed without dinner.

When Henry arrived the gentlemen enjoyed their meal, and afterwards roamed through the ruins until two o'clock in the morning.

CHAPTER XXII.

BALBEK.

FRIDAY, May 9, 1868.

THE beauties of the gigantic ruins of Balbek have been sung and described in every language; a poet or artist could pass months here, and at almost every step find some new cause for admiration; but our hours were numbered, for our passage was engaged for the steamer to leave Beyrout on the following Sunday, and all we could give to Balbek was *four hours.*

Four hours! hardly enough time to take a walk among the ruins; enough though to permit me to recognize every stone in the description Lamartine gives; and which I here translate for the benefit of my friends, as a remembrance of his poetry and his genius; for since our return the cable has brought the announcement of his death!

"I had crossed the summits of Sannin, covered with eternal snow (the highest peak of Lebanon), and had come down from the Lebanon, crowned with its diadem of cedars, into the naked and arid desert of Heliopolis at the end of a fatiguing day. At the horizon yet far from us, on the extreme distance of the black mountains of Anti-Lebanon, an immense mass of yellow ruins, gilded by the setting sun, was detaching itself from the shadows of the mountains. Our guides were showing it to us with their fingers, and exclaiming 'Balbek! Balbek!' It was indeed the marvel of the desert, the fabulous Balbek, coming forth all dazzling from her unknown sepulchre to relate to us of ages of which history has lost the memory.

"We were advancing slowly, restrained by the tardy step of our tired horses, our eyes fixed on those gigantic walls, on the beautiful and colossal columns, which seemed, the nearer we approached them, to spread, enlarge, and elongate. A profound silence was kept throughout our caravan, for each was afraid to lose a single impression of that hour by communicating what he felt.

"At last we arrived at the first stumps of columns, at the first blocks of marble, that earthquakes, accidents, and Arabs have scattered to more than a mile from the monuments themselves, like dried leaves tossed and rolled far from the tree after the tempest.

"We followed our route between the desert on our left and the undulations of the Anti-Lebanon on our right, walking along some cultivated fields, and the bed of a large torrent which winds between the ruins, and on the shore of which are some handsome walnuts.

"The Acropolis, or the artificial hill which supports all the great monuments of Heliopolis, appeared here and there between the boughs, and above the tops of the large trees; at last it was entirely disclosed to our sight, and all of us, as though touched by electricity, halted. No pen, no pencil could describe the impression that this single look imparted to the eyes—to the soul. Under our feet, in the bed of the torrent, in the midst of the fields, around the trunks of the trees, blocks of red and gray granite, of red porphyry, of white marble, of yellow stone, bright as the marble of Paros; shafts of columns, chiselled chapiters, architraves, volutes, cornices, entablatures, pedestals, fallen statues with faces to the ground, scattered parts which yet seem palpitating,—all these a confused mass, grouped in heaps, disseminated and gushing out in all parts as the lava of a volcano which had vomited the remains of a vast empire, so that you can scarcely find a path to cross the sweepings of art which cover all the ground. The iron-shod hoofs of our horses slipped and crackled at every step in the smooth acanthus of the cornices, or on the snow-white bosom of a female torso: only the winding waters of the river of Balbek find their way among these beds of fragments, and wash with their murmuring foam these broken marbles which obstruct their course.

"Above these fragments, forming dams of marble, is the hill of Balbek, a platform a thousand paces long by seven hundred feet wide, all built by the hand of man in cut stones, of which some measure fifty to sixty feet in length by fifteen to sixteen in height, while the greater part are from fifteen to thirty feet long. This hill of cut granite appeared to us from its eastern extremity, with its profound bases and its incommensurable casings, where three pieces of granite form one hundred and eighty feet of development and nearly three thousand feet of surface, with the large openings of its subterranean vaults, where the water of the river was engulfed, while the whistling of the wind mingling with the murmuring of the waters produced sounds similar to the far-off volley of the great bells of our cathedrals.

"On that immense platform the extremities of the great temples were presented to our view, cut out of the blue, pink, and golden colors of the horizon. Some of these deserted monuments seemed intact, and looked as if just finished by the hand of the workman; others presented partial remains still standing,—isolated columns, bits of leaning walls, and dismantled fronts. The eye lost itself in the shining avenues of colonnades of these various temples, and the too high horizon prevented us seeing where that world of stone ended.

"The six gigantic columns of the great temple, carrying still majestically their rich and colossal entablatures, dominated all that scene, and lost themselves in the blue sky as an aërial altar for the sacrifice of giants.

"The day after we arose with the sun, whose first rays striking on the temples of Balbek gave to these mysterious ruins the brightness of eternal youth.

"After a hasty breakfast, we went to examine what we had as yet but cursorily observed. We slowly approached the artificial hill, so as to be able to observe well the different masses of architecture which compose it, and soon arrived by the northern part under the shades of the gigantic walls which enclose the ruins. We passed the torrent of Balbek by the bridges that time has thrown there, and went up by a narrow and steep breach to the terrace overtopping the walls. Every stone that our hands touched, that our looks measured, called forth our admiration, and we could not refrain from exclamations of surprise and wonder.

Each of the stones of that enclosure wall was from eight to ten feet in length by five to six in width, and as much in height. These enormous blocks rest without cement one on the other, and almost all have the remains of sculpture of an Indian or Egyptian epoch.

"You can at a glance perceive that these huge ashlars have been used primarily for an entirely different purpose than that of forming a wall of terraces and enclosures, and that they were the precious material of primitive monuments which later have been taken to enclose the Grecian and Roman temples.

"It was an habitual, and, I believe, even a religious custom of the Ancients, when a sacred edifice was thrown down by war or time, or when more advanced arts required its renewal to perfect it, to use the same materials for the accessory construction of the restored monuments, so that the stones which the shadows of the gods had touched would not be profaned by common usage; and also, out of respect for their ancestry, that the human work of different epochs should not be buried and lost, but bear witness to the piety of man and the successive progress of the arts.

"Arrived on the summit of the breach, our eyes scarce knew where to rest. There were everywhere marble doors of a prodigious height and width, windows or niches bordered with the most admirable sculptures, arches covered with the most exquisite ornaments, pieces of cornices, of entablatures, of chapiters, as thick as the dust under our feet; all mystery, confusion, disorder; masterpieces of art, remains of the inexplicable marvels around us. No sooner did we look with admiration on one side, than a new wonder would attract us on the other. Each interpretation of the form or of the religious sense of the monuments was destroyed by a succeeding one; and in that labyrinth of conjectures we were entirely lost.

"You cannot reconstruct in thought the sacred edifices of a time, or of a people, of which you do not know either the religion or the manners. Time carries its secrets with it, and leaves its enigmas to baffle and deceive the human mind. We quickly renounced the attempt to build any system on the *ensemble* of these ruins, and contented ourselves with looking and admiring, without understanding anything but the ability and genius of man, and the strength of the religious idea which had been the incentive to move such masses and accomplish so many *chefs-d'œuvre.*

"We were still separated from the second scene of the ruins by interior constructions which debarred us the view of the temple. We were, according to all appearances, but in the dwelling of the priests, or on the ground of some private chapels consecrated to unknown usages.

"We leaped over these monumental constructions, far richer than the enclosure walls, and the second scene of the ruin was beneath our eyes. Much larger, much longer, and much more decorated than that we had just left, it offered to our view an immense oblong platform, whose level was often broken by remains of more elevated pavements, and which seemed to have belonged to temples entirely destroyed, or perhaps without roofs, so that the sun, which was adored in Balbek, could shine upon its altar.

"All around that platform were a series of chapels decorated with admirably sculptured niches, friezes, cornices, and compartments, of most elaborate work, but the work of an epoch already corrupt. You feel there the imprint of a taste surcharged with ornaments of the Greeks and Romans. But to feel that impression, you must already have the eye inured to the contemplation of the pure monuments of Athens; any other eye would be fascinated by the splendor of the form, and the finish of the ornaments. The only fault is too much richness; the stone is crushed down by its own luxury, and the laces of marbles run in all directions on the walls.

"There are yet eight or ten of the chapels entire, which seem to have been always as they are now, open on the oblong square which they surround, and where the mysteries of Baal were probably accomplished in full daylight.

"I will not try to describe the thousand objects of surprise and admiration which each one of these temples offers to the eye of the spectator. I am neither a sculptor nor an architect; I do not even know the name that the stone should bear in such or such a place, in such or such a form; I would speak badly in an unknown tongue; but that universal language which the beautiful speaks to the eye even of the ignorant, which the mysterious and the antique speak to the soul of the philosopher, I *do* understand, and never as strongly as in that chaos of marbles, of forms, of mysteries which encumber that marvellous yard.

"In combining by thought the remains of the temples of Jupiter Stator at Rome, of the Coliseum, of the Parthenon, one could represent to one's self this architectural scene, the prodigious agglomeration of so many monuments, of so much richness and so much work, in only one enclosure and under a single glance, in the midst of a desert and on the ruins of a city almost unknown.

"It was with much regret that we tore ourselves from that scene and walked towards the south, where the first of the six gigantic columns rose as a pharos above that horizon of ruins.

"To get to it we were obliged to cross again the exterior enclosure walls, some high porches, pedestals, and foundations of altars, which everywhere obstructed the space between us and it. At last we arrived at its base. Silent is the language of man when what he feels surpasses the ordinary measure of his impressions. We remained mute, contemplating these six columns, and measuring with the eye their diameter, their elevation, and the admirable sculpture of their architraves and cornices; they are seven feet in diameter and more than seventy feet in height, and are composed some of two and some of three blocks, but so perfectly joined together that you can hardly discover the line of junction; the sun's rays were then striking on their side, and we sat for a moment under their shade; large birds, similar to eagles, frightened at the sound of our steps, flew away from above the chapiters, where they have their nests, and soon returning, alighted on the acanthus of the cornices, striking them with their beaks, and moving their wings as if they were animated ornaments of the marvellous ruins.

"These columns, that some travellers have taken for

the remains of an avenue, one hundred and four feet long and fifty-six feet wide, leading formerly to a temple, appear to me to have been the exterior decoration of this edifice.

"In carefully examining the smaller temple, which stands nearly entire near by, you will see that it was constructed from the same design; and I consider it probable that, after the ruin of the first temple by an earthquake, the second was constructed on the same plan, and for its erection some of the material of the first was employed; only that the proportions, too gigantic for a degenerating epoch, were diminished; that the columns broken in their fall were used, but these that had been spared were left as a sacred remembrance of the ancient pile; if it were otherwise, other ruins of great columns would still subsist near the six now standing. Everything indicates, on the contrary, that the vacant space which surrounds them was cleared of remains from time the most remote, and that the rich façade was still used for ceremonies of religion.

"We had opposite, on the south side, another temple placed on the bank of the platform, at about forty paces from us. It is the most entire and most beautiful monument of Balbek, and, I might almost dare to say, of all the world. If you would re-erect one of the columns of the peristyle rolled on the side of the platform, and another, the head of which is still leaning on the intact walls of the temple—if you were to remove to their right places some of the enormous ornamental compartments which have fallen from the roof into the porch—if you were to raise again one or two sculptured blocks of the inner door, and readjust the altar with the *débris* which is scattered on the enclosure, so that it would take back its form and place,—call back the gods, bring back the priests and the people,—they would recognize their temple as complete, as intact, the polish of the stones as brilliant in the dazzling light, as the day that the architect delivered it for its intended use.

"The proportions of this temple are inferior to the one of which the six colossal columns formed a part. It is surrounded by a portico, supported by columns of the Corinthian order; each of these columns is about five feet in diameter by forty-five in height, and are each composed of three blocks; they are nine feet from each other, and at the same distance from the inner wall. On the chapiters of the columns is extended a rich architrave and an admirably sculptured cornice. The roof of the peristyle is formed of large blocks of concave stones, cut with the chisel in compartments, and which variously represent either the face of a god, a deity, or a hero. On one side we recognized a Ganymede carried away by Jupiter in the form of an eagle. Some of these blocks have fallen to the ground in the midst of the columns. We measured them, and found them to be sixteen feet square, with a thickness of about five feet. Such are the tiles of this monument.

"The inner door of the temple, formed also of enormous blocks, has a width of twenty-two feet. We could not measure its height, as other blocks have fallen in that place and filled it half up. The appearance of the sculptured stones which composed the façade of that door, and its disproportion with the remainder of the edifice, make me suppose that it is the door of the great fallen temple which has been inserted here. The mysterious sculptures which decorate it are, to my mind, of an entirely different period from the Antonine epoch, and of a work infinitely less pure. An eagle, holding a caduceus in its claws, spreads its wings on the opening, and from his beak run festoons of ribbon or chains, which are supported at their extremity by two cherubs.

"The interior of the building is decorated with pillars and niches of the richest, but surcharged sculpture; and we gathered some of the fragments which lay scattered on the floor. There are some niches perfectly intact, and which seem to have just left the workshop of the sculptor.

"Not far from the entry of the temple we found immense openings and subterranean staircases, which led to inferior constructions whose usage you can designate; everything is equally large and beautiful; these were, without doubt, the dwelling of the pontiff, the college of the priests, the halls of the initiations, perhaps also royal dwellings. They received the daylight from the top or by the sides of the platforms to which these rooms lead. Fearing to lose ourselves in the labyrinths, we only visited a small part of them; they seem to exist throughout all the extent of this mamelon.

"The temple that I have just described is placed at the south-western extremity of the monumental hill of Balbek, and forms the angle of the platform.

"In coming out of the peristyle we found ourselves on the brink of the precipice, and could measure the cyclopean stones which form the pedestal of that group of monuments. This pedestal is about thirty feet above the level of the plain of Balbek, and is constructed of stones whose dimensions are so prodigious, that if it were not attested by travellers worthy of belief, the imagination of men of our days would be crushed under the improbability. The Arabs themselves, every-day witnesses of these marvels, do not attribute them to the power of man, but to that of genii, or supernatural force. When one considers that these blocks of cut granite are sixty feet long by fifteen to sixteen wide, and an unknown thickness, and that these enormous masses are elevated on each other some thirty feet above the level of the ground; that they have been taken from far-off quarries, brought there, and raised to such an elevation, to form the platform for the temple, one recoils before such a proof of human strength! Science in our days cannot explain it, and one is not astonished that the ignorant should fall back on the idea of the supernatural.

"These wonders are evidently not of the same date as the temple; they were mysteries to the ancients as they are to us; they are of an unknown epoch, and may be antediluvian; they have probably sustained many temples, consecrated to various and successive religions. The ordinary observer will recognize five or six generations of monuments, belonging to various epochs, on the hill of the ruins of Balbek.

"Some travellers and some Arab writers attribute these primitive constructions to Solomon, three thousand years before the Christian era. He built, it is said, Tadmor and Balbek in the desert. The history of Solomon fills up the imagination of the Orientals, but that supposition, so far at least as concerning the gigantic monuments of Heliopolis, is not at all likely. How a king of Israel who did not even possess a seaport ten leagues from these mountains; who was obliged to borrow the marine of Hiram, king of Tyre, to bring him the cedars of Lebanon—how could he have extended his dominion above Damascus, and even unto Balbek? How could a prince, who, wishing to elevate the Temple of Temples, the house of the only God, in his capital, and who employed but fragile materials, which could not resist time, nor leave any durable trace, have raised at one hundred leagues from his people, in unknown deserts, monuments built with imperishable stone? Would he not sooner have employed his strength and his riches in Jerusalem? And what remains in Jerusalem which indicates similar monuments to those of Balbek? Nothing. It cannot then have been the work of Solomon.

"I rather believe that these enormous stones have been moved either by that first race of men that all primitive history calls giants, or by those of the antediluvian period.

"We are assured that not far off, in a valley of the Anti-Lebanon, there have been discovered human bones of an immense size; and '*that*' rumor has such consistency among the neighboring Arabs that the Consul-General of England in Syria, Mr. Farren, a man of superior intelligence, proposes to go without delay to visit these mysterious sepulchres. The Oriental tradition, and even the monument raised on what is said to be the tomb of Noah, not far from Balbek, assign this locality as a *sojourn* of that patriarch. The first men of his descendants might have preserved for some time the size and strength that humanity had before the total or partial submersion of the globe; these monuments may be their work. Even supposing that the human race has never exceeded its present stature, the proportions of human intelligence may have changed. Who tells us that this younger intelligence had not invented mechanical processes perfect to move, as an atom of dust, these masses that an army of a thousand men could not stir to-day? However it may be, some of the stones of Balbek are the most prodigious masses that ever man has moved! The largest stones of the pyramid of Egypt do not exceed eighteen feet, and these are but exceptional blocks, placed for the purpose of special solidity in certain parts of that edifice.

"In turning the angle north of the platform, the walls which support it are also in fine preservation, but the masses of the materials which compose it are less wonderful, though the stones, generally speaking, are twenty to thirty feet in length by eight to ten in width. The walls, much more antique than the superior temples, are covered with a gray tint, and pierced here and there with holes at their junctions. These openings are bordered with swallows' nests, and tufts of shrubs and pellitory flowers hang therefrom. The dark, grave color of the stone of the base contrasts with the bright and splendid tint of the walls of the temples, and the rows of columns on the summit.

"At sunset, when the rays play between the pillars, and gush out as waves of fire between the volutes and the acanthus of the chapiters, the temples glitter like silver on a pedestal of bronze.

"We went down by a breach formed at the southern angle of the platform, and there some columns of the small temple have rolled, with the architraves, into the torrent which runs along the cyclopean walls. The enormous shafts, or pieces of columns grouped every way in the bed of the torrent, and on the steep declivity of the ditch, will remain, without doubt, eternally, where time has shaken them. Some walnut and other trees have germinated between these blocks, covering them with their branches, and embracing them with their wide roots; but the most gigantic trees look like reeds grown up yesterday near these trunks, twenty feet in circumference, and of these pieces of acanthus, of which one only covers half the bed of the stream.

"Not far from there, on the northern part, an immense mouth in the side of the platform opened before us, which we entered. The daylight which penetrated there by the two extremities illuminated it sufficiently, and we followed it in its length of five hundred feet, running under the entire extent of the temples, and being about thirty feet in height. The vault is formed of blocks which even surprised us by their mass, after those we had just contemplated. We could, however, form no idea of its object. At the western extremity this vault has a branch more elevated and still larger, which extends to the platform of the small temple, and which we first visited. We found there the full light of day, the scattered torrent running among innumerable pieces of architecture rolled from the platforms, while handsome walnut-trees are growing in the dust of these marbles. The other ancient edifices of Balbek, disseminated before us in the plain, attracted our attention, but nothing could interest us after what we had travelled over."

Such were the marvellous ruins we were unfortunate enough to have but four hours to examine. There were several encampments of voyagers more happy than ourselves; one with the American flag was that of Church, the artist, who was occupied taking sketches.

We left Balbek at one o'clock, and a gallop of four hours brought us back to Stoura, a distance of thirty miles, where we again met the Johnson family, encamped near the house of Mr. Andrews; and, worn out with the exertion and fatigue of the last two days, we were glad to retire.

CHAPTER XXIII.

BEYROUT—THE STEAMER—RETROSPECT—RHODES—SMYRNA—EPHESUS—CONSTANTINOPLE—ST. SOPHIA—BOSPHORUS—BLACK SEA—GOLDEN HORN AND SWEET WATERS—ATHENS—THE ACROPOLIS—PARTHENON—ELEUSIS—MESSINA.

SATURDAY, May 10, 1868.

E left Stoura at half-past nine in the morning, in the coupé of the diligence, for Beyrout. A very interesting ride it was, with varied, handsome scenery, and frequent views of the Mediterranean.

Beyrout is the ancient Berytus, situated in Phœnicia. The city is on an elevation, declining gently towards the sea: its base is backed by the Lebanon Mountain, and some masses of rock, which advance into the waves, support the Turkish fortification, while the roadstead is closed by a point of land protecting the waters from the westerly wind, and all the suburbs and surrounding hills bear a rich girdle of gay and well-built villas, with large luxuriantly planted gardens. The climate is all that can be desired, combined with a rich soil producing limitless vegetation. Silk mulberry-trees, of which immense quantities are here grown for the culture of cocoons, are planted from stage to stage on artificial terraces; fig, orange, and lemon trees, and plantations of pines and firs, raised by the emir Fakhr-ed-Din, give to the city a beautiful appearance, while the high mountains of the chain of Lebanon form the background. There are no monuments, and, apart from its lively aspect, it possesses nothing worthy of notice.

Sunday, May 11.

The hotel where we lodged was filled with travellers, part of whom were to take the steamer for Smyrna or Constantinople; and when we left Beyrout and arrived on board, we found it crowded not only with first but with many second class passengers.

Half of the upper deck was taken for the use of the Turkish women and their children, so that it left but a narrow space for our accommodation; but as the sea was uncommonly smooth, and the company on board exceedingly agreeable, we forgot all the inconveniences we would so much have felt in any other case. We again met here a part of the French party we had first seen at Djenin; also the Count and Countess Rapp.

Several of these young men, Mr. Leon Bonnat, one of the most distinguished of our French painters, Mr. Ernest Journault, also a painter, Mr. Goupil, and some others, had accompanied the great painter Jerome in his travel to Egypt and Petra. Between conversation and reading, while the steamer was gliding swiftly on the smooth water, with continuous fine weather, the time passed pleasantly and rapidly, and it was the first time I had ever really enjoyed a sea voyage.

My "*diary*" is ended; our journey is drawing to a close. We have floated along that river whose wondrous ruins of by-gone ages confound the imagination of the historian; whose history, plainly written on the imperishable stone, is easily read, but, alas! in a language utterly dead; the manners and customs of whose people so wonderfully assimilate to those of their predecessors as we see them depicted on the temple walls.

We have roamed through the land and left our feeble footprints on the "*sacred soil*" trodden by our Saviour; rested in that land of Caanan which the children of Israel found overflowing with milk and honey after their sojourn of forty years in the desert; passed over the condemned ground near the sites of the accursed cities of Sodom and Gomorrah; stood with mingled awe and reverence on the shore of the Sea of Miracles; gazed on the gigantic constructions of unknown, perhaps antediluvian races; and are speeding northward with the almost bewildering recollections branded on our brains.

We visited Cyprus, and Rhodes, interesting by its street of chevaliers, the walls of whose houses still retain the escutcheons of the ancient families of France, Spain, Italy, and Germany.

In Smyrna, beautifully situated, surrounded by a rich country, with a bright and azure sky, we remained two days; one of which was spent in visiting the bazars and the bridge of the caravans, which is one of the greatest curiosities of Smyrna, as the brook which runs beneath it is the Meles, on whose shore it is said Homer was born.

The next day was occupied with an excursion to the ruins of Ephesus. As nearly all the passengers by our steamer were desirous of making this visit, a special train was engaged, and we were soon "*on the rail,*" speeding at a rapid rate through a fine productive country towards the site of this once celebrated city. The ruins occupy a large extent of ground, but ingenuity is at fault in the attempt to locate the celebrated temple of Diana, one of the seven wonders of the world.

The remains of an immense aqueduct—shafts of fallen marble columns—broken statues—bases, plinths, and cornices—sarcophagi—pavements—gateways—are scattered over acres in confused masses, overgrown with grass and bushes, or half buried in the accumulated dust of ages.

Perhaps the most interesting of these ruins is that of an immense theatre, the auditorium of which is scooped out from a hill-side, and capable of accommodating an audience of one hundred thousand.

Commerce made Ephesus the great and wealthy city which it once was; but an earthquake has probably altered the lay of the land, for what appears to have been a quay is at the present time several miles from navigable water.

Leaving Smyrna the following day, we skirted along the coast of Asia Minor, near the plain where once stood Troy; passed the island of Tenedos, behind which the Grecian fleet hid while trying the ruse of the wooden horse; and the promontories whereon are the tombs of Achilles and Patroclus; made the passage of the Dardanelles, where Leander swam from Cestos to Abydos for love, and got his Hero; and Byron swam for fame, and got—a cold; and arrived at Constantinople on Tuesday, May 18th.

Constantinople is admirably situated on seven hills. On one side the Sea of Marmora, on another the Golden Horn and the Bosphorus add to its enchanting aspect. But the interior of the city does not correspond with its external appearance. The streets are long, narrow, and so badly paved that it is impossible for Europeans to walk through them for any length of time. There are a great many horses, numerous sedan-chairs with porters, but few carriages.

On our arrival the hotels were so crowded that we could not at first obtain rooms, but after hunting for an hour or two we succeeded in securing an excellent suite, of which Tom, Aline, and I took possession, while the gentlemen of our party found accommodations in a house opposite.

Having hired a carriage by the day, we thus visited without fatigue all objects of interest in and about the city. Our guide conducted us first to the Seraï, a palace which was built by Mahommed II. The gardens are beautiful; but the palace itself possesses nothing of interest. We afterwards visited the ancient Church of St. Irene, constructed by Constantine the Great, and which to-day is transformed into an armory; thence to St. Sophia, the celebrated mosque of which we had heard so much.

Having been told that it was handsomer than St. Peter's in Rome, every one of the party, excepting myself, having seen the latter, naturally anticipated something still grander. As is often the case, when one expects too much, disappointment follows. It is certainly a magnificent mosque. The materials employed in its construction are of excessive richness, while the cupola is admirable; but I much prefer the Cathedral of Milan; and all the gentlemen gave the preference to St. Peter's at Rome.

After having seen St. Sophia, we next visited the Mosque of Suleiman, then that of Achmed, and the tomb of the Sultan Mahmoud, and that of Roxalana, celebrated in the "Arabian Nights," and several others.

In returning we saw the obelisk of Theodosius, a monolith of pink granite, brought from Egypt; the serpentine column, in bronze, which is believed to be the one which at the Temple of Delphos supported the tripod of Apollo; and the burnt pyramid, which has lost all its gilding, and threatens daily to fall, a mass of ruins. We descended into the cistern of the thousand and one columns, which really has only two hundred and twenty-four.

During our sojourn at Constantinople we employed one day in making a charming excursion on the Bosphorus. Its waters are bordered on either shore by elegant palaces and villas, the hills beyond covered with trees and vegetation. No English, Italian, or American lake can rival the Bosphorus in beauty.

At Bayuk-Deré, where the steamer left us, we took a small boat, were rowed to the Black Sea, and returned the same evening to Constantinople.

From the tower of Galatea a magnificent view is obtained over the city. The bazars are similar to those of Cairo and Damascus.

Friday is the Mussulman's Sunday. The inhabitants go to the Sweet Waters of Europe, as a place of recreation to pass the day, taking their lunch there, protected from the hot rays of the sun by the fine old trees that border the shore, and presenting, by the diversity and brilliancy of their costumes, a *coup d'œil* truly fairy-like. Having hired a caïque—a long and narrow boat, in which it is necessary to sit in the Oriental fashion if you do not wish to be upset—we were rowed through the Golden Horn and up the valley of the Sweet Waters. The river was crowded with these singular crafts, and we there met an elegant one, richly decorated, belonging to the French Ambassador, occupied by Mr. Bonnat and his friends.

On the 23d of May we left Constantinople on board the French *messagerie* steamer, and having been favored with a smooth sea, landed on the 25th at the Piræus; whence a drive of three-quarters of an hour brought us to Athens.

Little is left of ancient Athens but its Acropolis, which overlooks the modern city, giving it a grand and imposing appearance. The city is entirely European in character; its streets are all wide, straight, macadamized, and have handsome sidewalks. The palace of the king is surrounded by fine gardens. The inhabitants are cleanly, presenting a lively, intelligent appearance, many wearing the Albanian costume.

We spent the day after our arrival on the Acropolis, though many persons content themselves with a few hours' visit to the ruins. On the southeast side of the Acropolis, on the right bank of the Ilissus, we visited the remains of the Temple of Jupiter Olympus, commenced by Pisistratus, 590 B.C., and which was the largest of the temples of Athens; but sixteen columns remain standing, isolated on the plain.

Passing under the triumphal arch of Adrian, we approached the Acropolis, stopping at the Theatre of Bacchus, of which, six or seven years ago, but few remains were visible; but since then it has been excavated by a Prussian commission, and now you see a great portion of it as it was in the time of its splendor, exposing to view the auditorium, with the lower tiers of benches, as well as the arm-chairs of marble used by the priests and the nobles, and on which you can still read the owners' names, while a little higher than the others is a chair with the name of the Emperor Adrian inscribed on its front. The stage has disappeared, the statues are broken, the sculptures destroyed, and you see but fragments of what was once the perfection of art.

Passing still further on, we arrived at the Odeon of Herod Atticus, on the southern declivity of the Acropolis, and which was erected by him in honor of his wife Regallia.

From the top of the Acropolis we beheld before us the Areopagus, between the Acropolis and the Hill of the Nymphs; to the left the Pnyx, where the popular assemblies of the Athenians took place, and Demosthenes swayed the public mind for peace or war; and in the far distance, in an opening between some of the hills, we could see the Acropolis of Corinth. Around us were the beautiful ruins of the Propylons, the Temple of Victory, the Erechtheion, and the Parthenon. Beyond, and towards the north, a short distance below the Areopagus, were the Temple of Theseus, the modern city occupying the plain, with its white houses, and gardens, while in the distance beyond, and in a line with the king's palace, were Mounts Hymettus, celebrated still, as of yore, for its honey, Lycabettus, and the Pentelicon, whose quarries produce the most pure and beautiful marble of the world.

The temples and buildings are in a far more ruinous condition than any of us had supposed; but that which remains is grand, sublime! Still, at the risk of being condemned for want of good taste, we one and all agreed that the ruins of Balbek were finer, although they have not the same celebrity. Aware that the Parthenon is considered the most perfect specimen of architecture in the world, each hesitated to express an opinion; but when questioned, first one, then another, finally all, agreed to the fact that we were disappointed. Certainly the Parthenon is seen under great disadvantages, for what the wars and earthquakes spared, it was ordained that the English should destroy, and England has nothing to boast of in her Elgin marbles.

We passed two entire days among the ruins, and on the third, while some of the gentlemen made the ascent of Mount Pentelicus, whence there is an admirable view, Tom hired a carriage, and with Aline and myself went to visit the ruins of Eleusis, following the Via Sacra, by which route the processions annually passed on their way to celebrate these ancient mysterious rites.

At Eleusis we found the remains of a temple, which were only discovered four years ago, but what we saw bore evidences of great beauty. Although much smaller than the Parthenon, it was undoubtedly much more ancient.

A fine view greeted our eyes from the hill of the Acropolis. Before us lay the Gulf of Salamis, where Xerxes with his thousand ships was defeated by the Greeks 480 years B. C., one of the decisive battles in the world's history.

After a week's sojourn in Athens we took the steamer for Marseilles, in company with Mr. Leon Bonnat, and stopping a few hours in Messina, several days in Marseilles and in Cannes, where we visited some friends, arrived in Paris the 11th of June, after an absence of six months and fifteen days.

THE END.

NEW BOOKS
And New Editions Recently Published by
CARLETON, Publisher,
NEW YORK.

N.B.—THE PUBLISHER, upon receipt of the price in advance, will send any of the following Books by mail, POSTAGE FREE, to any part of the United States. This convenient and very safe mode may be adopted when the neighboring Booksellers are not supplied with the desired work. State name and address in full

---

Victor Hugo.

LES MISÉRABLES.—The celebrated novel. One large 8vo volume, paper covers, $2.00; . . . cloth bound, $2.50
LES MISÉRABLES.—In the Spanish language. Fine 8vo. edition, two vols., paper covers, $4.00; . . cloth bound, $5.00
JARGAL.—A new novel. Illustrated. . 12mo. cloth, $1.75
CLAUDE GUEUX, and Last Day of Condemned Man. do. $1.50

Miss Muloch.

JOHN HALIFAX.—A novel. With illustration. 12mo. cloth, $1.75
A LIFE FOR A LIFE.— . do. do. $1.75

Charlotte Bronte (Currer Bell).

JANE EYRE.—A novel. With illustration. 12mo. cloth, $1.75
THE PROFESSOR.— do. . do. . do. $1.75
SHIRLEY.— . do. . do. . do. $1.75
VILLETTE.— . do. . do. . do. $1.75

Hand-Books of Society.

THE HABITS OF GOOD SOCIETY; with thoughts, hints, and anecdotes, concerning nice points of taste, good manners, and the art of making oneself agreeable. The most entertaining work of the kind. . . . 12mo. cloth, $1.75
THE ART OF CONVERSATION.—With directions for self-culture. A sensible and instructive work, that ought to be in the hands of every one who wishes to be either an agreeable talker or listener. . . . . 12mo. cloth, $1.50
ARTS OF WRITING, READING, AND SPEAKING.—An excellent book for self-instruction and improvement . . 12mo, cloth, $1.50
HAND-BOOKS OF SOCIETY.—The above three choice volumes are also bound in extra style, full gilt ornamental back, uniform in appearance, and put up in a handsome box. Price for the set of three, ... $5.00

Algernon Charles Swinburne.

LAUS VENERIS, AND OTHER POEMS.— . 12mo, cloth, $1.75

Mrs. Mary J. Holmes' Works.

LENA RIVERS.—	A novel.	12mo. cloth,	$1.50
DARKNESS AND DAYLIGHT.—	do.	do.	$1.50
TEMPEST AND SUNSHINE —	do.	do.	$1.50
MARIAN GREY.—	do.	do.	$1.50
MEADOW BROOK.—	do.	do.	$1.50
ENGLISH ORPHANS.—	do.	do.	$1.50
DORA DEANE.—	do.	do.	$1.50
COUSIN MAUDE.—	do.	do.	$1.50
HOMESTEAD ON THE HILLSIDE.—	do.	do.	$1.50
HUGH WORTHINGTON.—	do.	do.	$1.50
THE CAMERON PRIDE.—	do.	do.	$1.50
ROSE MATHER.—	do.	do.	$1.50
ETHELYN'S MISTAKE.—*Just Published.*	do.	do.	$1.50

Miss Augusta J. Evans.

BEULAH.—A novel of great power.		12mo. cloth,	$1.75
MACARIA.— do. do.		do.	$1.75
ST. ELMO.— do. do. *Just Published.*		do.	$2.00

By the Author of "Rutledge."

RUTLEDGE.—A deeply interesting novel.		12mo. cloth,	$1.75
THE SUTHERLANDS.— do.		do.	$1.75
FRANK WARRINGTON.— do.		do.	$1.75
ST. PHILIP'S.— do.		do.	$1.75
LOUIE'S LAST TERM AT ST. MARY'S.—		do.	$1.75
ROUNDHEARTS AND OTHER STORIES.—For children.		do.	$1.75
A ROSARY FOR LENT.—Devotional Readings.		do.	$1.75

Captain Mayne Reid's Works—Illustrated.

THE SCALP HUNTERS.—	A romance.	12mo. cloth,	$1.75
THE RIFLE RANGERS.—	do.	do.	$1.75
THE TIGER HUNTER.—	do.	do.	$1.75
OSCEOLA, THE SEMINOLE.—	do.	do.	$1.75
THE WAR TRAIL.—	do.	do	$1.75
THE HUNTER'S FEAST.—	do.	do.	$1.75
RANGERS AND REGULATORS.—	do.	do.	$1.75
THE WHITE CHIEF —	do.	do.	$1.75
THE QUADROON.—	do.	do.	$1.75
THE WILD HUNTRESS.—	do.	do.	$1.75
THE WOOD RANGERS.—	do.	do.	$1.75
WILD LIFE.—	do.	do.	$1.75
THE MAROON.—	do.	do.	$1.75
LOST LEONORE.—	do.	do.	$1.75
THE HEADLESS HORSEMAN.—	do.	do.	$1.75
THE WHITE GAUNTLET.— *Just Published.*		do.	$1.75

A. S. Roe's Works.

A LONG LOOK AHEAD.—	A novel.	12mo. cloth,	$1.50
TO LOVE AND TO BE LOVED.—	do.	do.	$1.50
TIME AND TIDE.—	do.	do.	$1.50
I'VE BEEN THINKING.—	do.	do.	$1.50
THE STAR AND THE CLOUD.—	do.	do.	$1.50
TRUE TO THE LAST.—	do.	do.	$1.50
HOW COULD HE HELP IT?—	do.	do.	$1.50
LIKE AND UNLIKE.—	do.	do.	$1.50
LOOKING AROUND.—	do.	do.	$1.50
WOMAN OUR ANGEL.—	do.	do.	$1.50
THE CLOUD ON THE HEART.—		do.	$1.50

Orpheus C. Kerr.

THE ORPHEUS C. KERR PAPERS.—Three vols.	12mo. cloth,	$1.50
SMOKED GLASS.—New comic book. Illustrated.	do.	$1.50
AVERY GLIBUN.—A powerful new novel.—	8vo. cloth,	$2.00

Richard B. Kimball.

WAS HE SUCCESSFUL?— A novel.	12mo. cloth,	$1.75
UNDERCURRENTS.— do.	do.	$1.75
SAINT LEGER.— do.	do.	$1.75
ROMANCE OF STUDENT LIFE.—do.	do.	$1.75
IN THE TROPICS.— do.	do.	$1.75
HENRY POWERS, Banker.—*Just Published.*	do.	$1.75

Comic Books—Illustrated.

ARTEMUS WARD, His Book.—Letters, etc.	12mo. cl.,	$1.50
DO. His Travels—Mormons, etc.	do.	$1.50
DO. In London.—Punch Letters.	do.	$1.50
DO. His Panorama and Lecture.	do.	$1.50
JOSH BILLINGS ON ICE, and other things.—	do.	$1.50
DO. His Book of Proverbs, etc.	do.	$1.50
WIDOW SPRIGGINS.—By author "Widow Bedott."	do.	$1.75
FOLLY AS IT FLIES.—By Fanny Fern.	do.	$1.50
CORRY O'LANUS.—His views and opinions.	do.	$1.50
VERDANT GREEN.—A racy English college story.	do.	$1.50
CONDENSED NOVELS, ETC.—By F. Bret Harte.	do.	$1.50
THE SQUIBOB PAPERS.—By John Phœnix.	do.	$1.50
MILES O'REILLY.—His Book of Adventures.	do.	$1.50
DO. Baked Meats, etc.	do.	$1.75

"Brick" Pomeroy.

SENSE.—An illustrated vol. of fireside musings.	12mo. cl.,	$1.50
NONSENSE.— do. do. comic sketches.	do.	$1.50

Joseph Rodman Drake.

THE CULPRIT FAY.—A faery poem.	12mo. cloth,	$1.25
THE CULPRIT FAY.—An illustrated edition. 100 exquisite illustrations. 4to., beautifully printed and bound.		$5.00

Children's Books—Illustrated.

THE ART OF AMUSING.—With 150 illustrations. 12mo. cl., $1.50
FRIENDLY COUNSEL FOR GIRLS.—A charming book. do. $1.50
THE CHRISTMAS FONT.—By Mary J. Holmes. do. $1.00
ROBINSON CRUSOE.—A Complete edition. . do. $1.50
LOUIE'S LAST TERM.—By author "Rutledge. do. $1.75
ROUNDHEARTS, and other stories.— do. . do. $1.75
PASTIMES WITH MY LITTLE FRIENDS.— . . do. $1.50
WILL-O'-THE-WISP.—From the German. . do. $1.50

M. Michelet's Remarkable Works.

LOVE (L'AMOUR).—Translated from the French. 12mo. cl., $1.50
WOMAN (LA FEMME).— . do. . . do. $1.50

Ernest Renan.

THE LIFE OF JESUS.—Translated from the French. 12mo.cl.,$1.75
THE APOSTLES.— . . do. . . do. $1.75

Popular Italian Novels.

DOCTOR ANTONIO.—A love story. By Ruffini. 12mo. cl., $1.75
BEATRICE CENCI.—By Guerrazzi, with portrait. do. $1.75

Rev. John Cumming, D.D., of London.

THE GREAT TRIBULATION.—Two series. 12mo. cloth, $1.50
THE GREAT PREPARATION.— do. . do. $1.50
THE GREAT CONSUMMATION. do. . do. $1.50
THE LAST WARNING CRY.— . . do. $1.50

Mrs. Ritchie (Anna Cora Mowatt).

FAIRY FINGERS.—A capital new novel. . 12mo. cloth, $1.75
THE MUTE SINGER.— do. . do. $1.75
THE CLERGYMAN'S WIFE—and other stories. do. $1.75

Mother Goose for Grown Folks.

HUMOROUS RHYMES for grown people. . 12mo. cloth, 1.25

T. S. Arthur's New Works.

LIGHT ON SHADOWED PATHS.—A novel. 12mo. cloth, $1.50
OUT IN THE WORLD.— . do. . . do. $1.50
NOTHING BUT MONEY.— . do. . . do. $1.50
WHAT CAME AFTERWARDS.— do. . . do. $1.50
OUR NEIGHBORS.— . do. . . do. $1.50

Geo. W. Carleton.

OUR ARTIST IN CUBA.—With 50 comic illustrations. . $1.50
OUR ARTIST IN PERU.— do. do. . . $1.50
OUR ARTIST IN AFRICA.—(*In press*) do. . . $1.50

John Esten Cooke.

FAIRFAX.—A Virginian novel. . . 12mo. cloth, $1.75
HILT TO HILT.— A Virginian novel. do $1.50

How to Make Money

AND HOW TO KEEP IT.—A practical, readable book, that ought to be in the hands of every person who wishes to earn money or to keep what he has. One of the best books ever published. By Thomas A. Davies. 12mo. cloth, $1.50

J. Cordy Jeaffreson.

A BOOK ABOUT LAWYERS.—A collection of interesting anecdotes and incidents connected with the most distinguished members of the Legal Profession. 12mo. cloth, $2.00

Fred. Saunders.

WOMAN, LOVE, AND MARRIAGE.—A charming volume about three most fascinating topics. 12mo. cloth, $1.50

Edmund Kirke.

AMONG THE PINES.—Or Life in the South. 12mo. cloth, $1.50
MY SOUTHERN FRIENDS.— do. do. $1.50
DOWN IN TENNESSEE.— do. do. $1.50
ADRIFT IN DIXIE.— do. do. $1.50
AMONG THE GUERILLAS.— do. do. $1.50

Charles Reade.

THE CLOISTER AND THE HEARTH.—A magnificent new novel—the best this author ever wrote. 8vo. cloth, $2.00

The Opera.

TALES FROM THE OPERAS.—A collection of clever stories, based upon the plots of all the famous operas. 12mo. cloth, $1.50

Robert B. Roosevelt.

THE GAME-FISH OF THE NORTH.—Illustrated. 12mo. cloth, $2.00
SUPERIOR FISHING.— do. do. $2.00
THE GAME-BIRDS OF THE NORTH.— do. $2.00

Love in Letters.

A collection of piquant love-letters, selected from the amatory correspondence of the most celebrated and notorious men and women of History. By J. G. Wilson. $2.00

Dr. J. J. Craven.

THE PRISON-LIFE OF JEFFERSON DAVIS.—Incidents and conversations during his captivity. 12mo. cloth. $2.00

Walter Barrett, Clerk.

THE OLD MERCHANTS OF NEW YORK—Piquant personal incidents, bits of biography, estimates of wealth, and interesting events in the lives of nearly all the leading Merchants of New York City. Four volumes. 12mo. cloth, $1.75

H. T. Sperry.

COUNTRY LOVE vs. CITY FLIRTATION.—An amusing, satirical Society poem, illustrated with twenty superb full-page drawings by Augustus Hoppin. 12mo. cloth, $2.00

Miscellaneous Works.

WARWICK.—A novel by Mansfield Tracy Walworth	$1.75
REGINA, and other Poems.—By Eliza Cruger.	$1.50
THE WICKEDEST WOMAN IN NEW YORK.—By C. H. Webb	50
MONTALBAN.—A new American novel.	$1.75
MADEMOISELLE MERQUEM.—A novel by George Sand	$1.75
THE IMPENDING CRISIS OF THE SOUTH.—By H. R. Helper	$2.00
NOJOQUE—A Question for a Continent.— do.	$2.00
TEMPLE HOUSE.—A novel by Elizabeth Stoddard.	$1.75
PARIS IN 1867.—By Henry Morford.	$1.75
THE BISHOP'S SON.—A novel by Alice Cary.	$1.75
CRUISE OF THE ALABAMA AND SUMTER.—By Capt. Semmes.	$2.00
HELEN COURTENAY.—A novel, author "Vernon Grove."	$1.75
SOUVENIRS OF TRAVEL.—By Madame Octavia W. LeVert.	$2.00
VANQUISHED.—A novel by Agnes Leonard.	$1.75
WILL-O'-THE-WISP.—A child's book, from the German	$1.50
FOUR OAKS.—A novel by Kamba Thorpe.	$1.75
THE CHRISTMAS FONT.—A child's book, by M. J. Holmes.	$1.00
ALICE OF MONMOUTH.—By Edmund C. Stedman.	$1.50
THE LOST CAUSE REGAINED.—By Edward A. Pollard.	$1.50
MALBROOK.—A new American novel.	$1.75
POEMS, BY SARAH T. BOLTON.	$1.50
LIVES OF JOHN S. MOSBY AND MEN.—With portraits.	$1.75
THE SHENENDOAH.—History of the Confederate Cruiser.	$1.50
MARY BRANDEGEE.—A novel by Cuyler Pine.	$1.75
RENSHAWE— do. do.	$1.75
MEMORIALS OF JUNIUS BRUTUS BOOTH—(The Elder Actor).	$1.50
MOUNT CALVARY.—By Matthew Hale Smith.	$2.00
LOVE-LIFE OF DR. ELISHA K. KANE AND MARGARET FOX.	$1.75
PROMETHEUS IN ATLANTIS.—A prophecy.	$2.00
TITAN AGONISTES.—An American novel.	$2.00
CHOLERA.—A handbook on its treatment and cure.	$1.00
THE MONTANAS.—A novel by Sallie J. Hancock.	$1.75
PASTIMES WITH LITTLE FRIENDS.—Martha Haines Butt.	$1.50
LIFE OF JAMES STEPHENS.—The Fenian Head-Centre.	$1.00
TREATISE ON DEAFNESS.—By Dr. E. B. Lighthill.	$1.50
AROUND THE PYRAMIDS.—By Gen. Aaron Ward.	$1.50
CHINA AND THE CHINESE.—By W. L. G. Smith.	$1.50
EDGAR POE AND HIS CRITICS.—By. Mrs. Whitman.	$1.00
MARRIED OFF.—An Illustrated Satirical Poem.	50
THE RUSSIAN BALL.— do. do.	50
THE SNOBLACE BALL.— do. do.	50
AN ANSWER TO HUGH MILLER.—By Thomas A. Davies	$1.50
COSMOGONY.—By Thomas A. Davies.	$2.00
RURAL ARCHITECTURE.—By M. Field. Illustrated.	$2.00

www.ingramcontent.com/pod-product-compliance
Lightning Source LLC
Chambersburg PA
CBHW021203230426
43667CB00006B/538